HAUSA THEATRE IN NIGER

CRITICAL STUDIES ON
BLACK LIFE AND CULTURE
(Professor Henry-Louis Gates, Advisory Editor)
VOL. 16

GARLAND REFERENCE LIBRARY
OF THE HUMANITIES
VOL. 761

Critical Studies on Black Life and Culture
Professor Henry-Louis Gates, Advisory Editor

Charles T. Davis
Black Is the Color of the Cosmos

Margaret Perry
The Harlem Renaissance

Josephine R.B. Wright
Ignatius Sancho (1729–1780), an Early African Composer in England

Richard Newman
Black Index

Allan Austin
African Muslims in Antebellum America

Alan P. Merriam
African Music in Perspective

Alan Dundes
Mother Wit from the Laughing Barrel

Jeffrey C. Stewart
The Critical Temper of Alain Locke

Romare Bearden and Carl Holty
The Painter's Mind

George Campbell
First Poems

John M. Janzen
Lemba, 1650–1930

William Robinson
Phillis Wheatley and Her Writings

Sam Dennison
Scandalize My Name

Irma E. Goldstraw
Derek Walcott

Obi Maduakor
Wole Soyinka: An Introduction to His Writing

Janet Beik
Hausa Theatre in Niger: A Contemporary Oral Art

Eddie Meadows
Jazz Reference and Research Materials

Linda Rae Brown
Music, Printed and Manuscript, in the James Weldon Johnson Memorial Collection of Negro Arts & Letters, Yale University

Ishmael Reed
God Made Alaska for the Indians

Betty Kaplan Gubert
Early Black Bibliographies, 1863–1918

HAUSA THEATRE IN NIGER
A Contemporary Oral Art

Janet Beik

GARLAND PUBLISHING, INC. • NEW YORK & LONDON
1987

© 1987 Janet Beik
All rights reserved

Library of Congress Cataloging-in-Publication Data

Beik, Janet, 1953–
   Hausa theatre in Niger.

   (Critical studies on Black life and culture ; vol. 16)
(Garland reference library of the humanities ; vol. 761)
   Bibliography: p.
   Includes index.
   1. Theater—Niger. 2. Folk-drama, Hausa—Niger—
History and criticism. I. Title. II. Series: Critical
studies on Black life and culture ; v. 16. III. Series:
Garland reference library of the humanities ; v. 761.
PN3000.N54B45   1987   792'.0966'26   85-45119
ISBN 0-8240-8703-8 (alk. paper)

Printed on acid-free, 250-year-life paper
Manufactured in the United States of America

CONTENTS

List of Acronyms.....................................vii
Acknowledgments......................................ix
Map of Niger..xii
Photographs..xiii
Introduction..1
Chapter I: A HISTORY OF THE THEATRE IN NIGER..........7
    Traditional Theatre..............................8
    Literary Drama..................................19
    French Theatre in Niger.........................29
    Popular Theatre in Niger........................35
    Endnotes..47
Chapter II: THE TROUPES AND THEIR REHEARSAL
           PROCESS.....................................59
    The Development of a Theme......................63
    The Arrangement of Scenes.......................69
    The Distribution of Roles.......................76
    The Role of the Director........................82
    Actor Training in Rehearsal.....................87
    The Rehearsal Process...........................93
    Improvisation in Performance...................110
    Endnotes.......................................115
Chapter III: PLAY STRUCTURE.........................131
    Narrative Patterns.............................139
    Social Drama Form..............................151
    Endnotes.......................................159
Chapter IV: CHARACTERS IN ACTION....................165
    Serious Characters.............................172
    Comic Characters...............................184
    Central Characters.............................200
    Endnotes.......................................219
Chapter V: PERFORMANCE: THE TROUPES AND THEIR
          AUDIENCES..................................239
    Endnotes.......................................259
Conclusion: GADO K'ARHIN ALLA.......................265
    Endnotes.......................................275
Bibliography..277
Recorded Interviews.................................287
Recorded Plays......................................289
Appendix..291
    ALHAJI SHAGALI.................................292
    BA GA IRINTA BA................................295
    'DAN KWANGILA..................................298
    DARAJAR K'ASA AL'ADARTA........................302
    GADO K'ARHIN ALLA..............................306
    KOWA YA BUGI RUWA IDONAY.......................309
    KUSKURE KARATU NE..............................312
    TALALA MAI KAMAN SAKE..........................316
    WALWALE..320
Index...323

ACRONYMS

BDRN	Banque du Développement de la République du Niger
BIAO	Banque Internationale de l'Afrique de l'Ouest
CEG	Collège d'Enseignement Général
CELHTO	Centre d'Etudes Linguistique et Historique par Tradition Orale
IRSH	Institut de Recherches en Sciences Humaines
MJC	Maison des Jeunes et de la Culture
OPEN	Office des Petites Entreprises Nigériennes
ORTN	Office de Radiodiffusion-Télévision du Niger

ACKNOWLEDGMENTS

>Wannan ba da suna ne kam, banza da wohi, don mutum guda ba shi iya yi komi. Ba ya yiwuwa.
>(This giving of only one name is ridiculous, it's worthless, because one person alone can't do anything. It isn't possible).
>
>>Mahamadou Lido
>>Actor, Mainé Soroa Troupe

More people than I can name have helped with this project. I thank them all--the actors of the Hausa troupes, the people of Niger who welcomed me and my work, and the scholars and friends there and here who helped to shape my writing.

My research was funded by a Fulbright Hays Doctoral Dissertation Research Abroad Fellowship and facilitated by equipment from the Laboratories for Recorded Instruction, University of Wisconsin--Madison, and tapes from the Archives for Traditional Music, Indiana University. I am especially grateful to Frances Rothstein of the UW Fellowships Office and Anita Eikens of LRI for their administrative and technical help.

In Niger, the staff of the Institut de Recherches en Sciences Humaines (IRSH) of the University of Niamey provided assistance in obtaining official clearance, affiliation, and letters of introduction for my research. The staffs of the Centre d'Etudes Linguistique et Historique par Tradition Orale (CELHTO) and of the Office de Radiodiffusion/Télévision du Niger (ORTN) generously assisted me in using their archives and in recording and copying tapes of plays. I thank the directors of these offices, Djibo Hamani of IRSH, Dioulde Laya of CELHTO, and Mochtar Diallo and Mamane Bakabé of

ORTN, for their gracious encouragement of my research.

To Aboubacar Mahamane, the Hausa transcriber of CELHTO, I owe profound thanks for many hours of interviews, recordings and transcription. I hope that someday he will write his own study of the Hausa theatre.

Of the many theatre people who shared their time, creativity and laughter with me, I would like particularly to thank the members of the Troupe Amadou 'Dan Bassa, the Radio Club Troupe and the ORTN Troupe of Zinder, the Troupe Théâtrale de Mainé Soroa, and their leaders--Yazi Dogo, Oumarou Nainou, Abdou Louché, Alhaji Abdousalam Adam, Sani Na'Awa, Mamman Manzo, Alhaji Zoubeirou Lawal and Mahamadou Lido. I remain a pupil of their masterful work.

In my travels through Niger, I am grateful to Susan McCoskrie, Francie Pouch, Carol Terris, Karen Martensen and the other Peace Corps volunteers who shared their homes with me, to Lesley Mortimer who nursed me back to health, and to Tom, Barbara, and John Hale who cheerfully welcomed me at all the odd times I appeared in Niamey. My thanks also to Djibo Aman of Zinder for crucial commissions, to his wives Abou, Nana, and Sarkina for food, friendship, and the daily news, and to Abou's brother, Sanoussi Nakata, for help with transcription.

The writing of my dissertation in Madison was primarily funded by a Knapp Fellowship from the University of Wisconsin. To the members of the Department of African Languages and Literature I owe many years of guidance, encouragement, and support. I thank Neil Skinner, my advisor throughout my graduate career and the chairman of my dissertation committee, for his sage counsel and wry wit. I thank Linda Hunter for her careful reading of draft chapters and her refreshing sense of perspective, Harold Scheub for his unbounded enthusiasm and incisive critiques, Edris Makward for his thoughtful comments and comparisons. I would also like to thank James Moy and Phillip Zarilli of the Department of Theatre and Drama for their theoretical suggestions and inspiring questions. To Richard Ralston and Nellie McKay of the Department of Afro-American Studies, I extend warm thanks for sharing their time, humor, and wisdom about all things academic.

I am deeply grateful to Connie Stephens who first suggested that I study the Hausa theatre and who has followed the progress of this project from one continent to the other, adding her keen insight and ever-practical suggestions at many points of transition.

For the final manifestation of the thesis, I thank Mimi and Bill Berry, friends in need, for their word processor and for the generous donation of their time teaching me to use it and rescuing lost files. For its reincarnation as a camera-ready manuscript, I thank Barbara Peters, a friend indeed, for the final editing and solving the endless glitches in transformation from one computer program to another. Thanks also to Jeff Jordan for his technical assistance.

And for my family and extended family of friends who smiled, wrote, and called to say "hello" and **"du courage"** throughout this journey, I reserve very special thanks.

As the dissertation slowly became a book, I am grateful to Skip Gates for his kind recommendations, to Julia Johnson, Pamela Chergotis and the staff of Garland Press for their patience and cheerful suggestions.

Chapter two was originally presented as a paper at the African Literature Association's (ALA) annual meetings in 1983 at the University of Illinois (Urbana). It was subsequently published by the ALA and is reproduced with their permission from AFRICAN LITERATURE IN ITS SOCIAL AND POLITICAL DIMENSIONS, eds. Eileen Julien, et al. (Washington D.C.: Three Continents Press, 1985) (copyright ALA).

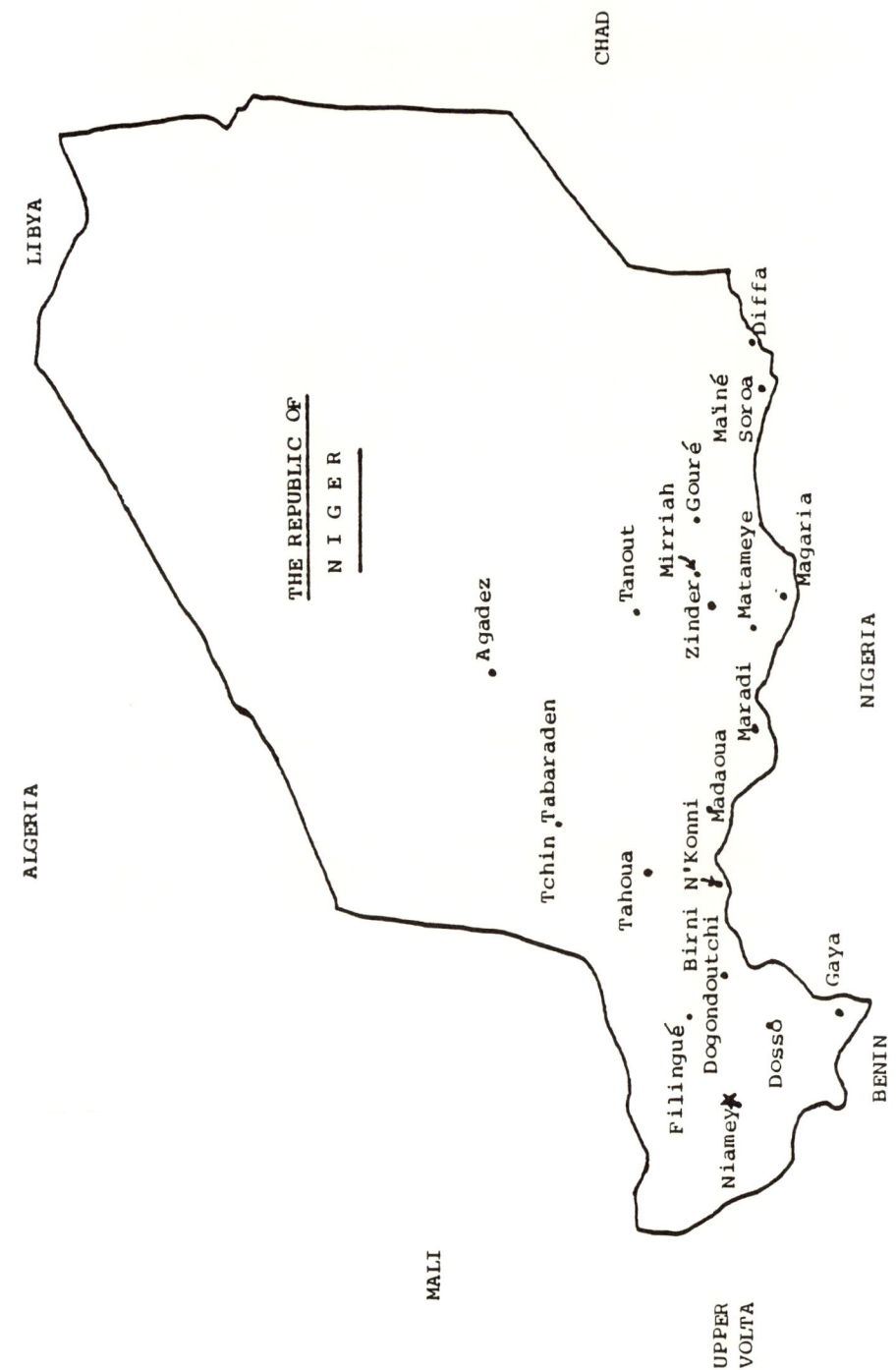

Wasan Kara, Zinder, Niger, June 1981. Actor Sinni Sanda as Nigeria's President Shagari speaking to the crowd.

Actor/Director Yazi Dogo of the Troupe Amadou 'Dan Bassa of Zinder.

Actor/Director Alhaji Zoubeirou Lawal of the Maine Soroa Troupe. He was awarded the prize for Best Actor for his portrayal of Alhaji Shagali in the 1981 Diffa Festival.

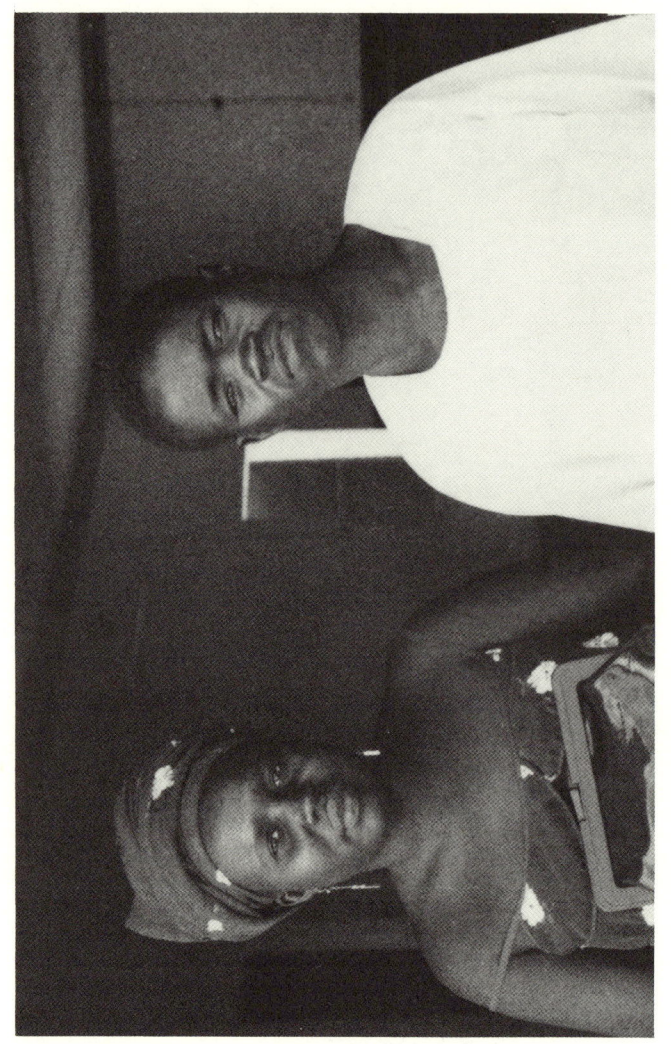

Actors Ladi Saley and Mamman Lawal of the Troupe Amadou 'Dan Bassa of Zinder.

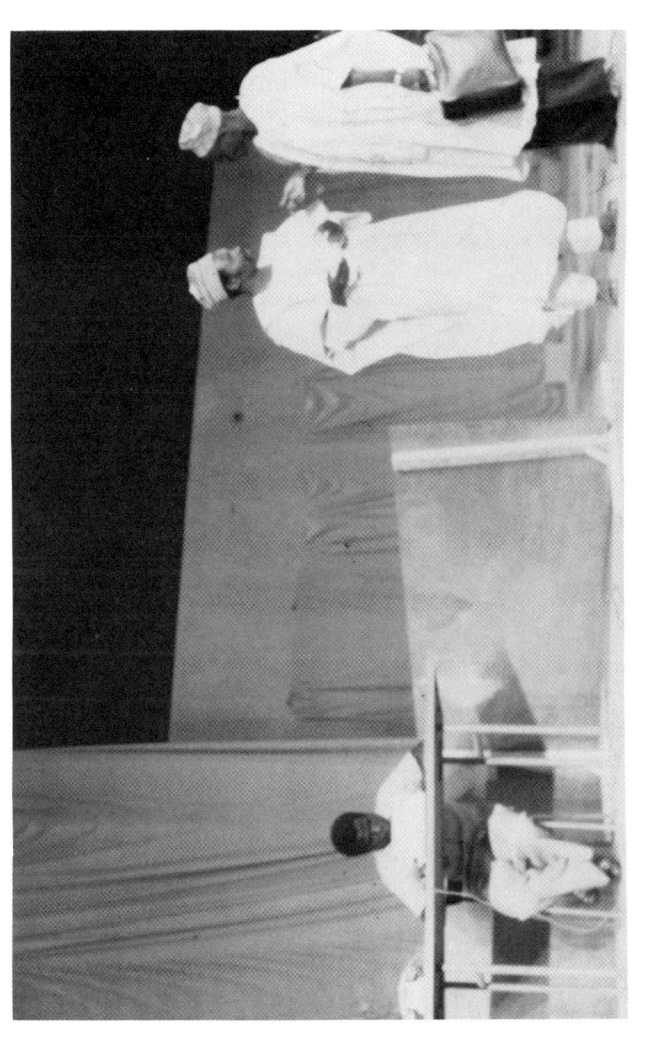

Alhaji Rangama and Alhaji Gimshik'i discuss how to get a loan quickly at the bank. *Dan Kwangila*, Scene 3, performance by the Maradi Troupe at the Diffa Festival, April 1981.

Walwale attends the town meeting to discuss the pump project for the village school; he sits at the edge of the meeting among the women and refuses to contribute to the project. *Walwale*, Scene 1, performance by the Agadez Troupe at the Diffa Festival, April 1981.

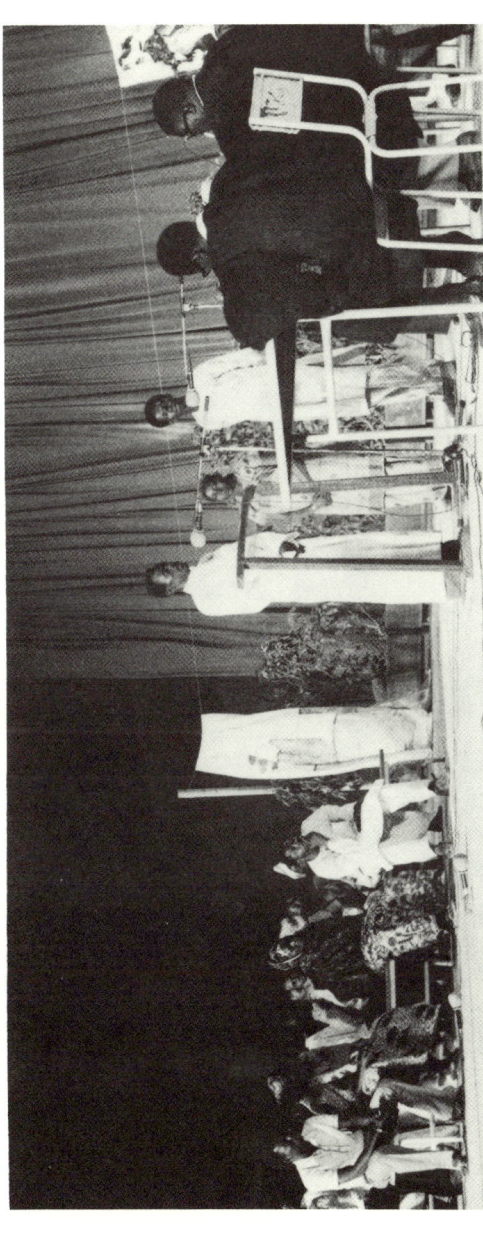

Talala faces the judges to account for his abuse of his late brother's estate. To his left stands his niece, who brought the complaint against him, and the court clerk. Seated in the background are Talala's nephew, his widowed sister-in-law, and the other witnesses. *Talala Mai Kaman Sake,* Scene 7, performance by the Troupe Amadou 'Dan Bassa of Zinder at the Diffa Festival, April 1981.

Horsemen in the Diffa Festival parade.

The stage at Tahoua, typical of the acting spaces in Niger's larger towns. This theatre was built for the 1977 Festival.

INTRODUCTION

The first Hausa play I attended was quite by accident. I had been teaching English in Dogondoutchi, Niger, as a Peace Corps volunteer for a full year (1976-77) without realizing that my secondary students performed plays regularly at the **Maison des Jeunes**. One day, the other American teacher and I saw a sign in the market for a play that evening, asked about it, and decided to go. We arrived too late to get seats, but some of our students made room for us in the second row. Children of all ages crammed around us struggling to see the stage, a cement platform about a foot high in front of the **banco** house that served as the town's **Maison des Jeunes**. Dogondoutchi had no electricity at the time; the stage was lit by a row of oil lamps across the front and by the moon and stars. Young and very noisy, the audience was a most appreciative one; it was extremely difficult to hear the dialogue amid the laughter, shouts, and comments of the spectators. I cannot recall clearly the story of this play, but one scene--a group of men praying--remains utterly vivid in my memory as the funniest moment in the theatre I have ever experienced. The male student actors, dressed in their fathers' robes, lined up behind the prayer leader to perform the ritual Muslim prayers together--bending, bowing, and touching their foreheads to the ground. In the midst of this solemn ritual arrived a drummer with a group of dancing girls. One by one, the back row of pious men began to twitch in time to the beat, at first within the motions of the prayer but gradually sliding into the dance. The back row, then the middle row, then the front row, and finally the prayer leader himself were converted by the music from prayer to dance. Without a word of dialogue, they all danced offstage, leaving the audience in riotous laughter. Whether these students had even seen such a scene, or had created it on their own, I do not know, but their performance held the fine edge between parody and blasphemy.

I returned to Niger three years later to study this thriving theatrical tradition, of which the student plays are only a secondary part. My year of research (1980-81) took me all over the country to collect and record as many of the plays as I could and to interview their creators. I found Nigeriens everywhere--government officials, theatre people and audience members alike--to be quite enthusiastic about my work; they felt their theatre to be important and were pleased to have it preserved on tape and in photographs as well as in a written form for the first time. My intentions were to begin to document this tradition, very little of which has been recorded, and to investigate the creative process behind the plays--how they are developed; where their themes, plots and characters originate; to what extent western drama and the oral tradition have influenced them.

My research divided into five periods of different sorts of work. In December 1980 and January 1981, I travelled to five of Niger's seven **départements** to gather information about the active Hausa troupes. Much of the information I obtained in these meetings and interviews was of a general nature--facts about the troupes (the number of members, their age range, whether women and children were included, actors' other occupations, etc.); how the group worked (the director's role, communal decisions, who chooses themes for the plays); definitions of plays as a genre and how they differ from **ballets** and storytelling; and the purposes of theatrical productions both for the performers and for their audiences. At this time, the troupes were unwilling to discuss their current work for the national festival that April because of the competition involved with other troupes I would be meeting.

In March 1981, I observed the preliminary competition, held in Tanout, among the troupes of the Zinder Département for the performance categories of drama, dance, song and instrumental ensemble. Following these first public performances of their festival offerings, I was permitted to attend the month of final rehearsals by the troupes chosen to represent the **département**.

Introduction

In April, The National Festival of Youth and Culture was held in Diffa with performance competitions each evening among the seven **départements**, which I photographed and recorded on tape. Following the festival, I arranged interviews with the three leading troupes (from Maradi, Mainé Soroa, and Zinder) about their plays. In these interviews, as in the earlier ones before the festival, Aboubacar Mahamane of the Centre for Oral Traditions in Niamey (CELHTO) provided invaluable assistance.

In June 1981, I settled in Zinder for six months to observe the work of the three theatre troupes there: the Radio Club Troupe, the ORTN (**Office de Radiodiffusion/Télévision du Niger**) Troupe which performs weekly serial plays on the radio, and the Troupe Amadou 'Dan Bassa of the **Maison des Jeunes**, probably the best known Hausa troupe in the country and the closest to a national troupe. Each of these troupes had work in progress, both rehearsals and performances, which they allowed me to observe. At the same time, I worked on transciptions of several plays, with constant opportunity to ask questions of the actors who had created them.

In October, I returned to Niamey to use the videotapes at the national television station (ORTN), the only recorded versions of some of the famous past plays. The results of all this research appear in the following chapters.

The current Hausa plays in Niger are called **teyatur** in Hausa, derived from the French **théâtre**, although the Hausa term common in Nigeria, **wasan kwaikwayo**, is also used. Play performances occur most often in the evenings and usually in conjuction with other events--songs, the traditionally based dance/dramas know as **ballets**, and/or instrumental pieces. The plays are not a traditional Hausa form, but one derived from western theatre during the colonial period. They are staged on raised platforms in front of a seated audience in outdoor auditoriums. Actors play fictional characters in a series of scenes, with breaks in between, that develop a story. Yet these are not typically western plays. There are no playwrights, no scripts, and often no directors. The troupes create their plays through communal work, largely through improvisation, drawing on their village traditions and backgrounds. A new, dramatic oral tradition is forming, with its own conventions of structure, characters, themes, and improvisational performance. This dynamic process has only just begun, yet the plays have already found mass audiences throughout the country, exciting prospects in local television, and a significant place in national development efforts as a means of instruction as well as entertainment. Troupes are springing up in communities in every region to perform live productions, and plays form an important and popular segment of radio and television programming.

    Chapter I outlines a background history of this theatre, sketching some of the traditional Hausa forms that contribute to the current plays--market comedy, satiric poetry, and the like--and some of the French theatre models Niger inherited from colonial times. Very little has been written on either of these topics. I have included as many specific references as I could find, relying on secondary sources because so few of the early plays were published and even fewer descriptions exist of actual performances. This chapter also discusses the movement toward theatre in national languages, primarily Hausa, in the 1970's, and the government's support for drama through the national festival competition and the community organizations, the **samariyas**, which sponsor the majority of the contemporary troupes.

    Chapter II explores the rehearsal process of the theatre troupes whose plays I recorded in 1980-81. It is based on interviews with members of fourteen different troupes and my observations of rehearsals by the three troupes in Zinder. While each troupe exhibits a unique style, a common pattern of work appears in their discussions of how they develop their plays. After determining a central theme, the troupe arranges a scenic framework, assigns roles, and works out the details of characters and actions through improvisation. The chapter presents each step of this process as expressed by the troupe members and as I saw it unfold in rehearsals.

    Chapter III examines the structure of the plays--their use of stock scenes and repetition,

Introduction 5

their links to the narrative tradition, and their relation to current social conflicts.

Chapter IV discusses different character types and their functions within the plays. Most roles can be broadly defined as comic or serious types, with the central characters combining the two. Recurring character types show direct descent from the oral narrative tradition in their actions if not always in name.

Chapter V attempts to put the plays into their proper milieu--performance. The troupes perform before two different types of audiences: their own communities and the more diversified national audiences viewing the festival or television productions. Such performance elements as the language of the play, its costumes, settings, properties, and even the themes, comedy and improvisational style of acting may change in relation to the expected audience for any given performance.

My conclusion focusses on a single play, GADO K'ARHIN ALLA, the only Nigerien Hausa play published to date and considered by many, myself included, to be the best yet produced.

In the Appendix, I have included synopses of the major plays I discuss in these chapters, along with lists of their characters. I have translated all of the Hausa and French quotations into English in my text, but the original languages are included in the notes following each chapter.

A note on the Hausa transcriptions:

Three different orthographies of Hausa are now used in Niger: the French spellings of personal and place names, the UNESCO system (whose most obvious characteristic is the doubling of long vowels) originally adopted by the Oral Traditions Centre (CELHTO) and the Nigerien **Alphabétisation** campaign, and the Nigerien standard based on the Kano dialect.

I have used all three at different times, aware that this creates inconsistencies but trying to remain faithful to the source. Thus, I have kept the common (French) spellings of names, since that is how their Nigerien owners generally spell them. For texts printed in the UNESCO system, I have reproduced the original transcriptions. The following example illustrates the three systems:

> Aboubacar Mahamane (how he normally writes it)
>
> Abuubakar Mahamman (UNESCO system, used for his publication of GAADOO K'ARHIN ALLAA)
>
> Abubakar Mahamman (Nigerian standard)

In 1980, a conference to standardize Hausa transcriptions between Niger and Nigeria adopted most of the Nigerian conventions, dropping the doubled vowels, and using **ai** for **ay**, **au** for **aw**, etc. ("Final Report: Meeting of Experts on the Harmonization of the Orthography of the Hausa Language," Organization of African Unity, CELHTO, Niamey, January 1980).

In my own, as in Aboubacar Mahamane's transcriptions of the 1981 festival plays, these conventions were used. Thus, a character named **Suleman** may be played by an actor named **Souleymane**. I have kept the transcriptions true to Nigerien dialects in sound, however, rather than substituting the standard Kano forms. The most frequent example of this would be **h** or **hw** replacing Kano **f** (**hwa'da** for **fa'da**, **lahiya** for **lafiya**, and so on).

The glottalized consonants **b, d, k,** which are printed as hooked letters in standard Hausa texts, appear here with apostrophes: **'b, 'd, k'**.

CHAPTER I
A HISTORY OF THE THEATRE IN NIGER

    Hausa theatre in Niger follows patterns similar to those of drama described in other parts of Africa. Anthony Graham-White's survey, THE DRAMA OF BLACK AFRICA, categorizes theatrical performances into three types: traditional, literary, and popular, the latter two both emerging from the traditional.(1)
    Traditional drama in his schema refers to a wide range of performances which contain such common elements as: the integral role of music, dance and song; the use of improvisation and interaction between the performers and the audience; the use of masks and costumes more often than scenic elements; stock characters; repetition; and a grounding in well-known mythology. He notes that these elements are characteristic of traditional drama in many places outside of Africa as well and that they describe the drama but do not define it.(2)
    Literary drama is based on written scripts as in the western tradition, whereas popular drama tends to be improvised. Graham-White describes popular drama as similar to the traditional drama in its methods of developing a performance, particularly through improvisation, and its use of local languages. However, it has developed as a primarily urban entertainment with the aim of profit in attracting mass audiences, unlike traditional drama which was free and accessible to all.(3)
    The current Hausa theatre in Niger falls into this category of popular theatre with roots in traditional theatrical forms and influenced by exposure to western literary drama and performance conventions.

Traditional Theatre

Discussions of traditional African performances define and classify them in a variety of ways but generally agree as to what constitutes the dramatic in traditional life. E.T. Kirby approaches African theatre on the basis of enactment, a performer representing another being or character before an audience.(4) He then describes seven categories of African performance with examples from all over the continent.

1) Simple enactments (such as hunting pantomime or women acting out proper household conduct for young girl initiates)

2) Ritual and ritualized enactments (abstract symbolic actions)

3) Storytelling performances (including songs, the audience as chorus, and the representation by the storyteller of characters in the story through voice, gesture, etc.)

4) Spirit-cult performances (characterized by the "theatricalization of persons possessed by particular spirits")(5)

5) Masquerades and masquerade enactments

6) Ceremonial performances ("formalized action presented to sanction political, social, or religious concepts... but it is not inherently symbolic as is ritual action")(6)

7) Comedies (short farces or satiric skits).

Each of these types of performance could be found in traditional Hausa society, as for many other peoples.

A History

From an historical perspective, Robert Cornevin includes early accounts of African theatre by French explorers, missionaries, and colonialists, in LE THEATRE EN AFRIQUE NOIRE ET A MADAGASCAR.(7) These accounts include dance performances, representational ceremonies, pantomime, praise-singing, performances by **griots** (oral historians and poets) and buffoons, games, storytelling, puppetry, and Mandingo theatre in Mali with stories enacted by male actors and musical accompaniment by an orchestra and a choir of women.(8) Among these descriptions recorded at random by Europeans, the only one specifically referring to the Hausa people is an account of puppets cited by Labouret and Travélé in 1928 from their travels through the savannah belt of West Africa. Their original note:

> On the other hand, in certain Hausa villages in the French colony of Niger, one can see wooden puppets appearing in real performances in the markets during the important Muslim festivals. The puppeteer sits hidden behind his robe; through its opening, with an invisible hand, he presents the ordinary characters of comedy--the husband, the wife and the lover. This practice appears to come from North Africa.(9)

Two reviews of specifically Hausa theatrical forms have been written, one for Nigeria and the other for Niger. Ibrahim Yaro Yahaya's paper, "Nazari Kan Yanayin Wasan Kwaikwayon Hausa" ("An Investigation of the State of Hausa Plays"), presented at a Hausa Language Conference in Kano, Nigeria, in 1978, presents a definition of Hausa drama and briefly discusses a range of dramatic customs in traditional Hausa society.(10) According to Yahaya, the term **wasan kwaikwayo** from **wasa** (song, game, joke) and **kwaikwayo** (to imitate) explains itself: it is partly play and partly an imitation of real life, a way for people to understand things, both good and evil.(11) He lists a variety of traditional customs to demonstrate the antiquity of drama in Hausa life, including the following:

A. Children's Games

1) **Langa** (a game boys play in pairs holding one foot with one hand and trying to knock the other down). This becomes drama when played by teams organizing a match for an audience, with the champion gaining recognized sovereignty over the neighborhood or village, and the other boys on his team acting as his attendants and warriors.

2) **'Dan Akuyana** (the goat). Children gather in a circle, representing the granary, while one child (the goat) in the center tries to butt his way out.

3) **Bikin 'yar tsana** (celebration of the dolls). Girls act out the rites of marriage for their dolls.

4) **Wasannan Tashe** (games during the Islamic month of fasting). These games, played in the evenings after the fast has been broken, include boys dressing up as old bearded men and begging from house to house, or boys acting as herbal doctors peddling their charms and bits of bone, seeds, roots and the like, from door to door. Girls act out the

A History

marriage of Mairama and Daudu, a bride and groom.

B. Adults' Theatrical Customs

1) **Bori** (the spirit possession cult). Each spirit requires certain accoutrements for the person it enters and the possessed person acts in stylized ways. For example, Malam Alhaji (the Muslim pilgrim) is received by his initiates who are dressed all in white with prayer beads, and who perform the ablutions before prayer and other characteristically Islamic movements.

2) **Dabo-Dabo** (puppets). The performers create a special space in the marketplace or other public area, marked by cloth or robes hung on sticks, within which they sit to manipulate the puppets. The puppets are characters such as young lovers, the false **malam**, or boxers.

3) **Kalankuwa** is a festival after the harvest for young, unmarried men and women to choose leaders for their respective organizations. The **sarkin samari**, the leader of the young men, appoints a court modeled after that of the real village **sarki** and hears court cases (complaints) from the

youth. Communal work projects, dances and celebrations also occur during the several days of the festival.

4) Other examples Yahaya mentions without elaboration include the **'yan kama** and **'yan gambara** (itinerant, comic poet-musicians); the **wasan sarki** (court fool); and the **'yan hoto** or **nabiso** (a group of dancers who perform knife tricks and like entertainments).(12)

Yahaya does not demonstrate specifically how these traditional forms relate to current theatre practices, but his main point is clear: a wealth of play and imitative activities form a strong background to present-day Hausa culture, providing a variety of resources for the theatre to use, consciously or not.

Dan-Inna Chaibou's master's thesis, "La Théâtralité en Pays Hawsa," written in 1978-79, is the only critical work on Hausa theatre in Niger I have yet discovered.(13) Chaibou compares traditional and modern forms of Hausa theatrical performance in order to see whether twentieth century theatre can take inspiration from traditional forms to seek a fusion.(14) He purposely uses the term **théâtralité** instead of **théâtre** to include a wide range of performances, rejecting western definitions of theatre which would exclude much of the traditional African experience.(15) Chaibou divides traditional Hausa theatrical forms into two categories, the sacred and the secular. For the sacred drama, he describes two different performances in detail, without by any means claiming these to be the only types.

The first of these performances, the **kora**,(16) is a traditional religious ceremony which Islam has eliminated in most Hausa regions. Chaibou's description comes from Tahoua in north central Niger, one of the areas where it still occurs. The verb **kora** means to expel, and the performance is organized in order to expel the evil spirits from the village. According to Chaibou, the **kora** takes place on the last Thursday before the Islamic month of fasting, a month during which non-Islamic manifestations are forbidden to occur. It begins in front of the house of the **sarkin bori** (the head of the spirit possession cult), where musicians, **bori** initiates and non-initiated spectators gather. The music for each spirit is played and the initiates become possessed, each dressed in the apparel appropriate to his or her spirit and dancing, gesturing, or moving in accordance with that spirit's demands. At the peak of the mounting intensity, the **sarkin bori** gives a signal for the **kora** to begin and the entire crowd--spirits (inhabiting their human "mounts") and spectators alike--travels all over town to each place where the evil spirits dwell. In Tahoua there are six such locations, all rocky outcrops. At each stop, the possessed actors wage a battle with the spirits of the rocks, using arrows, knives, sabres, and other weapons to drive them out. At the final stopping point, the initiates sacrifice a calf in secrecy, away from the crowd, and the **sarkin bori** informs the spectators what they should do to insure peace for the coming year (private sacrifices, etc.). Exhausted, the possessed actors cough three times, the signal for the spirits to depart, and the initiates regain their own personalities. The **kora** ends with this departure of the good spirits after the bad have been driven off, but human celebrations continue into the night with feasting, dancing, and rejoicing at the commencement of another peaceful year.(17)

The second type of performance Chaibou discusses is the coronation of a regional chief (**sarki**), a ceremony that is subject to precise rites whose origins are lost in time.(18) The specific coronation Chaibou describes took place in Filingué, in the Kourfay region of Niger, northeast of Niamey. The ceremony traditionally occurs forty days after the death of the former **sarki**, and one week after the election of his successor from among the male relatives of the royal family. The entire village assembles in front of the **sarki's** house, including musicians, praisesingers, and representatives from other communities in the region. Everyone has an assigned place to sit or stand according to his rank and position. At the arrival of the **sarki** led by the **doka**, the cult official who will install him, the crowd is silent and the ritual begins.

The **sarki** follows the **doka** three times around a white mat, and the **doka** dresses him in special robes with two attempts before completing each gesture on the third trial. The **sarki** sits on the mat, again with two gestures before he completes the act, and raises his hand three times to stop the praises and songs being performed for him; this indicates that he is not vain or swayed by the flattery. Feasting and musical praise performances continue long after the actual installment rite has ended. Chaibou explains the major symbols in the ceremony in this way: three is the ritual number for males (four for females), the white mat symbolizes royalty, while the black, white and red garments are consecrated to **Sarawniya**, the spirit protector of the chief (black stands for a bull, white for milk, and red for blood). Chaibou states that the actions and ritual represent the agreement by the gods to aid a man in his duties, to delegate part of their power to him. This in turn raises the status of the **sarki** above his people and gives him unique rights and privileges. He is no longer to be addressed by his name but by his title, **sarki**, or **Biya Muradi** ("May your wishes be fulfilled").(19)

Chaibou analyzes both the coronation and the exorcism ceremonies in terms of their theatrical and ritual elements. He sees the **kora** as theatrical in its essential elements: actors, spectators, and the imitation of war. It is ritual in that all the participants believe in the efficacy of the ceremony, that they are in fact expelling spirits from the town. Nor are the actors conscious of imitating war, because they are in a state of possession. This fact for Chaibou marks it as ritual.(20) For the coronation ceremony, Chaibou defines as theatrical the fact of two actors performing before the public, not with dialogue but with ritual gestures charged with significance. Here, both the **sarki** and the **doka** are aware that they are performing, unlike the possessed initiates during the **kora**, but their performance is regulated by the dictates of tradition. Their roles, however, are not separated from their social roles; the **doka's** role in the community includes the duty of installing the **sarki**, and the **sarki** assumes his ruling role during the ceremony.(21) Again, as in the **kora**, ritual unites integrally with the theatrical. This combination leads Chaibou to describe these events as sacred because of the role of the spirits/gods and because of their social functions in the community.(22) Yet they are theatre, nonetheless.

Ritual material of this sort has been used as the basis for modern theatre, most notably by Wole Soyinka who puts Yoruba ritual at the center of the action in plays such as THE STRONG BREED, and DEATH AND THE KING'S HORSEMAN.(23) Similarly, the enthronement of a **sarki** forms the core of GAADOO K'ARHIN ALLAA (Inheritance, Strength from God), the best known Hausa play and the only one published to date in Hausa in Niger.(24)

Chaibou describes the hunter's praisesinging as practiced in the Arewa region in south central Niger, a region where traditional religion retains a stronghold and where hunting has survived longer than in other areas. Traditional beliefs make the successful hunter a hero, for hunting is a battle between two forces of nature, two sets of spirits, the man's and the animal's; to kill a wild animal requires spiritual powers, knowledge of certain secrets, as well as physical prowess. Poets appear in the wake of these hunter-heroes to sing their praises. Known as **mai komo** or **mai gurumi**, these poets accompany themselves on a guitar-like instrument (the **komo** or **gurumi**). With the decline of hunting in recent years, the poets can no longer make a living from hunters' praises alone; many work on farms or have taken up other forms of praisesinging, diversifying their repertoires.(26)

The text Chaibou analyzes, "Na Giamma," was performed by Maida, a **mai komo** originally from the Arewa, a man born into the trade. He sings both material which was passed on to him and his own creations; he now praises the local chief in addition to the few hunters in the Filingué area where he lives. "Na Giamma" praises 'Danladi, a local hunter, the husband of Giamma. Chaibou's recording of Maikomo Maida's performance was in front of 'Danladi's house before a number of spectators.

The poem follows Maikomo from Filingué to Zinder in search of 'Danladi who has promised him an animal to sacrifice for the Muslim festival. Maikomo arrives in the middle of the night, but 'Danladi, a man of honor, immediately takes him out into the bush to find a bull elephant, in order to fulfill his vow. They see several other animals first, but none will do except the elephant. Maikomo portrays himself, the poet, as a coward in all these adventures, adding further glorification to 'Danladi's strength and courage when they finally see a herd of elephants and 'Danladi kills ten with one blow. So huge is one of the beasts that one hundred men, called by Maikomo for the purpose, are needed to skin it before 'Danladi can present the meat and organs to Maikomo.(27)

Music and mime form essential parts of this performance as Chaibou describes it. The instrumental accompaniment of the **komo** emphasizes intense moments of the narration and the singing emphasizes the poetry, the beauty of the rhymes.(28) The **mai komo** mimes certain gestures of the characters in the story (one of whom is himself), and he uses stylized movements for certain repeated segments; for example, he extends his hand each time he chants the line, "Wuce ba nan ba" ("Go on, it's not here"), as they pass each of the animals in the bush.(29) Chaibou also points out that the **mai komo's** voice changes between the straight narration and the direct speech of the characters; thus, the poet assumes the character's role.(30) According to Chaibou, the poet represents the actions of his narrative-song before his audience, but he evokes the action in the imagination of his audience rather than concretely portraying the actual movement as in western theatre.(31) For this, the form of the poetry, its rhythm, the type of musical accompaniment, the performer's voice, and the familiar patterns and subjects all aid the theatrical evocation of the story in the audience's imagination. Chaibou's account here echoes Harold Scheub's analysis of a consummate storyteller in "Body and Image in Oral Narrative Performance."(32) There may be only one actor, but he creates an entire world for his audience through poetry, voice and gesture.

A second traditional type of poet, the **'dan kama**, reigns supreme in comedy. Chaibou describes the **'dan kama** (literally, one who catches/tricks, pl. **'yan kama**) as a **griot**, the embodiment of comedy, a juggler, dancer and player with words, a popular performer obsessed with food.(33) Typically, the 'dan kama arrives in a village with his troupe, is received by the head of the griots, and then parades around the public square on market day to perform. His characteristic garb consists of hitched-up trousers, with no shirt, and he carries a wooden sword and a tambourine under his arm, which he also uses to catch money, cola nuts and other items thrown to him. He performs a series of songs in succession, but the principal theme of all of them is food; while singing he uses his sword to snatch food from the wayside vendors to the delight of his audience.(34)

In his study, Chaibou includes three poem-songs from a 'dan kama. The first is an imitation of the prayer of blind men begging for alms; the 'dan kama, however, begs not for pardon for his sins but for food and drink.(35) The second piece presents the 'dan kama as the hero of food. He takes a well-known praise poem to a wrestler, Ado, and compares himself to Ado.(36) The various foods are all afraid of the 'dan kama, but even champions like Ado cannot resist hunger and are dependent on food; therefore, the 'dan kama, ruler of food, proclaims himself the true champion.(37) The third song gives advice to a man who complains that his son does not know how to eat cassava.(38)

The 'dan kama plays everything to comic effect. His chorus supports him musically and in the performance of his jokes; they sometimes imitate other characters, but only briefly, as Chaibou says--a mere wink at the spectators.(39) The 'dan kama imitates other people, as in the first piece where he pretends to be the blind man, but the pretense is always transparent, a parody. The 'dan kama primarily portrays his own role, the ultimate glutton, with traits stylized to the extreme.(40)

Chaibou analyzes the comedy of these performances in terms of the character of a 'dan kama himself, marked by his exaggerated traits: gluttony, greed, boastfulness, etc. The words he uses are comic, often burlesques of serious poetry, as are his gestures: uninhibited antics with abrupt reversals of mood and pace, as he dances, juggles, imitates people, and throws himself at the vendors throughout the marketplace.(41) Chaibou contrasts the exuberance of the 'dan kama's play to the concise, stylized and poetic recitation of the **mai komo**,(42) but both are inherently theatrical.

Another study of the **'dan kama**, C.G.B. Gidley's "'**Yankamanci**--the Craft of the Hausa Comedians," uses written records of performances in the 1920's and compares them to material of the 1960's, the period of his study.(43) Gidley's account of a performance by Haji Katsina in 1928, written by a student who later became the Emir of Abuja, notes material similar to Chaibou's account: imitations of a Qur'anic scholar, a porter and country dancers. In addition, it includes two reportedly true stories of rather elaborate impersonations, practical jokes on men in power. In the first, Haji Katsina went to visit the Chief of Wamba, a newly converted Muslim who was known for his hospitality to religious scholars. Haji Katsina posed as a dignified scholar, received a warm welcome, and, on being received by the **sarki** himself, suddenly pulled out his drum to perform--a surprise and delight for the entire court. The second story concerns a visit by Haji Katsina to the Emir of Lafiya, a man renowned for his seriousness. When Haji Katsina's usual performance failed to make the Emir laugh, he suddenly drew his sword when a noble warrior arrived at the court. The famous fighter fled in fear, and then the Emir laughed.(44) According to Gidley, impersonations on this scale have become far less common, less likely, given the spread of radio, television, and general education, since people cannot be fooled so easily. Gidley claims an educative function for these traditional ruses, which became the subject of gossip long after the joke was discovered.(45) In recent years, parodies of popular songs, which are spread by the radio and recordings, have become the main feature of performances by the **'yan kama**. Gidley dates the decline of the craft with World War II and the subsequent introduction of modern forms of entertainment. However, **'yankamanci** has not died out; the comic poets now appear on radio and television in Nigeria.(46)

Gidley's analysis of the craft of a **'dan kama** emphasizes spontaneous performance and the ability to improvise.

> To succeed...a **'dan kama** has to have a retentive memory, well stocked with pieces of acceptable

> nonsense, and with facetious
> comment, interspersed with songs;
> to employ these materials to good
> effect he needs a ready wit and
> dramatic talent.(47)

Each performance may last quite a long time and should appear constantly spontaneous, while the **'dan kama** must avoid giving offence to anyone in a changing audience. Gidley states that the **'dan kama** needs a good knowledge of everyday affairs and a good sense of humor, along with a watchful sense of the audience's reaction and a skillful manipulation of it.(48) A successful **'dan kama** thus requires natural talent and training during actual performances with audience interaction.

Chaibou's conclusions concerning the traditional Hausa theatre echo Gidley's sense of the skill of life-long artists. Chaibou considers secular spectacles, as he has defined them, more elaborate than the religious ones because there is greater aesthetic research, a constant quest for new and better material, a more profound relationship between an artist and his art. The secular artist is conscious of performing and must vary and improve his repertoire to continue making a living from it, whereas the sacred spectacles have their own justification, the sanction of the gods.(49) Yet, in Chaibou's view, both secular and sacred traditional theatre have functions within the society, expressing social preoccupations and enlisting the participation of the entire group. Both inspire interaction between the performer and the public; both retain an integral unity of the different arts--music, poetry, dance and imitation. In these respects, traditional African theatre is different from western theatre. Unfortunately, Chaibou concludes, colonialism relegated this traditional theatre to the level of folklore, now found only in the countryside, and introduced a new and dominant form of spectacle, the modern theatre.(50)

Literary Drama

European written drama was introduced in Africa through the colonial missions and schools. Colonialism manifested itself somewhat differently in the French and British territories, but it brought exposure to western art forms, including theatre, to both.

In comparing the theatre of the British and French colonies in Africa, Anthony Graham-White discusses the crucial difference in colonial educational policies.(51) In the British territories, vernacular drama developed alongside vernacular education, whereas few performances in African languages are recorded in the French territories where all education was conducted in French. French education and policies emphasized acculturation, the assimilation of Africans into the Empire, but the French institutions also offered more support to the arts than did the British system. Graham-White argues that on the whole, drama in the French colonies was better developed than in the British. His list of published plays supports this claim: before 1957, four full-length and twenty-seven short plays were published in French, compared to three long and three short plays published in English.(52) The most influential plays of the colonial period, in Graham-White's view, were those of the elite French teacher's college, the William Ponty School in Senegal. In addition, the French government sponsored cultural centers and tours throughout the West African territories by local and metropolitan theatrical troupes. British support of theatre was, in general, much less extensive and more sporadic.(53)

Yet after independence, drama in English began to flourish while French African drama declined. Graham-White credits this change to the number of French West African states created and the absorption into the new governments of the few educated people. Here again, the French educational system, with its elitist emphasis, left its mark on the theatre and other arts. French-speaking poets and playwrights were needed as administrators, and the first two francophone universities, in Dakar and Abidjan, had no theatre departments, unlike their English counterparts in Accra and Ibadan.(54) One further reason Graham-White suggests for the relative lack of French African drama at the time of independence is the Négritude movement's popularity. He feels Négritude was better suited to poetic than to dramatic expression, in its philosophical emphasis, mystical values, and nostalgic descriptions.(55) Whatever the blend of factors and differences, the colonial records clearly indicate that African drama in French developed earlier than that written in English. Yet the francophone theatre did not maintain its momentum after independence, just as anglophone productions and published plays began to proliferate.

Ibrahim Yaro Yahaya's outline of Hausa literary theatre in Nigeria echoes Graham-White's study. Yahaya states that written plays were introduced to Northern Nigeria in the twentieth century with the arrival of European schools. English drama was part of the curriculum, and plays also provided recreation for the students. Hausa plays soon followed the English models. Prior to this experience, there were no written plays in Hausa, due largely to the dictates of Islam and the monopoly of writing by religious scholars.(56) Yahaya lists fourteen Hausa plays published in Nigeria between 1930 and the date of his paper, 1978, two of which are Hausa translations of plays by Shakespeare and Tawfik al'Hakim.(57)

To date, Niger has only one published Hausa play, GAADOO K'ARHIN ALLAA (1973), which is not a literary creation but rather a transcription of an improvised performance. The contrast between the Hausa communities in Nigeria, a former British colony, and Niger, a former French colony, bolsters Graham-White's conclusions concerning colonial education and African languages. Theatre in Niger followed the French route, with the Hausa dramatic tradition there diverging from that of its Nigerian neighbors.

In his detailed history of the francophone African theatre, Robert Cornevin states that as soon as schools were established in the French colonies at the end of the nineteenth century, the teachers organized dramatic performances for Christmas, Easter, and the distribution of prizes at the end of the school year.(58) Although there remain few records of the earliest such performances, Cornevin's sources note that they were usually scenes from the Bible or history and always in French. As early as 1913 at the teacher-training school in St. Louis, theatre using French texts was encouraged by the director of the school as a remedy for the students' boredom while far away from home.(59) Cornevin also includes descriptions of Church plays in Dahomey, Togo, Cameroun and

Gabon. In the latter two colonies, some local subjects were done as well as French themes, with experiments using folklore and even local languages. Nonetheless, all the pieces were performed during Christian holidays and for the benefit of European audiences and a few educated Africans.(60)

One of the early school theatres, that of the **Ecole Normale de William Ponty** in Senegal, is cited in all the theatre histories of West Africa as a major influence on African theatre in French. The Ponty school was one of the few secondary institutions established in the French colonies, and students from throughout the West African Federation attended it. Cornevin details an account of the Ponty theatre at some length, and Bakary Traoré centers a major part of his analysis on the work of this school in THE BLACK AFRICAN THEATRE AND ITS SOCIAL FUNCTIONS, the first major study of the African theatre by an African, published in 1959 before the majority of West African nations attained independence.(61) While Cornevin's sources, primarily the French administrators and visitors to the school, stress the initiative of the students in creating their plays at Ponty, Traoré's account emphasizes the control and imposing presence of the French faculty and spectators over the students' creativity.

Traoré cites the educational reform of 1933 to "reintegrate" the African students with their backgrounds as the precipitating factor for this theatre. Students at the Ponty School were given holiday assignments to investigate the life and customs in their villages; it was also suggested that they write "indigenous" plays in French for the festival at the end of the school year. The first such play, in 1933 by the Dahomean students, was such a success that original plays became a part of all the festivals in succeeding years. Each regional group of students produced a play drawn from history or folklore; all the writing, acting, and directing were done by the students, to the lavish praise of their audiences, Europeans and assimilated Africans who could follow the French.(62) Plays were taken on tour to towns throughout West Africa and even to Paris in 1937 for the **Exposition Coloniale**. In 1939 the young women at the **Ecole Normale de Rufisque**, the sister school to William Ponty, began to produce plays as well, and they later joined the Ponty students for a production in 1948, the first mixed troupe on record. But by 1948, a change in colonial education which granted French diplomas at schools like Ponty caused the neglect of extracurricular theatre in the more intense scholastic competition.(63)

Cornevin's chapter, "Du Théâtre scolaire au 'théâtre universitaire' de Ponty," includes copious documentation of the Ponty phenomenon. He credits Charles Béart, teacher and later director at the school, as the "father of African theatre."(64) Although there is a small controversy over whether this "indigenous" theatre began at the Bingerville School or at William Ponty, Béart was associated with both schools. Cornevin records two versions of the beginning of this student drama: one on laundry day and the other a student protest over buttons for their new uniforms. In both stories, the students began an impromptu satire of military and village characters, with Charles Béart observing the fun from his window. Béart was then inspired, according to his memoirs, to institute theatre as a regular extracurricular activity for the boys. Béart described the students' satire as a re-invention of the **Commedia dell'Arte**.(65)

Béart's objectives in promoting education and the arts at Ponty were, as Cornevin notes, global. Cornevin quotes Béart's article, "Le Théâtre indigène et la culture franco-africaine," as saying:

> Not only do we seek to create material well-being, but we also want to develop all the artistic powers that the race possesses. Therefore, in our schools, we have given an important place to arts and crafts preserving tradtional skills. To further assure their development, we have special establishments where professional European artists immerse themselves in indigenous techniques in order to allow them to evolve without becoming corrupted.(66)

Béart further described the theatre as an excellent lesson in French, the opportunity for students to expand their command of the language by seeking to express traditional proverbs, songs, and the like, in French.(67) Béart's paternalistic, colonial outlook gives credence to Traoré's argument that the plays were not as indicative of the students' thought as they were of the guidance of their French patrons.

The dialogues of the Ponty plays were in French, although the songs, which formed an integral part of the dance and action, were usually in the common local language of the regional groups of students. According to Cornevin's sources and plot synopses, the plays were about historical situations or were representations of traditional customs such as coronations, circumcisions and weddings. Some plays presented current problems and concerns of the students, as in the conflict between an educated daughter and her parents when they arrange a traditional marriage for her. With respect to sets and costumes for these performances, Cornevin's quotations from journalists and administrators who witnessed the plays suggest that the costumes were the traditional clothing of the students from their own wardrobes, and the scenery consisted of painted backdrops (one report described two alternating scenes, one "sunny" and one "sad").(68) Traoré records that the students rejected the use of masks as a policy; they preferred to place emphasis instead on the verbal elements of the plays.(69) He notes elsewhere that scenery was far less important in traditional African theatre than costumes,(70) a characteristic which is reflected in the descriptions of the Ponty theatre.

Traoré's analysis of the Ponty theatre indicates the strong influence of French models in the students' emphasis on the written play over improvisation, the structuring of the plays into acts and scenes with intervals, and the development of plots with an eye to cause and effect, an exposition/development/denouement structure after the seventeenth century French classics.(71) The African elements--songs, dances, costumes, themes--apparently were subordinated to the overall western form. This emulation of French theatre would also explain the students' rejection of masks, which were strong symbols of traditional cultures.

Cornevin stresses that although the Ponty productions were student affairs, those students were not ordinary youths. The students at the Ponty School were the elite of West Africa, chosen by a rigorous selection process and usually several years older than their French counterparts. The Ponty School trained not only teachers but administrators and pre-medical students, who later became the leaders, doctors and administrators of their respective countries.(72) The theatre these students produced was correspondingly important: their audiences included the Governor-General and other high administrative officials of the French West African Federation.(73) Moreover, the Ponty performances in Paris in 1937 received exceptional praise from the French press; although, as Cornevin remarks, it was a time when patriotic loyalty to France was reassuring in the face of Germany's growing power in Europe.(74) The Ponty theatre thus achieved importance in several spheres as a symbol of imperial success, unity, and the French ideal of assimilation.

In contrast to the contemporary adulation, Traoré's evaluation emphasizes the elitism and control exercised in the school environment at Ponty. He claims that this theatre did not accurately reflect the merit of the African elite, nor did it express the need of students to rediscover African values. The school authorities exercised control and censorship of the productions and kept the students divided into regional and ethnic groups; moreover, they promoted the "Ponty spirit" of elitism.(75) Traoré asserts that this became a class theatre cut off from the masses and reflecting the official French version of history rather than any sort of nationalism, as when the plays attacked traditional customs or portrayed African rulers as bloodthirsty tyrants.(76) In Traoré's view, the Europeans were attracted by the exoticism of the plays, the masses of people had no access to the French but were merely drawn to the color and movement, while the French authorities favored the plays as "happy colonization."(77) Traoré concludes that the Ponty theatre was a controlled activity encouraging the colonial status quo.(78)

Cornevin, quite differently, concludes his review of the Ponty theatre as follows:

> From the point of view of the battle for African unity, for the great French West African Federation, the Ponty theatre provided a measure of common culture.
> Whatever the criticisms directed at it by Bakary Traoré and certain French educators immediately after the war, the Ponty theatre was a resounding success. It was a diversion, an occasion to meet and to work together, a pilgrimage to traditional sources--all at the same time. From 1936 to 1946, this theatre stamped an entire generation of students who were to become the politicians of the Fourth Republic, the presidents and ministers of independent Africa.
> This theatre had a rippling effect through the eventual administrative careers of the actors. Sent back to their own countries or to other parts of the Federation to be teachers, doctors and clerks, these former "Pontians" revived the dynamism [of the theatre] in schools out in the bush.(79)

Cornevin even quotes Traoré as conceding the success of the Ponty theatre in creating a community among the various regions of the federation through the students' vacation tours.(80) The Ponty theatre inspired controversy as well as a burst of theatrical activity. Cornevin includes both laudatory and sharply critical statements by former students about their experiences with the Ponty theatre. Yet this theatre and the widespread exposure it enjoyed provoked vital discussions about the purpose of African theatre, its treatment of history and the oral tradition, its appropriate themes, its accommodation (or not) of European spectators.(81) The nature and value of its success may remain moot, but the Ponty theatre itself undeniably forms the starting point for the literary theatre in French West Africa.

After the decline of the Ponty theatre during World War II, the next surge of francophone theatre in West Africa came with the establishment of cultural centers in the French colonies and annual competitions among them during the 1950's. According to Cornevin and Traoré, school drama died at Ponty when it became a "cramming school" where French degrees and the chance for advanced study in France became more important than theatrical diversions.(82) All students beyond the **baccalauréat** degree went to France, where several African theatrical troupes were formed.(83) But in Africa itself, theatrical activity in French declined; in Cornevin's words, mediocre troupes, cut off from Ponty inspiration, stagnated and disappeared until the renewal of the mid-1950's.(84)

The appointment of Cornut-Gentille as Governor-General of French West Africa in 1953 gave great impetus to the local cultural centers in the colonies. A few such centers had existed previously, but within two years of Cornut-Gentille's tutelage, one hundred and seventeen became active.(85) In November 1953, a meeting of the center directors from all the colonies was held to assess the activities of their centers. In view of the reports presented and the general popularity of the theatre expressed by the directors, the convention decided to reserve part of the cultural bulletin, TRAITS D'UNION, for theatre articles, the publication of plays, and advice to playwrights and actors. The center directors also called for an annual theatrical competition among the centers, which, Cornevin declares, gave great momentum to theatre in French West Africa until the breaking apart of the Federation in 1958.(86)

The rules for the competitions, which were held only in 1955, 1956, and 1957, called for each center to prepare a performance by no more than twenty-five participants, with a maximum length of ninety minutes. The compositions had to be original and in French, except for the songs which could be traditional. Regional eliminations were judged by juries whose members were listed by title. The territorial finals were recorded for broadcasting by Radio Dakar; then quarter-finals, semi-finals, and the **grande finale** were held in designated towns.(87) Indicative of the lasting influence of these competitions is the fact that this organizational framework still exists in Niger's national festivals. Instead of territorial eliminations, a system of regional competitions leading to the national event has been established, and the time limit, number of participants, the juries and the sense of competition remain essentially the same.

Cornevin briefly describes some of the plays during the three years of colonial competitions and includes a quotation from the editor of TRAITS D'UNION on the importance of the competitive setting as a stimulus for the best possible artistic efforts.(88) A wide variety of theatrical activity blossomed, both for the competitions and outside of them, but attention largely remained focussed on Dakar, the Federal capital, where the theatre audiences included highly influential colonial figures and the press. Dakar hosted the final competitions, and it became the ideal of every "bush" troupe to perform there.(89)

Nonetheless, the most famous theatrical troupe during the 1950's was not from Dakar or even in Senegal, but from the Ivory Coast. The **Cercle Culturel et Folklorique de la Côte-d'Ivoire**, established in 1953, benefitted from the earlier experiences of F.J. Amon-d'Aby and Coffi Gadeau, two of its leaders. These former Ponty students had established **Le Théâtre Indigène de la Côte-d'Ivoire** after their graduation in 1937.(90) This first troupe was the only one of its kind in Africa, according to Cornevin, marking the Ivory Coast as the only country to maintain an active and dynamic theatre during World War II.(91) The **Cercle Culturel** succeeded the **Theatre Indigène**, adding Bernard Dadié to its leadership and placing political consciousness in the forefront of its aims. This new troupe won the Federation competitions in 1955 and 1956 and had immense success in the **Théâtre des Nations** in 1956 and 1960, including a tour of France.(92) Exposure to the work of this theatre by way of the French West African competitions must have had an effect on the troupes from other regions. Many of the francophone playwrights published later were first exposed to theatre in the French schools and through these colonial competitions, including Cheik Ahmed Ndao and Abdou Anta Ka of Senegal, as well as Bernard Dadié himself.

Yet the cross-fertilization of competitions, cultural centers, TRAITS D'UNION and federal

A History

financial support for theatre ended with the dissolution of the French West African Federation. With Independence, each country began its own theatre history.

French Theatre in Niger

Dan-Inna Chaibou's brief history of the modern theatre in Niger begins with the Ponty school, which he credits as the source of propagation of (western style) theatre in francophone Africa. The first known performances of plays in French in Niger were those of the Ponty students on tour during their school vacations. By 1940, the **Amicale des Fonctionnaires de Niamey**, a club for the literate few, had a theatre troupe whose purpose was diversion for its actors and spectators, mainly French administrators and the tiny local African elite.(93)

Among Cornevin's descriptions of the colonial theatre competitions in the 1950's, he includes the following information for Niger in 1956:

> ...in Niger the **Samariya** youth, the French Scouts, the Veterans, the theatrical group of the Friends of Niamey, and the Elmina Renaissance were outclassed by the **Amicale** of Niamey with its dances **Atchapouga**, **Karoua**, the legend of **Kabrin Kabra**, and the comedy **Sona** from the Ponty repertoire.(94)

The **Amicale** (association) of Niamey won out over the five other theatre groups listed, then surpassed Dahomey in the regional finals, but lost to the troupe from the Ivory Coast in the final competition in Dakar. In 1957, Niger presented LA CHEVRE and LE PHARE DES PALMES, which Cornevin describes as portraying two men stranded in a lighthouse on the African coast, facing their destiny.(95) These plays lost to Dahomey's production in the first series of competitions for that year.

Two of the Nigerien plays produced during this period of the competitions appeared in TRAITS D'UNION: L'AVENTURE D'UNE CHEVRE (in July-August

1955), and LA LEGENDE DE KABRIN KABRA (in 1957), both by Mahamane Dandobi.(96) Dandobi, a Ponty alumnus, was director of the theatre section of the **Amicale** of Niamey at the time he wrote these plays. His first play, L'AVENTURE D'UNE CHEVRE, was performed in Bobo Dioulasso. In its four brief scenes, a farmer offers the goat of the title to three different men as collateral for loans from each. He obtains his money, only to abandon the goat for his creditors to fight over. In the end, they learn that he even stole the goat.(97)

Cornevin merely records the title of KABRIN KABRA, and I was unable to find a copy of it, but Chaibou characterizes it as an historical play from the Arewa legend (of the south central region of Niger), which tells of a cruel monarch who killed all the old men in his territory and was in turn destroyed by a stag.(98) Two other plays from the colonial era are summarized by Chaibou; apparently these have never seen print. The first, MARIAGE, presents a comparison between two couples, the happy **évolués** and the **non-évolués** who lack love and proceed to divorce. The second, ELECTIONS, concerns the 1946 elections for territorial deputies, and shows the colonial administration intervening to quell the corruption and infighting by local rivals.(99) As Chaibou notes, these plays were heavily influenced by colonialism and present a very different picture of history from the post-independence plays.

The limited repertory of plays in the early 1950's is suggested by the report of the Nigerien Center directors at the 1953 convention, as quoted by Cornevin:

> In Niger, Zada Niandou and Ly Souleymane lamented that the repertory has hardly been revised for the two annual performances: BAKARY DIAN, THE ELECTIONS OF 1946, COMPARISON OF THE MARRIAGES BETWEEN AN ENLIGHTENED COUPLE AND AN UNENLIGHTENED COUPLE, THE WIFE'S BETRAYAL, etc. (100)

The two annual performances cited here in 1953 rapidly expanded into the active competition reported among six different troupes in 1956 (see above), testifying to Cornevin's assertion that

the Centers and competitions caused a surge of theatrical activity in French West Africa.
   One other western theatrical model to appear amid these early African troupes came by way of the tours by French actors and companies in the colonies. The earliest such tour in Africa which Cornevin records took place in 1949-50 under the direction of Pierre Ringel, a comedian whose company performed variety shows including works by Molière.(101) However, Ringel's stops did not include Niger, probably because it was a distant and comparatively unpopulated bush outpost for the French, requiring difficult overland travel to reach.
   Following the independence of the French West African nations in 1960 came a stream of French troupes on tour, a part of the new cultural diplomacy. Cornevin includes notes on fourteen French tours in Africa between 1963 and 1968, only five of which reached Niamey (and only one of which ventured beyond Niamey to Maradi within Niger). The repertoires of these French companies were mainly comedies and farces, although one of the tours to Niamey included Anouilh's ANTIGONE as well as Molière's LE MALADE IMAGINAIRE, and another played Sophocle's ANTIGONE as well as Molière's LES FOURBERIES DE SCAPIN.(102)
   In addition to the road shows, several French artists conducted theatre workshops in Africa. From Cornevin's account, the only one of those to include Niger was the conference tour by Jacques Scherer, who visited eleven nations in less than three months (17 November 1965 to 3 February 1966). Cornevin presents a chart of statistics which show Scherer's activity in all eleven countries. During his stay in Niger, he apparently conducted one lecture for eighty people, three colloquiums for twelve people, three private interviews, one interview for the press, one visit to a ministry, and he also saw one play, read one, and heard twenty-one plays improvised orally.(103) While this list suggests an impressive amount of activity in a very brief time, it would be difficult to judge the impact of such a flying visit on the Nigerien theatre; Professor Scherer probably learned more than he taught.
   Niger's theatre after independence saw a gradual shift away from French models and toward popular forms of theatre. Plays were, from its

institution in 1964, a part of the **Semaine de la Jeunesse** (Youth Week) during December (10th to 17th), the annual celebration of the date of independence. Chaibou claims that the potential of theatre as a propaganda vehicle and political tool was recognized by the new government, but that the early productions retained an elite character.(104) Only a few plays were in local languages and the majority of the people had no access to those in French. With the arrival of the second regime in 1974, the week-long youth festival has celebrated the anniversary of the **prise de pouvoir** each April, and plays performed in national languages have been encouraged.(105)

The shift from French to national languages found its theorist in André Salifou, the Nigerien historian and playwright. Chaibou writes that Salifou was one of the first to advocate the use of Nigerien languages in the theatre, and Cornevin states that the Nigerien theatre owes its revival to him.(106) Salifou's play TANIMOUNE was the first full-length Nigerien play in French to be published (1973) and the only one to date.(107) According to a letter written by Salifou to Cornevin, the **Amicale** of Zinder asked him to compose a play for the national competition in 1967 while he was working on his thesis on the history of Zinder (known as Damagaram in the nineteenth century). He did so; the resulting play entitled TANIMOUNE ET L'EMANCIPATION DU DAMAGARAM won the national prize and was then presented in Niamey for a group of African heads-of-state who were meeting there at the time. Salifou asked for their critiques as well as the comments of friends in France, and subsequently revised the text, which was later published in France by Présence Africaine.(108) After its success in Niger, the play was performed at the Pan African Festival in Algiers in 1969 to an audience of six or seven hundred people despite scorching heat,(109) an event which Salifou describes as a stimulant to his efforts:

> For me, Algiers was a stimulant, a great moral vitamin. I have hoped to contribute to the creation of a truly Nigerien theatre, a desire strengthened by the success that TANIMOUNE achieved in Algiers. The

> Nigerien authorities now seem more determined than ever to help me make my small mark in this field.(110)

In writing about TANIMOUNE, Salifou emphasizes two fundamental aspects of his vision of theatre: the presentation of history to the people and the use of local languages. The play represents the story of Tanimoune, the ruler of Damagaram in the nineteenth century who threw off the rule of the Empire of Bornu and consolidated a small Hausa empire in the region around present-day Zinder. Salifou's letter to Cornevin admits that the play does not portray historical reality as such, but that is not its purpose; the specialists, he writes, can read his thesis. Rather, he wants to reach the masses of people, those who cannot read, to teach them their history.(111) In the introduction to the published play, Salifou explains the double purpose of the African historian: first, to dig out the buried African past from the colonial rubble, and then to bring it to the awareness of his compatriots.

> The Nigeriens capable of reading a work written in French--even the slightest text that records a part of their history--still represent only a handful of the privileged. And the others? just because they do not know the language of Vaugelas, must they be starved of the knowledge of their past?...
> An historical play portrayed simply on stage has a much greater chance of affecting the illiterate than a text to which they have no access. But in the end, nothing is resolved. African authors continue to face a fundamental problem: **that of language.** There is no doubt that the same illiterate spectator--interested in the performance of a play he cannot read--will be infinitely more inspired by a

play in a language he understands
perfectly: his own.(112)

   In this passage lie Salifou's basic goals for his theatre, the teaching of history to the people and the use of local languages to make it fully accessible. He goes on to discuss the problem of language in wider terms: the problem of the African writer's audience and the need to use colonial languages to reach beyond one country's borders; the problem of the aftermath of colonial education which has instilled French so deeply into the system that many Africans still find it easier to express themselves in French than in their mother tongues; and the problem of European publishing companies' continuing dominance over African literary production. Excusing himself for having to write his play in French, Salifou pleads a strong case for the use of African languages, not only in the theatre but in education.(113) The issue of the languages to be used for education is still under debate in Niger as in much of Africa, but Nigerien languages have definitely taken over the theatre.
   André Salifou's work with national theatre in Niger extends far beyond his published play and philosophy. In the introduction to TANIMOUNE, he describes his work with unwritten, improvised theatre productions:

     Theatre in African languages,
   as I have participated in it,
   has never been written.
     First, the actors listen
   attentively to the creator of the
   idea which the scene will be
   improvised around.... Next, the
   rehearsals begin. Things generally move quickly because there
   is no text to read or explain.
   They also go quickly because in
   improvisation, the African actor
   feels particularly comfortable
   expressing himself in his mother
   tongue.(114)

   This type of improvised drama has become the most commonly performed in Niger. Few plays are produced now in French, and fewer still appear in

A History

written form either before or after their production. Salifou was cited as the mentor of the Zinder theatre troupe by their director in 1981. Not only did Salifou work directly with the troupe while he was living in Zinder, but he personally aroused interest in theatre among the current leaders of the troupe, and also gave them a name, **K'ungiyar Amadou 'Dan Bassa** (the troupe of Amadou 'Dan Bassa), after a famous historical ruler of the region.(115) In 1980 the first feature-length Nigerien film in Hausa (with French subtitles), SI LES CAVALIERS ETAIENT LA..., was written by Salifou and performed by members of the Zinder troupe; the film portrays the insurrection of Amadou 'Dan Bassa against the French conquerors. André Salifou is at present Director of the **Ecole de Pédagogie** at the University of Niamey, but he remains a strong influence in Nigerien theatre, which has not only adopted national languages, as he hoped, but has become a truly popular theatre.

Popular Theatre in Niger

The **amicales** of colonial times have disappeared in Niger and have been succeeded by three types of theatre troupes--those of the students, the **samariyas**, and the radio troupes. These troupes create popular theatre, based on improvisation, rather than literary drama.

Like their predecessors in the colonial schools, students' performances primarily provide entertainment for local events, to celebrate holidays and to commemorate visits by important people or sports teams. These performances are now less likely to be French skits or Ponty re-runs than the students' original improvisations in their own languages based on topical subjects. Students at the beginning secondary level (**Collège d'Enseignement Général** or CEG) are the most likely to produce plays; by the time they reach the **Lycées** or **Ecoles Normales**, they devote themselves more exclusively to their studies in order to pass the highly competitive exams, still modelled after the French system.(116)

The **samariyas** are local youth groups which organize community projects. As Chaibou notes, the **samariyas** existed before colonization, but fell into disuse during French rule. With the military regime in 1974, the **samariyas** have been revitalized as the basis of political action, local cadres for national development. The organizations include both formally educated and uneducated people of all ages although the former usually provide the leadership and the latter the majority of the membership.(117) Theatre troupes have become one of the more visible activities of the **samariyas** in the annual competition for the national arts festival, but not every **samariya** has a theatre group and some of the troupes perform **ballets** rather than plays.

Ballets are neither traditional dances nor western ballets, but they are theatrical performances in Chaibou's broad sense. According to Chaibou, the dance performances called **ballets** were introduced to Niger by students from the Ponty School and then popularized by the **amicales** and the later theatre troupes. The **ballets** are inspired by cultural traditions, particularly dances, but they are original, choreographed creations. Chaibou defines the **ballets** in this way:

> Today they can be defined as productions in song, dance, and mime drawn from certain rituals or the facts of daily life characteristic of this country.(118)

In colonial times, the **ballets** were used primarily to vary the spectacle and were often of non-Nigerien origin. More recently they demonstrate the artistic and cultural traditions of Niger as part of the government's efforts to revalidate national culture. Chaibou describes **ballets** on such themes as collective labor (**gayya**), circumcision, demonstrations of manhood (**sharo**), a spirit possession ceremony (**girka**), and a festival of the butchers' caste (hawon k'afo).(119) **Ballets** include performances by musicians and singers as well as dancers and are often thoroughly rehearsed and minutely choreographed. In Chaibou's evaluation:

> The ballets are a successful synthesis of theatre, mime, song and dance. They preserve our cultural and artistic heritage which is threatened with

extinction by the adoption of new ways of life, and which the plays sometimes denounce.(120)

Ballets and plays (pièces théâtrales) are usually performed together and Nigeriens easily categorize a performance as one genre or the other. Yet the fine lines of distinction are not so clear. Dance and music predominate in the **ballets** although the plays may contain both as well. Dialogue and action are more generally characteristic of the plays; however, most of the **ballets** include some dialogue and many portray a story, as in the Gaya **Ballet** of 1981 which re-enacted an historical battle and the preservation of a village by a Muslim scholar.(121) Directors of both dance and drama troupes told me that the **ballets** are based on tradition, either customs or history, while the plays focus more on the problems of modern times. Counterexamples arise immediately: there are many historical plays, notably TANIMOUNE. Others develop around traditional customs, such as GAADOO K'ARHIN ALLAA whose central subject is the installation of a chief.

The categories are further blurred by the instrumental ensembles, which are often performances by traditional musicians, but which may include dance and song as well. Two of the instrumental ensembles at the 1981 Festival took their themes from the **Société du Développement**, the government's most recent development plan, and the International Year (1981) for the Handicapped.(122) Such contemporary topics would normally be the realm of the plays. All three genres--**ballets**, plays, and instrumental ensembles--overlap to some degree, although I would not classify most of the instrumental performances as theatre.

Abdoullahi Bagoudou, the theatre director in Gaya, whose troupe performed the historical **ballet** described above, explained the difference between **ballets** and theatre in this way:

> The **ballets** appear like the plays, but **ballets** are very complex with everything that goes into them. They begin with a little play but have dance and songs as well. The dance and words show that, for example,

>an old man does this and an old woman does that, so it is like a play. But the songs have to explain what is going on, what is intended. You have to have songs [in a **ballet**].
>
>In a play, you can put in dancing but it's not necessary. The same for songs, they're not essential. Sometimes if you're doing something [for a play] that requires a song, if you use history that has a song in it, then you must put the song in, but only for a minute or two.(123)

Certainly both the **ballets** and the plays are theatrical, with the difference being one of emphasis rather than kind--the ballets emphasizing music and dance, the plays their spoken dialogue and themes.

The government of Niger has influenced both these performance genres and the **samariya** troupes which create them through its sponsorship of the arts, particularly for the national festivals. The directors of village and town **Maisons des Jeunes**, the youth centers which house theatre and other recreational activities, are government employees. Often they are the men who organize the **ballets** and plays although some towns have a separate theatre director. The performers are not paid salaries for their theatre work; they remain amateurs with full-time occupations elsewhere in the community. But there are significant rewards for performance, including costumes (usually clothing which actors can add to their personal wardrobes), travel, local fame, and the chance to appear before national audiences at the festival and on television.

Television became nationally broadcast only in 1979 in Niger, but it has rapidly saturated the country. The government has funded television sets in the **Maisons des Jeunes** and other public centers throughout the country, using solar-battery-powered sets in locations without electricity. Watching the evening broadcasts is usually a community activity with dozens of people gathered around a single publicly or privately owned television.

Although the broadcasts as yet occur only four evenings a week (usually from 8:00 to 12:00 p.m.), the majority of the programs originate in Niger and are produced in any of five national languages (Hausa, Zarma, Fulfulde, Kanuri and Tamashek) as well as French. The Festival of 1979, held in Dosso, provided some of the first material for broadcast throughout the nation, and festival events from each year since then form an important part of the programming during the year, with frequently repeated segments of the songs, dances, instrumental pieces and plays. The Zinder theatre troupe was asked very early to perform its repertoire for television videotapes,(124) and other regional troupes have also had plays videotaped for broadcast. Despite its recent arrival, television has added a dynamic new dimension to theatre in Niger. Although its impact lies outside the scope of this study, it would be a significant subject for future investigation.

Niger's National Youth Festival, le **Festival National de la Jeunesse**, held annually the week of April 15th,(125) has become the focus of a large portion, though by no means all, of the country's theatrical activity. The festivals provide a competitive forum for the best troupes from each regional division (**département**) of Niger for the categories of: song, dance (**ballet**), instrumental ensemble, and drama. In the months before the festival, the seven regions sponsor their own competitions among the **samariyas** of their towns and villages. The organized nature of these competitions has affected the local troupes' efforts in a number of ways. Official guidelines have been established to limit the number of performers which the troupe may bring to the festival under government sponsorship (twenty-five for drama troupes), to limit the time of the performances (ninety minutes for plays, thirty for **ballets**), and to stress the qualities which will be judged by the juries.(126) Conforming to these standards has tended to homogenize the presentations by different troupes. In turn, non-festival productions are influenced by the models of the festival plays, which enjoy not only widespread performance and exposure but a great deal of national prestige.

Somewhat distinct from the **samariyas'** popular theatre and the students' efforts which imitate it are the improvised plays of the national radio station, the **Office de Radiodiffusion-Télévision du Niger** (ORTN). The television emissions of ORTN are of quite recent date, but the radio station has broadcast plays since its inception in 1962. Most of the weekly series of plays in Hausa are now produced by the ORTN troupe of Zinder although there is also a Hausa radio troupe in Tahoua. While some of the membership in the past has overlapped among the ORTN troupe, the Radio Club troupe, and the troupe of the **Maison des Jeunes** in Zinder, their organizations remain distinct and their work separate. The Radio Club (the name is misleading) now produces both stage plays and plays for television, much like the **samariya** troupes throughout the country. The ORTN troupe of Zinder specializes in radio serials that are totally improvised; a theme is chosen, parts assigned, and the actors go on the air. This troupe has produced plays for television as well, including KARA DA KIASHI, a seven-hour serial drama, but I am not aware of any live stage productions by them.(127) My study concentrates on stage productions rather than the serial radio plays although I will draw occasional comparisons where applicable.

Chaibou classifies the modern Hausa plays he studied in the mid-1970's as historical or social/contemporary dramas. Western divisions of tragedy and comedy, he claims, are not applicable to these plays; rather, they combine the two:

> The plays are generally a mixture of pathos and comedy. Even when evoking painful situations they always find a way to make the spectator laugh.(128)

Within his historical and social categories, Chaibou presents brief plot summaries of the plays he observed. He provides little data, however, on the dates or productions of these plays. Since Chaibou's work remains the only record for most of these plays, I have summarized his descriptions for their comparative value, with as much production information as he includes. He credits a few of the plays to specific authors; these can be assumed to be from written scripts. The rest are apparently the work of **samariya** troupes, many for the national festivals, given the glowing accounts of the new military government which Chaibou

A History

describes. His historical plays include Salifou's TANIMOUNE, and three others about the pre-colonial period:

> RABAT presents the victorious resistance of the Manga people against expansionists from Rabat in the nineteenth century.
>
> YAKIN SHIHIRUN [The War of Shihirun] portrays Namaylaya, ruler of Filingué, repulsing the troops of the Tuareg chief Firhoun.
>
> SONNI ALI BER (by Boubou Hama) depicts the conquests and state construction by the famous Songhai leader of the title.(129)

These plays laud the traditional rulers as heroes who struggled for the liberation of their people, in direct contrast to the historical plays during colonial times which degraded the African past.(130) Chaibou continues his list of historical plays to include three which present aspects of the colonial period:

> TCHIWAKE [a man's name in Hausa, literally "the bean eater"], performed by the troupe from Filingue, reveals the conditions of French recruitment of African soldiers to fight in Indochina.
>
> SI LES CAVALIERS ETAIENT LA (by the Zinder troupe) portrays the attempted uprising by Amadou 'Dan Bassa, its subsequent discovery, and his exile.
>
> LAMPOO [Hausa form of the French l'impôt, "the tax"], by the Filingué troupe, traces the adventures of a young peasant under the oppressive taxes and forced labor during both the

colonial period and the Diori regime (1960-76).(131)

Chaibou notes that the current plays portray the French ideal of assimilation as a force that both alienated Africans and deprived them of their heritage; the newer plays emphasize French exploitation in the colonies. These perspectives reverse those of the colonial plays which affirmed French values; as Chaibou notes, the **amicale** members who produced the early plays were the rare African beneficiaries of colonial policies.(132)

Yet the post-independence plays are not only critical of the French; they examine the current society to satirize its faults as well. These plays Chaibou classifies as social or contemporary dramas and he describes them as being about daily life and current problems, stressing action rather than deep psychological analysis of their characters.(133) His synopses in brief:

'YAN ZAMANI [Children of the Present Age], performed by a troupe from Niamey, presents young university students in the big city who all take up alcohol and prostitutes and reject traditional culture, except one.

INDA NA SANII (If I Had Known), by the troupe from Agadez, preaches against emigration during the time of the drought, through the story of a young man who goes to Libya only to find life there more difficult than at home, where the new government helps him to find a job upon his return.

HANNU BIDI NA KANKA [Hand, Look to Yourself], by the troupe from Tahoua, follows a young farmer, fresh from government training, as he sets up a model field to show his neighbors new methods of agriculture with outstanding results.

CALOO (Rodents) presents a village suffering from the famine, and rodents are eating their young crops long before harvest. Some of the villagers leave, but those who stay receive relief from the government.

ARMEE (Marriage), by a **samariya** troupe of Niamey, creates the conflict between a young girl, who wants to continue her studies, and her father, who tries to marry her off to the rich man of his choice. Her uncle, an enlightened man, intervenes, allowing her to marry the young government worker she loves.

SHEERIN KI, BUSHIA [Chaibou says that this title comes from a proverb, "Your curses, Hedgehog, will fall on your back"], presents a portrait of the corruption of the first independent government under President Diori, as it grows richer while the people suffer during the drought. The play shows the effects of the government's policies on one starving village and ends with the radio announcement of the **coup d'état.**

L'IMPOT EST MORT (written in French by Oumarou Idé). A peasant tries to get his advance tax payment back after learning that the tax has been abolished. The corrupt local chief and government official plot to silence the peasant and keep the village taxes, their source of livelihood.

GAADOO K'ARHIN ALLAA [Inheritance, Strength from God], by the Zinder troupe (1973), portrays the period before the election of a new chief. Various candidates are shown, but the one chosen is the successor named by the former **sarki**. [Here, Chaibou is slightly inaccurate: it is not the **sarki's** favorite son but the government's choice who succeeds him.]

ALHAJI MAY BONDOL [Alhaji Bundle] shows a seemingly respectable man who, in fact, trafficks in drugs, with the complicity of the customs agents at the border. He supplies young people with the drugs and incites them to debauchery, but he is duly unmasked and imprisoned.

RIKITTAA (Confusion), written in Hausa by Ada Mahamane, portrays the sort of merchant who plunges into business, squandering his resources, speculating, taking loans but failing to make his payments or deliver his goods on time. Alhaji Rikittaa uses his loan to buy a Mercedes, fails in his obligations, and flees before a judgement can be brought against him.(134)

Chaibou recognizes the political function of these plays which glorify the military regime that had recently taken power at the time they were produced.(135) Nonetheless, the plays also confront current problems: juvenile delinquency, the changing status of marriage, traditional caste divisions, the exodus to large cities or to other countries from the farm, the high cost of living in large towns, the red tape of government, the embezzlement of public funds, problems of succession and inheritance, the racketeering of merchants.(136) The plays aim to spotlight these faults for the public, to lead people to correct what is wrong in present-day society. Chaibou states that the plays work by exaggerating the evil characters on stage; this is the reason, he claims, that the productions are nearly all comic. The purpose of the comedy is to ridicule, to make people laugh at the wrongdoer, but also to warn them against behaving in a similar manner.(137)

In this respect, the modern theatre merely carries on a traditional function of Hausa literature: moral instruction. A not-uncommon feature of Hausa narratives and a dominant one for the poetry is that of didacticism.(138) Nigerien theatre troupes intend their plays to be instructional, and government influence has broadened the educative function to include the political elements of nationalism and economic development efforts. Balancing this didacticism is the other major characteristic of the plays--comedy. The successful combination of the didactic with the comic provides a key to the tremendous popularity of current theatre productions in Niger. Audiences fight their way into crowded theatres. They go to be entertained, but the public as well as the members of the troupes and the government sponsors feel the theatre to be important, a tool in nation-building, a place to learn as well as to laugh. Yazi Dogo, the director of the Troupe Amadou 'Dan Bassa of Zinder, expressed the character of the new theatre in this way:

> At the time when we didn't understand the usefulness of the theatre, we put on plays and everybody laughed and left. That was how it was then. We would arrange things with no meaning, we'd work things up just so people would laugh.
> But now, people's consciousness has begun to understand the theatre, what it's becoming. That's what we're looking for, the right words that people can make use of. Just as they instruct people on the radio, or what they write in the journals, the advice--that's what we're doing in the theatre.
> Now, whenever we're about to begin a new play, we examine what its purpose is to be. Shall we do it just for laughs? or so that people can work with what we

say? We've seen that the usefulness in it is greater when people will work with what they've seen us do. It's like a lesson we're drawing in the play. That's what we've learned.

But then, given that, if a person sits for an hour or an hour and a half, watching, not moving his body, not laughing--that's no good. So in our arrangement, we mix it up a little, we put a few funny things in so that people enjoy it. Yes, that's it.(139)

A master of understatement, Yazi Dogo the actor is known nationwide for his comic talent; the "few funny things" in the Zinder troupe's plays have made them one of the most popular troupes in the country, famous for their uproarious spectacles but also highly regarded for the sophistication of their themes. His statement is deceptively simple, for the right mixture of comedy and instruction, enough to spark an explosion of popular theatre throughout a new nation, does not happen everyday. It is happening in Niger.

This, then, is the Hausa theatre explored in the following chapters--popular, widespread, improvised, topical, political, instructive, comic, changing. It has roots in traditional forms stretching far into the past, but it also has been profoundly affected by the colonial experience, exposure to western art forms and the legacy of French education. A new theatrical tradition is rising out of this multifaceted heritage, one which must face the realities of a developing nation in the present world and develop along with it.

ENDNOTES: CHAPTER I

1. Anthony Graham-White, THE DRAMA OF BLACK AFRICA (New York: Samuel French, 1974), p. 2.
2. Graham-White, p. 32.
3. Graham-White, p. 3.
4. E.T. Kirby, "Indigenous African Theatre," THE DRAMA REVIEW, 18, No. 4 (December 1974), pp. 22-35.
5. Kirby, p. 27.
6. Kirby, p. 32.
7. Robert Cornevin, LE THEATRE EN AFRIQUE NOIRE ET A MADAGASCAR (Paris: Le Livre Africain, 1970).
8. Cornevin, Chapter 1, pp. 11-43.
9. Henri Labouret and Moussa Travélé, "Le Théâtre Mandingue (Soudan français)," AFRICA, I, no. 1 (January 1928), p. 96. (Cited by Cornevin, p. 23). The original French quotation:

> Par contre, dans la colonie française du Niger et dans certaines villes Haoussa, on peut voir sur quelques marchés, lors des grandes fêtes musulmanes, une représentation véritable dans laquelle paraissent des poupées de bois. L'opérateur est assis, dissimulé par sa blouse; il présente par l'échancrure de celle-ci et d'une main invisible les personnages ordinaires de la comédie: le mari, la femme, et l'amant. Cette pratique semble venir de l'Afrique du Nord.

10. Ibrahim Yaro Yahaya, "Nazari kan Yanayin Wasan Kwaikwayon Hausa" (An Investigation of the State of Hausa Plays), A Paper Presented at the Conference on Hausa Language and Literature, July 1978 (Kano, Nigeria: Center for the Study of Nigerian Languages, Bayero University College).
11. Yahaya, p. 1.
12. This list is my summary and translation from Yahaya, pp. 1-7.

13. Dan-Inna Chaibou, "La Théâtralité en Pays Hawsa," Memoire de Maîtrise, Université Nationale de Côte d'Ivoire, 1978-79.
14. Chaibou, pp. 2-4.
15. Chaibou, p. 1.
16. Chaibou uses the UNESCO system of transcription, including double vowels (**koora**), but I have followed standard Kano Hausa usage, most of whose conventions were adopted in Niger in 1980. See "Report of the Meeting of Experts on the Harmonization of the Orthography of the Hausa Language" (Niamey, Niger: Centre for Linguistic and Historical Studies by Oral Tradition/CELHTO, January 1980).
17. Chaibou, pp. 14-17.
18. Chaibou, p. 20. Chaibou uses the French term **chef**, instead of the Hausa **sarki**, throughout his description, although he uses the Hausa title **doka** for his partner in the ceremony. I have used the Hausa titles for both the **sarki** and **doka**.
19. Chaibou, pp. 20-22.
20. Chaibou, pp. 17-18.
21. Chaibou, pp. 23-4.
22. Chaibou, p. 24.
23. Wole Soyinka, THE STRONG BREED, in THREE SHORT PLAYS (London: Oxford University Press, 1969), and DEATH AND THE KING'S HORSEMAN (London: Eyre Methuen, 1975).
24. GAADOO K'ARHIN ALLAA (Wasan Kwaykwayoo na Zinder a 1973) (Inheritance, Strength from God, a Play by the Zinder Troupe, 1973), transcribed by Abuubakar Mahamman (Niamey: CELHTO, 1977).
25. Chaibou, p. 25.
26. Chaibou, p. 26.
27. Chaibou reproduces the text of this poem in Hausa and French, as well as giving a detailed analysis of it, pp. 27-58.
28. Chaibou, pp. 58-59.
29. Chaibou, p. 60.
30. Chaibou, p. 61.
31. Chaibou, p. 62.
32. Harold Scheub, "Body and Image in Oral Narrative Performance," NEW LITERARY HISTORY, VIII, no. 3 (Spring 1977), pp. 345-67.
33. Chaibou, pp. 65-6.
34. Chaibou, p. 66.
35. Chaibou, pp. 66-9.
36. Chaibou, p. 77.
37. Chaibou, pp. 70-3.

38. Chaibou, pp. 73-4.
39. Chaibou, p. 75.
40. Chaibou, pp. 76-7.
41. Chaibou, pp. 76-8.
42. Chaibou, p. 78.
43. C.G.B. Gidley, "'Yankamanci--The Craft of the Hausa Comedians," AFRICAN LANGUAGE STUDIES, 8 (1967), pp. 52-81.
44. Gidley, pp. 54-9. See also Chaibou's account of a **'dan kama's** practical joke, pp. 108-9.
45. Gidley, p. 59.
46. Gidley, pp. 59-60; 75.
47. Gidley, p. 80.
48. Gidley, p. 80.
49. Chaibou, pp. 79-80.
50. Chaibou, pp. 79-80.
51. Graham-White, pp. 61ff.
52. Graham-White, p. 60.
53. Graham-White, pp. 62-9.
54. Graham-White, pp. 106-8.
55. Graham-White, pp. 108-10.
56. Yahaya, p. 9.
57. Yahaya, p. 8.
58. Cornevin, p. 44.
59. Cornevin, pp. 45-6.
60. Cornevin, pp. 46-50.
61. Bakary Traoré, THE BLACK AFRICAN THEATRE AND ITS SOCIAL FUNCTIONS, Trans. Dapo Adelugba (Ibadan, Nigeria: Ibadan University Press, 1972); the original French edition: LE THEATRE NEGRO-AFRICAIN (Paris: Présence Africaine, 1959).
62. Traoré, pp. 31-3.
63. Traoré, pp. 34-5.
64. Cornevin, p. 52.
65. Cornevin, pp. 51-3.
66. Charles Béart, "Le Théâtre indigène et la culture franco-africaine," EDUCATION AFRICAINE (Dakar, 1937), pp. 3-4, quoted by Cornevin, p. 55. The original French:

> Nous ne cherchons pas seulement à créer du bien-être matériel, nous voulons aussi que se développent toutes les puissances d'art que la race possède: aussi avons-nous, dans nos écoles, fait une grande place à l'artisanat qui "conservera" les métiers d'art;

nous avons même, pour assurer leur développement, des établissements spéciaux où des artistes professionels européens se pénètrent de la technique indigène pour la faire évoluer sans qu'elle se corrompe.

67. Cornevin, p. 62.
68. Cornevin, pp. 60; 56.
69. Traoré, p. 61.
70. Traoré, p. 56.
71. Traoré, pp. 57-8.
72. Cornevin, p. 70.
73. Cornevin, p. 58.
74. Cornevin, p. 63.
75. Traoré, pp. 69-71.
76. Traoré, p. 74.
77. Traoré, pp. 77-8.
78. Traoré, p. 80.
79. Cornevin, p. 74. The original French:

Dans cette perspective du combat pour l'unité africaine, pour la grande fédération d'A.O.F., le théâtre de Ponty a, dans une certaine mesure, donné une infrastructure culturelle.... Quelles que soient les critiques adressées par Bakary Traoré et certains directeurs français de l'enseignement dans l'immédiat après-querre, le théâtre de Ponty fut un éclatant succès. A la fois distraction, occasion de se retrouver et de travailler ensemble, pèlerinage aux sources traditionelles, ce théâtre a marqué de 1936 à 1946 toute une génération de normaliens qui sont devenus les hommes politiques de la IVe République, les présidents et les ministres de l'Afrique indépendante.
     Ce théâtre eut un effet multiplicateur du fait du

> destin administratif des comédiens renvoyés dans leur pays d'origine ou dans la Fédération comme instituteurs, médecins, commis d'administration. Revivant dans les écoles de brousse au gré du dynamisme des anciens "Pontins".

80. Cornevin, p. 74.
81. See Cornevin's quotations from former Ponty students and administrators, pp. 68-74.
82. Cornevin, p. 73; Traoré, p. 35.
83. See Cornevin's Chapter III, "Théâtre africain et acteurs noirs en Europe (1946-60)," pp. 83-103.
84. Cornevin, p. 105.
85. Cornevin, p. 109.
86. Cornevin, pp. 110-12.
87. Cornevin, pp. 112-13.
88. Cornevin, pp. 114-17.
89. Cornevin, pp. 117-18.
90. Cornevin, pp. 75-80.
91. Cornevin, pp. 80; 120.
92. Cornevin, pp. 120-2.
93. Chaibou, p. 82.
94. Cornevin, p. 116. The original French:

> ...au Niger la jeunesse Samaria, les scouts de France, les anciens combattants, le groupe théâtral des amis de Niamey, la renaissance Elmina furent surclassé par l'amicale de Niamey avec les danses Atchapouga, Karoua, la légende de Kabrin Kabra, et la comédie SONA du répertoire de Ponty.

95. Cornevin, pp. 116-17.
96. Cornevin, pp. 123-4.
97. Mahamane Dandobi, L'AVENTURE D'UNE CHEVRE, in TRAITS D'UNION (Dakar, juillet--septembre 1955), pp. 76-83; and in LE THEATRE POPULAIRE EN REPUBLIQUE DE COTE-D'IVOIRE (Abidjan: Centre Culturel et Folklorique de Cote d'Ivoire, 1966), pp. 181-190; cited in Cornevin, pp. 124-5.
98. Chaibou, p. 93.
99. Chaibou, p. 93.

100. TRAITS D'UNION (Dakar, décember 1953--janvier 1954), pp. 13-22, as quoted by Cornevin, p. 110.

> Au Niger, Zada Niandou et Ly Souleymane déplorent que le répertoire ne se renouvelle guère pour les deux représentations annuelles: BAKARY DIAN, LES ELECTIONS DE 1946, COMPARAISON DU MARIAGE ENTRE EVOLUES ET NON-EVOLUES, TRAHISON DE LA FEMME, etc.

101. Pierre Ringel, MOLIERE EN AFRIQUE NOIRE (Paris: Presse du Livre Français, 1951); cited by Cornevin, pp. 105-6.
102. Cornevin, pp. 167-8.
103. Cornevin, p. 170.
104. Chaibou, pp. 82-3.
105. Chaibou, pp. 83-4.
106. Chaibou, p. 83; Cornevin, p. 216.
107. André Salifou, TANIMOUNE (Paris: Présence Africaine, 1973).
108. Cornevin, p. 217.
109. Cornevin, p. 216.
110. Letter from André Salifou to Robert Cornevin, 25 August 1969, quoted by Cornevin, p. 217. The original French:

> Alger a été pour moi une grande vitamine morale, un stimulant. J'ai aussi le souci de contribuer à la création d'un véritable théâtre nigérien et ce, d'autant plus que le succès remporté à Alger par TANIMOUNE semble avoir rendu les autorités nigériennes plus que jamais décidées à m'aider à poursuivre mon petit bout de chemin dans ce domaine.

111. Salifou Letter in Cornevin, p. 217.
112. Salifou, TANIMOUNE, pp. 7-8. The original French:

> Les Nigériens capables de lire un ouvrage--ou même le

> moindre texte--écrit en français et portant sur telle ou telle partie de leur histoire, ne représentent encore qu'une poignée de privilégiés. Et les autres? Devraient-ils, parce qu'ils ignorent la langue de Vaugelas, être privés d'une nourriture aussi importante et aussi riche que celle que pourrait leur offrir la connaissance de leur passé?.... Une pièce historique simplement mise en scène a beaucoup plus de chances de toucher les illettrés qu'un texte auquel il leur est impossible d'accéder. Mais, somme toute, rien n'est encore résolu. Un problème fondamental continue à se poser aux auteurs africains: **celui de la langue**. Il n'y a pas de doute, en effet, que le même spectateur illettré qui suit avec beaucoup d'intérêt la représentation d'une pièce qu'il est incapable de lire par lui-même, serait encore infiniment plus "saisi" par une pièce représentée devant lui dans une langue qu'il comprend parfaitement, dans sa langue à lui.

113. Salifou, TANIMOUNE, pp. 10-12.
114. Salifou, TANIMOUNE, pp. 9-10. The original French:

> Le théâtre en langue africaine, tel que j'ai eu à le pratiquer jusqu'ici, n'a jamais été écrit.
> Dans un premier temps, les acteurs écoutent attentivement l'auteur de l'idée autour de laquelle va être improvisée la saynète ... Puis, dans un second temps, les répétitions commencent. Les choses vont

généralement vite dans la mesure où il n'y a pas de texte à lire, à expliquer... Elles vont vite aussi parce que, dans l'improvisation, l'acteur africain s'exprimant dans sa langue maternelle se sent particulièrement à l'aise.

115. Interview with Yazi Dogo and Abdou Louché of the Troupe Amadou 'Dan Bassa, by David Hofstad for the Voice of America, Niamey, Niger, 30 October 1981.

116. During my two years of teaching at the CEG of Dogondoutchi, Niger, (1976-78), I was invited to several plays organized by the students to entertain visiting football teams from other schools; these performances were followed by dance parties. When I returned to Niger for research in 1980-81, I interviewed the student troupes at three CEG's and observed one student play at Tchin Tabaraden, performed in celebration of National Independence Day, 18 December 1981. Upon inquiring at some of the **Lycées** about student theatre groups, I was told that there were none. A former student of mine, who had been a key leader in the theatre troupe in Dogondoutchi, and who had gone on to the **Lycée Technique** in Maradi, informed me that the **Lycée** students had to study too much to put on plays. Chaibou notes student performances during vacation periods (p. 85); I was not aware of such performances.

117. Chaibou, pp. 85-6.
118. Chaibou, p. 89. The original French:

> Ils peuvent être définis aujourd'hui comme la mise en scène chantée, dansée et mimée de certains rites ou de quelque faits de la vie quotidienne propres au pays.

119. Chaibou, pp. 89-91.
120. Chaibou, p. 91. The original French:

> Les ballets sont un synthèse réussie entre le théâtre, la pantomime, le chant et la danse. Ils permettent de

conserver notre patrimoine culturel et artistique qui est menacé de disparition par l'adoption de modes de vie nouveaux, ce que dénoncent parfois les pièces théâtrales.

121. **Ballet** Entry of the **Département** of Dosso, by the Troupe from Gaya, director Abdoullahi Bagoudou, for the National Festival in Diffa, Niger, 9 April 1981.

122. Instrumental Ensemble Entry of the **Département** of Dosso, by the Troupe from Dogondoutchi, for the National Festival in Diffa, Niger, 9 April 1981; and Instrumental Ensemble Entry of the **Département** of Niamey, 7 April 1981.

123. Interview with Abdoullahi Bagoudou, conducted by Aboubacar Mahamane, Gaya, Niger, 10 December 1980. (The quotation is my paraphrased translation of his statement).

124. Yazi Dogo, Niamey, 30 October 1981.

125. In April 1982, after the festival had been held in each of the seven regional capitals of the country, the government announced that it would be biennial in the future.

126. The Government of Niger publishes a "Guide au Festival National" for the organizers and participants throughout the country. The play competitions at the departmental level in Zinder which I observed in March 1981, were judged for: choice of theme, direction, interpretation (of theme), setting and costume. **Ballets** were judged for: choice and development of theme, choreography, setting and costume, and music. Each of these categories could earn a maximum of five points, with twenty a perfect score, and with penalties (for going over the time limit, for example) subtracted from the total. Each judge evaluated the plays individually, and then the jury as a group determined the final order at the end of the week's performances. I believe this scoring system to be the standard one used nationally for the festival entries.

127. KARA DA KIASHI, by the ORTN Theatre Troup of Zinder, produced by Mamane Bakabé (Videotapes in the ORTN Archives, Niamey).

128. Chaibou, p. 92. The original French:

> Les drames sont généralement un amalgame de pathétique et de comique. Même dans l'évocation de situations pénibles on trouve toujours le moyen de faire rire le spectateur.

129. Chaibou, p. 94.
130. Chaibou, pp. 100-1.
131. Chaibou, pp. 94-5.
132. Chaibou, pp. 101-3.
133. Chaibou, p. 95.
134. Chaibou, pp. 95-9. The bracketed additions are mine.
135. Chaibou, p. 114.
136. Chaibou, p. 103.
137. Chaibou, pp. 103; 114.
138. See Neil Skinner, "Realism and Fantasy in Hausa Literature," REVIEW OF NATIONAL LITERATURES, II, no. 2 (1971), pp. 167-87.
139. Interview with Yazi Dogo, Zinder, Niger, 14 August 1981. His original statement:

> Da lokacin ba a gane amhwanin teyatur ba kurum dai a yi teyatur a yi dariya a tashi. Da, haka ake yi. Sai a tsara abubuwa ba su da ma'ana, ana gyaggyara abubuwa dai dan mutane su yi dariya shi ke nan. To yanzu ko hankalin mutane sun hwara gane teyatur, saboda teyatur ya zamanto ... tana muke bi, mu huddo maganganu dan mutane sun yi amhwani. Kamar yadda ake garga'di a **radio**, ko kuma ana rubuta cikin jarida cikin **journaux** haka, kamar kwansai. To. Shi ma a cikin teyatur ana yin hakanan. To. Shi ma har yanzu duk teyatur kin da za mu yi mu, sai mun dubi in muka yi shi mi ne ne amhwaninshi? Dan a yi dariya kawai za mu yin shi? Ko ko dan a yi aiki da abin da

muka gaya? Muka ga amhwaninshi ya hi a yi aiki da abun da aka gani ciki. Kamar shi ne **leçon** da za a **tirer** ciki. I. Shi ne muka gani. To.

Wani sa'in sai mu ce to, amma mutum yana zamna awa guda ko awa da rabi, yana kallo, bai motsa jikinshi bai yi dariya, ba da'di. To cikin tsari sai mu 'dan garwaya ka'dan, muna sa abubuwan dariya ka'dan don mutane su ji da'di. I. To.

CHAPTER II
THE TROUPES AND THEIR REHEARSAL PROCESS

    Each Hausa theatrical troupe has a unique style although the troupes share certain general characteristics. Their improvised work depends heavily on the group's personalities, their interaction, how well the members know one another, how long they have worked together, their shared experience in producing and performing plays. During my six months' stay in Zinder in 1981, I was privileged to observe meetings, rehearsals, and performances by three of the different troupes: the Troupe Amadou 'Dan Bassa of the **Maison des Jeunes** (MJC), the Radio Troupe of ORTN, and the Radio Club Troupe. In interviews with members of twelve other troupes in regions throughout the country, many directors, actors, dancers, administrators, and students shared insights with me about their work in the theatre, their organization and methods.
    Most troupes have thirty to forty members of whom the majority are young and middle-aged men. Some of the troupes will not work with children, the rest include them only in certain plays. Others have no old actors but use false beards and make-up to age younger actors for elderly roles. The student troupes, generally at the CEG level where the age range is from thirteen to eighteen or nineteen, are the most homogeneous in terms of age. Yet age is relative, and is not always known very precisely in Niger (especially for older people); it did not seem of particular concern for the troupes. They accept anyone who expresses interest in acting; the majority of those interested seem to be men in their twenties, thirties, and forties.
    Membership in the troupes remains voluntary and it fluctuates with each season and each project. There are no professional actors yet in

Niger; every actor has one or more occupations in the community and performs in his spare time. People from all walks of life join the troupes, although in Zinder, a city large enough to have several troupes, the educated **fonctionnaires** seem to congregate in the MJC troupe, while the Radio Club troupe has more traditional local people. Government service demands that **fonctionnaires** move frequently, so few are likely to remain long in their home region.(1) They may join a troupe in one town but not in another, depending on the town's activities, its composition and openness to strangers, and even its primary language. The **samariya** troupe of the MJC in Mainé Soroa, which often performs in Kanuri (Manga) at home and in Hausa elsewhere, included primarily local people, permanent residents of the town, whereas the troupe at the MJC in Zinder was a greater mixture--Hausa, Fulani and Kanuri people; office workers, farmers, merchants, teachers, nurses, traditional musicians, secretaries, prostitutes. The **samariya** in Dogondoutchi produced plays at one time under the direction of a schoolteacher, but when he moved away, they turned to **ballets**.(2)

The women in the troupes are perhaps their most volatile element. Traditional Hausa society confines women to roles in the home; Muslim seclusion, while not stringently practiced in most of Niger, remains an ideal--the higher a man's status and wealth, the less his wives and daughters will be seen in public. Increasing numbers of educated women are changing traditional patterns, but it is still rare to find married women, even as audience members, at public events, including the theatre. The exception to this rule appears in **bori** performances, which women attend and where initiated women become possessed by spirits; however, these initiates are often prostitutes or women otherwise set apart (by illness or infertility) from the typical role of wife and mother.(3) Women involved in modern theatrical performances, too, are either young, unmarried girls or women "who live alone" (**masu zama kansu**/divorcées/prostitutes). Most of the troupes have very few actresses, usually between five and ten, in comparison to the number of men, and they frequently need to recruit new women as the others get married or move away. Both the Radio Club Troupe and the MJC Troupe of Zinder lost key actresses to marriage

Troupes and Rehearsals 61

between two sets of performances of the same play, during the brief time that I was in Zinder.

Opinions among the directors, all men, differ over including women in the troupes. In Gaya, Director Abdoullahi Bagoudou prefers to work only with young girls:

> Here we put young girls in the theatre, because we don't put women ... we don't want to work with public women. It happens with those women ... a woman who lives alone and follows her own interests, we don't like to work with her because she would spoil our business. We would come and she'd see the area of her desire--here's what we want her to do, but there's where her inclinations go--it won't work. Therefore, we work with young girls, we don't let them go anywhere at all, they are a trust in our hands.(4)

When these young women marry, the Gaya troupe replaces them. In contrast, the **animateur** of the troupe in Matameye, Nawaki Abdou, stated that there are problems working with unmarried girls, especially when traveling; the young women his troupe prefers to work with are independent of families.(5) I only witnessed one play that had no women acting at all, but the director of that troupe (from Magaria) said that they did have women members in the troupe.

By bringing men and women to work together on a project, the current theatre presents a new and unusual social context in Hausa society. Traditionally, men's and women's activities, whether social, economic, religious, or political, remain quite separate, coinciding only when necessary even within the home.(6) Thus, theatrical performance, which requires joint efforts by men and women over a period of time, operates in a marginal realm of the culture, one which must create its own rules.(7) As a public event, this theatre is much closer to the men's world of tradition, and the women are venturing farther from their customary roles to participate. To date few have been willing to do so. As one of the Zinder actors explained to me, their troupe had only three women acting with them a few years ago, now there are seven. "Kansu ya hwara waiwaiye" (they are beginning to awaken).(8) Yet it is not only the women's consciousness that must change if more women are to enter the theatre world; the wider issue involves the social status and acceptance given to theatre, and women's participation in it, within the culture as a whole.

Similarly, but perhaps less revolutionary in this context, is the fact that work in the theatre promotes interaction among different classes and ethnic groups within the country. This has been one of the aims of the government of Niger in promoting theatre and the other cultural activities for the national festivals. Before the Diffa Festival in 1981, LE SAHEL, Niger's only newspaper, made this statement:

> However, besides being a celebration, the national youth festival is also a privileged moment for [artistic] expression and total communication through art, sport, and the contact between people physically, intellectually, and spiritually. The result is that the national youth festival is an essential opportunity for collective reflection, multiple exchanges, and real camaraderie.(9)

National attention, particularly for plays presented at the annual festival, has given prestige to the **samariya** troupes and to their actors, who express pride in being part of the theatre.

The troupes each have a nominal director, although they generally prefer to give him the title of **animateur** or **responsable**, to that of **metteur en scène**. Leadership arises from within the group; the director generally will have worked with the troupe for a long time, taken responsibility for production arrangements, and earned the respect of the group. He may call for the production of a new play, set rehearsal times, oversee the rehearsal and production details, but he is never alone in this work. Usually a small number of dedicated men assist him, make decisions with him and take his place when he is not present at rehearsals (a frequent occurrence among those I attended). Moreover, most if not all of the artistic decisions and many administrative ones as well are left open to comment, discussion, and change by the full troupe.

The Development of a Theme

Plays develop around a central theme or idea agreed upon by the troupe. The French word **thême** has become the standard term for this in Nigerien Hausa. Themes suggest themselves to members of the troupe. They may be historical or religious; they may relate to current local problems or political issues; but they always represent something of immediate concern to the community. For the national festival, nationalistic themes prevail, but plays intended only for the local audience will treat local issues. Alhaji Zoubeirou Lawal, the director of the Troupe of Mainé Soroa, described the plays for the national festival as demonstrating issues that people may not understand, such as Niger's development (**ci gaban k'asa**), its unity (**ha'da kan mutane**)--the sorts of issues discussed on the radio and in the journals. But for their local productions, they portray problems that are disturbing their town, such as drugs or gambling; the troup uses the plays to expose the wrongdoers, to show concerned citizens what they can and should do about people selling drugs, and to inform the miscreants that their designs are known. In his words:

> Don wasan kwaikwayon na **festival** da irin na **animer** gari wannan, daban suke. E.
> (Thus the plays for the festival and those that motivate our town are different.)(10)

For their theatre entry in the 1981 Festival, the Mainé Soroa troupe chose their theme from six suggestions. The theme that they developed, that of **entreprise**, was Alhaji Zoubeirou's idea. When asked why they selected that particular theme, he replied that it seemed the most appropriate for the festival that year in neighboring Diffa; the government had funded quite a lot of construction in their region before the festival, but some men took on the projects just to gain money, not caring that the buildings were meant to serve the people of the département. The troupe created their play around a greedy entrepreneur of that type to draw people's attention to the problem.(11) Also that year, the troupe from Maradi produced a play on the same theme; Maradi's play was awarded first prize at the festival and Mainé Soroa's took second place. It proved to be a timely topic indeed.

In answer to the same question about their choice of theme, the director and an actor from the Maradi troupe remarked that they often research ideas for a month or two, but that for that year they had only one meeting of the troupe and chose their theme from three ideas. The three they began with were: the entrepreneur, the Development Society, and the reform of education. They decided on the contractor, **'Dan Kwangila** (kept as the title of their play), because there were so many work-sites everywhere that were unfinished or where the work was badly done or unnecessarily delayed. They felt that demonstrating the problems of government construction projects would be the most instructive theme for their audience. But they incorporated the second theme of national development (**la Société du Développement**) into the play as well, particularly in the discussion in the first scene, because it bolstered their central theme.(12) Both Maradi's and Mainé Soroa's troupes mentioned the radio, the national newspaper, and statements by the government as sources for their inspiration.

In Zinder's Troupe Amadou 'Dan Bassa, four or five key members of the troupe meet to decide the theme they will center their play around, according to their director, Yazi Dogo. These actors follow events in the news carefully to discover things of concern to people; they find themes in speeches by the president and the ministers; they also frequently do historical topics. If they have two good themes, they will try to combine them into a play, but one always remains the most important; if they cannot combine them, they choose the one that is more suitable (**ya hi dacewa**) or more useful to people (**wanda ba da amhwani k'warai**). The troupe researches its themes: two or three members will talk to the important **malams** if the theme concerns religion; they will discuss ideas with the **sarki** (the Sultan of Zinder) if it concerns his court. Among troupe members information can be gleaned about many topics. For topics the troupe is uncertain of, the actors find people who can instruct them.(13)

Zinder's festival play in 1980, BA GA IRINTA BA (There's Nothing Like It), which was awarded first prize for theatre that year, takes education as its central theme, examining the problems within the educational system and their causes. In an official critique of the 1980 Festival in Niamey, Kélitigui A. Mariko praised the Zinder Troupe's complex treatment of their theme:

> The Zinder play takes off from everyday events and tries to point out the obligation for everyone, rich and poor, to respect the law. Through the behavior of Mamman Arrivé, who deals only with the banks and the chamber of commerce, many problems erupt simultaneously: relationships between teachers and the pupils' parents, relationships at the heart of the family, at the heart of the school, among the teachers, etc. As the play develops, new subjects are grafted onto the main theme....
>
> With the experience and finesse for which they are famous, the actors of the troupe have tackled numerous problems with mischief rather than bitterness, as would the man in the street.(14)

Director Yazi Dogo described the troupe's process in choosing their educational theme in this way:

> At the time when we were beginning to prepare the play that we gave the name BA GA IRINTA BA, a lot of us sat down and we asked each one to bring

themes in order to arrange our work for the festival. We met, everyone brought his [ideas], we examined them and said, "This one is okay, this one won't do."

Well! We thought about them and said, "Hey! There's one thing which concerns all of us, even the elders, even the government, and that is the problems of the students, the teachers, and the children's parents." So we said, "Yes, this is really appropriate, this is a good theme."

So we began to research it, to seek it out. Now, there are a lot of teachers in our troupe. They helped in the research, everyone brought his ideas; we collected them all, we arranged them, we took what was bothering the teachers, what was bothering the parents, and also what was bothering the kids themselves. Yes. Then we agreed, "Truly, it is necessary that we prepare something about this because of its usefulness to all of us--for the parents to understand, the teachers to understand, for the elders, also, to understand the problems at school." That's how it was.(15)

The school problems which the troupe knew so intimately and portrayed so well struck a responsive chord in nationwide audiences; the play has remained a favorite among their repertoire.

Extensive research may be carried out on a theme, particularly for plays or **ballets** that include historical events or traditional customs. The director of the troupe in Gaya, Abdoullahi Bagoudou, stated that he often travels some distance to gather information on his themes. He discusses his theatre topics with the experts of the particular craft (in one instance, blacksmiths); for historical facts, he goes to the place of origin to seek the truth. He obtains permission for these investigations both from the sous-préfet and from the **sarki**, the civil and traditional rulers, and he courts the elders who possess crucial information with frequent visits and cola nuts. His town of Gaya is located on the River Niger near the borders of both Benin and Nigeria, and as Abdoullahi sees it, before the Europeans came, the country was all the same; so he ventures over the borders and into the bush to collect ideas, information, history, customs, and themes. He himself has no formal education but feels that God gave him this work to do in the theatre. Yet, although he searches for themes so far afield, he brings his work back to his troupe and members of the community to discuss. When asked how he chooses themes, Abdoullahi replied:

> Harakan jama'a sai jama'a.
> (For the things of the community, there is only the community.)
>
> Whatever I have collected, when I get back I gather everybody together. Sometimes I act as though I don't know anything and I ask them ... "What should we do this year?" ... Then everyone states his opinion. I see if their opinions are appropriate and I tell them that, but if they're not appropriate, I carefully correct them, "You see, this is what prevents us from doing what you've said." ... "Now let's prepare such-and-such a thing. But from now on, watch closely, if you see that everything is correct, tell me, but it if isn't right, you must also tell me that." That's it--then we prepare and begin our work.(16)

Quite different from this meticulous research for the themes of **ballets** and historical plays is the weekly work of the Radio Troupe in Zinder. **La Voix du Sahel** (Voice of the Sahel), the national radio station (of ORTN), broadcasts an hour of Hausa drama every Sunday afternoon, most of the plays being performed by the Zinder troupe. Several members of this troupe have worked together for over fifteen years; they know each other well and seem to have no difficulty in constantly thinking up new themes for their plays. As Alhaji Abdousalam Adam, a longstanding member and former director of the troupe, expressed it:

> Researching themes is no trouble, because the **animateurs** get together, everyone has his own idea, something that he sees as necessary to bring to people's attention through a play.
> At the time we go [to the station], if the play we've been doing is nearly done, or if the day we're to finish it is the next week, then we'll say, "Okay, everyone come and bring his opinion on a theme to begin our new play with."
> When the time comes, one person, or two or three, will bring a theme, then we'll see which is most appropriate among ourselves, and we'll go on with it at that time.(17)

The five-hour serial play by the Radio Troupe which I watched in production, BABBAN RUMBU MATARSHI TUKUNYA (Big Corn-bin Whose Wife Is Cooking Pot), was created in August and September 1981 shortly before the harvest season. The play concerns the rich men who speculate on the crops, offering farmers advance money at a time when they lack cash and later collecting all of the harvest only to sell it back, at higher prices, to the farmers for food. As the troupe's director, Sani Na'Awa, informed me, the purpose of the radio play was to warn the farmers against taking money from speculators, at the very time they were likely to appear in the villages--just before the harvest and during the Muslim festivals, a time of extra expense for religious duties and festivities.(18) The topic was particularly timely as the rains that year had been meager and the harvest was expected to be poor; thus, advance sales of crops still in the fields would be disastrous for the farmers.

Troupes and Rehearsals

The Radio Troupe's play aimed to show the village people the true designs of speculators through the satire of Babban Rumbu, his wife Tukunya, and their agent Dila (jackal), whose intrigues are discovered by the head of the village **samariya** and foiled in the end.(19)

The Arrangement of Scenes

Once a theme has been determined, the troupe plots out a set of scenes around it. This first arrangement may be the work of one person or a small group; it may or may not be written down in brief outline form. But whatever its initial source, the descriptive list of scenes is presented to the troupe as a whole for discussion and modification, a process which continues throughout the rehearsals. The outline of scenes is not a set text, unlike the script in a conventional western play; rather, it remains a working frame, a basis for the changes made by the group in translating thematic ideas into human interaction on the stage.

The Maradi Troupe structures each of its scenes around a key phrase (**la phrase clef**) relating to the main theme. In a group interview, members of the troupe explained that several of the leaders in the troupe (**musamman**) work together to arrange the scenes before rehearsals begin. The troupe includes about thirty **fonctionnaires** and usually five of them do this preliminary work. For their 1981 play, 'DAN KWANGILA (The Contractor), they felt that a construction project follows a logical history: it must be announced, then awarded, money must be obtained, the government offices must be consulted on where and how the building will be constructed, then it will be built well or badly. From this sequence of real-life events, the troupe worked out eight scenes: 1) discussion of the contracts to be awarded, 2) seeking the contract, 3) finding funds, 4) arranging with the government workers to establish the site, 5) beginning the construction, 6) the work itself--good or bad, and (7 and 8) wrapping up what happens in the end. One actor emphasized that each scene is developed to its fullest potential; they discuss the scene at length, searching for the key phrase carefully, because that phrase begins everything. When they have prepared the first scene to its fullest extent (an **kai mak'ara**), they join it to the central idea of the next scene.(20)

In retrospect after their festival performance, the director and two actors in the troupe gave the following summary of the important points, the key phrases, of each scene of 'DAN KWANGILA. The bracketed additions are mine for clarification.

> Scene 1 is at the home of Alhaji Gimshik'i, a conversational meeting place. The group hears the government's radio announcement calling for bids for the construction project for clinics in the Maradi region. The men discuss the importance of people working together (**ha'da kansu**) for national development (**tsarin k'asa**). Alhaji Rangama [the **'Dan Kwangila** of the title] wants to try for the contract but is warned against it [as he knows nothing about building].
> In Scene 2, the troupe wanted to show that sometimes getting a contract is fair (**mai gaskiya**) but at other times it a case of corruption (**cin hanci**). Not everyone is corrupt, but the actors wanted both the public and the government to see that there are corrupt people. [The prospective contractor, Alhaji Rangama, goes to Niamey to visit a member of the committee which will award the contract; he brings a pile of presents, including a color television, to this man's house].
> Scene 3 presents the committee giving out the contract. The man whom Alhaji Rangama bribed makes certain his candidate is awarded the contract.
> Scene 4 takes place at the bank. It shows how rich people like Alhaji Rangama can get money very quickly [via "friends" and bribes], while government workers [here typified by a nurse and a teacher waiting days for small loans] do not receive any attention. The bank employees expect gifts to do their work.

Troupes and Rehearsals

In Scene 5, 'Dan Kwangila goes to the city planning office to learn the site for his construction. The official papers have not arrived from Niamey [to Rangama's annoyance].

People who have money often think they can do anything they like; 'Dan Kwangila is one of those people. He refuses to wait and barges into the director's office. [He also refuses to wait for the proper clearance from Niamey].

The scene also shows corruption among the government employees, such as the friend of the director who complains that his old vehicle has used up his gas allotment, when he has just given his coupons to the secretary outside the director's office [to go on a date with her].

Scene 6 shows the construction site and the problems with the work which has begun: not enough workers have been hired and those who have come have no skills. [Rangama will not pay the official wages]. One of the workers takes a complaint to the inspector.

In Scene 7, the inspector of [employee welfare] comes to the site and lists Rangama's faults: he has failed to hire Nigerien workers, he has failed to pay sufficient wages, and he has worked the laborers over-time. The inspector tells Rangama that he must pay all of them their back wages.

Here, the director of the troupe emphasized the troupe's portrayal of the bad character of contractors, while an actor explained that they also wanted to show the workers that they must report to the appropriate government officials so that they will not be cheated by unscrupulous employers.

After the inspector comes the director of city planning to inspect the foundation; he finds the worthless bricks. [Rangama has tried to save money by increasing the ratio of sand to cement]. Since the building is no good, it must be destroyed. This shows the necessity of work properly done.

Scene 8 portrays the destruction of 'Dan Kwangila: he loses his building [news arrives that it has been torn down]; he loses his money [his Yoruba accountant has gone to Kano with the workers' wages]; and he loses his senses [he has to be carried off by his wife's brother and his friend, Alhaji Gimshik'i].(21)

Using methods similar to those of the Maradi troupe, four or five people in Zinder's Troupe Amadou 'Dan Bassa take their theme and arrange it (**tsara**). Their director, Yazi Dogo, described this arrangement using the French terms **charpente** (skeleton, framework) or **plan**. The small group designs the actions and then brings the actors together to explain the plan to them. One of the difficulties with theatre in Hausa, Yazi stated, is that it is not written down. He added:

Sometimes we write the play down after we do everything, but we don't come with a written thing and say, "This is what we'll do," because there are always changes. Before you finish it, it will change two or three times. Yes.(22)

For the over-all arrangement, the troupe looks at the theme from beginning to end, what is necessary to present first and how it continues from there. They begin when they have two or three scenes in mind and then work through the rest. Sometimes they find no connection between two scenes, and they look at them calmly (**da hankali kwance**) to see what is to be done. They want the scenes to follow one another, but not to be confused (**rikice**). According to Yazi, history plays are no problem because the troupe knows the history and how events follow one another. But at times, they begin rehearsing a play and see that they have made a mistake (**kuskure**) and so they change the arrange-

Troupes and Rehearsals 73

ment and replace things to make it right (**daidai**).(23)

For ALHAJI SHAGALI (Alhaji Pleasure-seeking), Mainé Soroa's festival play in 1981, the director of the troupe, Alhaji Zoubeirou Lawal, wrote the original outline of scenes himself. He began with nine scenes but the troupe worked the play out finally in only six. In October, about six months before the festival, they began work, not only on their play but on a **ballet** and a song as well. Alhaji Zoubeirou suggested the idea for the play's theme, that of **entreprise**, so he developed the scenes (**tableaux**) for it, while others worked on the themes for the **ballet** and the song. The troupe began rehearsals with Alhaji Zoubeirou's original nine scenes, but several townspeople they had invited to observe it told him to remove some of them. He asked them to explain their ideas and the troupe consented to their suggestions. In Alhaji Zoubeirou's words:

> Even though I wrote it, I didn't say ... I didn't stop with what I did. It's not like that. When we do [a play], then we invite people to come and watch what we've done. Everyone watches and tells us his ideas, his opinions, and then we work with that. That's how it was for this one, we got [their opinions] and we took out three scenes. That's how it happened that we did six.(24)

One reason Alhaji Zoubeirou gave for inviting people from outside the troupe to observe their rehearsals was that he himself had the central role, Alhaji Shagali. He had not intended at first to act in the play, but when they could find no one else suited to play the comic lead, he took the part and asked some of the **fonctionnaires** in the town to come and critique him and the play since he could not see his own work and faults (**laihi**).(25)

Nonetheless, the actors in the Mainé troupe insisted on the group's role in creating the play. One of the senior actors, Mahamadou Lido, forcefully stressed the importance of the whole troupe as follows:

Now look, for this theme, Alhaji brought it, Alhaji Zoubeirou, for this play we've just presented. He had only one role in it. How many people were at the work-site? How many people were on the stage? If it weren't for them, it wouldn't work.
(A chorus of assent from others in the troupe: It wouldn't work.)
I myself think that if a person finds a theme, if it's done and done well, and they say it's So-and-So's--this giving of one name is ridiculous, it's worthless, because one person alone can't do anything. It isn't possible.(26)

Mahamadou reiterated Alhaji Zoubeirou's account of choosing this theme from six suggestions, although neither man would list the other themes, which they may use at a future time. Generally in their troupe, after everyone agrees on a theme, the person who brought the idea prepares his outline for the scenes. This time, the troupe saw that some of Alhaji Zoubeirou's scenes were like **tatsuniya** (fairytales, fantastic stories), things that are not shown in the theatre, so they left them out.(27) According to Mahamadou, they kept adjusting the arrangement and finally did the six most appropriate scenes.(28)

Alhaji Zoubeirou believes that audiences need fewer scenes now to understand a play than they did in the past. With increasing education, he feels, audiences know the ending to a play just after it has begun, so the troupe arranges only a few scenes. For the first Festival in 1976 in Zinder, the troupe performed eleven scenes; the next year they did ten; two years later they had nine; and then they reduced the current play to only six. He felt six scenes were sufficient for ALHAJI SHAGALI; people understood it.(29)

When I asked what they had eliminated from his original outline, Alhaji Zoubeirou replied that one scene they cut out showed Alhaji Shagali getting an advance allowance for the construction project,

buying a car and gallivanting about town while his
wives sit at home; the scene took a lot of time and
the audience understood his character without it.
The second scene which they eliminated presented
Shagali quarreling with his family and neglecting
them; the third showed Shagali going off with
people's money entrusted to him.(30) Instead of
the elaboration of Shagali's corruption through
those extra scenes, the troupe developed at length
the three central scenes of their performance--the
chaos of the construction site with the workers'
complaints, the food vendor not being paid, and the
sous-préfet's inspection (Scene 3); the scene at
Shagali's home where he tries to buy time on the
construction debts, consults his **marabout** for help,
and enrages his two wives (Scene 4); and the
climactic comic scene where Shagali visits Gimbiya,
a prostitute, who lures him into drinking too much
whiskey and escapes with his money as he falls into
a drunken sleep (Scene 5).(31) Alhaji Zoubeirou
judged his audience well in believing they would
know Shagali's character without the extra details
of the scenes that the troupe eliminated; the
performance aroused and sustained uproarious
laughter, particularly in the scene at Gimbiya's
house.

This comic emphasis in Mainé Soroa's treatment
of the construction theme appears as the central
difference between their play, ALHAJI SHAGALI, and
Maradi's 'DAN KWANGILA. The jury at the Diffa
Festival noted the similarity of their themes,
but nonetheless awarded them the two highest
prizes, with Maradi's first for the troupe's
composition and interpretation of the theme.(32)
The Maradi Troupe's play is more seriously political in its orientation, striking a different
balance between the didactic and the comic elements. When asked to compare the two plays,
members of both troupes hesitated to answer, but
agreed that the difference was slight. An actor in
Maradi noted the different number of scenes--
Maradi's eight as opposed to Mainé's five (as he
remembered them)--and the key scenes diverging when
Shagali went to the prostitute's house, whereas
'Dan Kwangila's foreign accountant left the country
with the project's money.(33) Speaking for the
Mainé Soroa Troupe, Alhaji Zoubeirou pointed to the
difference in the names chosen for the main character: their Alhaji Shagali truly lived up to his

pleasure-seeking name, while Maradi had its 'Dan Kwangila, stressing his role as contractor. But, he added, the two plays were close, like Hassan and Husaini (twins).(34)

The Distribution of Roles

Roles evolve along with the process of transforming the framework of scenes into actions on the stage. The core group of actors in a troupe usually create their own (major) parts; the director does not always act, but often he has a starring role as well. Typically the plays have large numbers of minor roles, and doubling parts is a common practice. The troupes rarely designate official understudies, but role substitutions occur frequently during rehearsals whenever actors are unable to attend, and sudden substitutes seem to cause no problem to performances. Having thoroughly worked through a sequence of scenes together, the actors usually can take nearly any role in the play.

Roles become assigned to actors during rehearsals, often by a trial and error process. The director or the leaders who have worked out the beginning scenic plan may name actors to certain parts for the early rehearsals. If the roles suit the actors, and if they perform them adequately, they will stay with them to develop them in the play. If the actors feel uncomfortable with the characters they are to play, or if the director or others in the troupe feel there is something wrong, they will try someone else in the role. Again, as in the scenic arrangement, the group's interaction appears central here. The consensus as to what is appropriate or fitting (**abin da ya dace**), and what is a mistake (**kuskure**) may have been difficult to define for an outsider like me, but it was very much a factor in the troupes' work.

One highly specialized instance of this consensus in assigning roles perhaps will best demonstrate how integral a part of the group process it is. Zinder's annual **Wasan Kara** (Harvest Play, literally, "game of cornstalks") involves the entire city community in a day-long series of events. The custom extends back to the traditional gatherings of young men and women following the harvest,(35) but it has taken on political overtones, at least since colonial times. Now the play generally depicts the leaders of Niger and of other African nations as well. In 1981 while I was in Zinder, the **Wasan Kara** portrayed the visit of Nigeria's President Alhaji Shehu Shagari to Zinder. The "characters" of the play were all famous people--President Shagari, Niger's own President Lt.-Col. Kountché, government ministers, the diplomatic corps, local leaders. A large part of the fun seemed to be the audience's recognition of their neighbors and friends in those eminent roles.

Alhaji Abdousalam Adam, Honorary President of the 1981 **Wasan Kara**, explained to me that the eighteen **samariyas** of the city of Zinder worked together to produce the performance. The leaders of each **samariya** met in a council not only to work out the program of events, which re-created a state visit with great verisimilitude, but also to assign the roles. Actors were selected from among the **samariyas** for their resemblance to the famous characters--by their features, how they walked, how they smiled, however they most closely appeared like one of the dignitaries needed for the play. Thus the representatives from eighteen **samariyas** chose a cast of several dozen players--presidents, ministers, ambassadors, local leaders, with accompanying military guards, newsmen and a band--from among the citizens of (potentially) the entire city.(36)

The actor chosen to play President Shagari, Sinni Sanda, a nurse at the hospital and an actor in the Troupe Amadou 'Dan Bassa, did indeed resemble him although Sinni is probably thirty years younger. Sinni came to ask me for help in composing and delivering President Shagari's speech in English; he had been told that he had to speak in English despite the fact that he had never had an English lesson in his life. That President Shagari and the people of Zinder all speak Hausa and would have no need of their divergent colonial languages appeared to be irrelevant to the purposes of the play. Instead, the key factors seemed to be that the actor look like the Nigerian president and that he make a speech in English. During the actual performance, the audience burst into such loud laughter as soon as Sinni began speaking, "Ladies and gentlemen...," that it hardly mattered what he then said since he could no longer be heard, even with a microphone. The town leaders knew what effect they wanted, what their audience expected, and they achieved it with thunderous success.(37)

On a smaller scale and with (presumably) less coincidental criteria than those of looking like Nigeria's president or the Chinese ambassador, the troupes pair their actors with the roles of each new play. For Zinder's Troupe Amadou 'Dan Bassa, most of whose members have worked together for quite a long time, certain types of roles have become the specialties of certain actors. As Yazi Dogo described the process of assigning roles, careful consideration is given to each actor's talents. The troupe gathers and the leaders who have worked on the theme explain their ideas, the framework of scenes, and the various roles they see in them. The actors consider this plan and begin contributing their ideas, what they can do to help develop it, bits of action to add in. Yazi stated that they do not just tell each actor what role he is to have, but they look at everyone and consider what is needed (**ya kamata**) for each role:

> We look among ourselves, who is necessary [for this]? Who is it who is needed for this role? We look carefully, we examine the face of the actor, we examine what he is to do.(38)

If the role has authority, like that of the traditional rulers (**ikon sarauta**), then Abdou Louché will take it; there is no question but that the role is his. For comic roles, they have Yazi himself or "Dodo" (Abdou Nagondja), or "Gliss" (Ibrahim Tando). If the character needs a way with words (**iya magana**), it goes to Alilio (Ali Kassoum) or Kailou (Kailou Bako). They want the role to suit the person so that the audience will feel that it is right/appropriate.(39)

New actors become incorporated into this troupe by two routes. Sometimes the troupe thinks of people in town who would be suited to certain roles for a theme and they ask them to join the troupe. If these townspeople are interested in the theatre, they may stay with the troupe; if not, the troupe will find others. For prospective actors who approach the troupe on their own, the second source of newcomers, the troupe looks at their character (hankali), their intelligence and abilities. They tell the new actor to watch their work for a while, and they wait before giving him a role. Yazi used the French term **stage** for this process, a training period, an apprenticeship. When a role comes up that the new actor might be able to do, they try him out in it; they show him what to do until he becomes accustomed to it (**har ya saba**). According to Yazi, they have no problem finding actors; many come to the troupe by themselves. Some "cannot do anything," but the rest stay with the troupe and learn.(40)

In two interviews in Maradi (January and April 1981), I received somewhat different replies to questions concerning how members of the troupe are cast. One of the actors, Chaibou Begu, explained that the director (**metteur en scène**) is the president of their rehearsals (**shugabancin répétitions**) and takes charge of all the preparations, including the assigning of parts to the actors. He added that this does not prevent the others from giving their opinions but that the director is in charge.(41) The troupe's director, who was not present at the first interview, replied that certain roles are "married" to certain people, "When you see him, you know it is right for him."(42) Chaibou then elaborated on this statement by the director, saying that the troupe has been working together for five years and everyone knows one another well; if there is a **sarki's** role, they have someone who does that, there is someone for a **mak'adi** (a drummer), a comic role, or whatever it might be. The troupe has no problem assigning parts, they have someone for every role.(43)

Members of the Troupe of Mainé Soroa gave me fuller descriptions of the process of matching actors to their roles. In Alhaji Zoubeirou's words:

> At the time we began preparations for the festival, we called together the young men and women, the actors of our troupe. Well, there it was, we had a theme, so what were we going to do? Everyone took his role, the one that was right for him, the one he could do or that she

could do. Then we ... if we're mounting it, then I, for example, will take the role of an **alhaji** or perhaps a **malam**. Then I see that everyone takes one.

Like the time that we put Gimbiya in this role of Gimbiya.(44) There was another girl we put in [the role], we saw that she couldn't do it, or if she did it, it wasn't right. So we put another one in, that didn't work, then we tried her [Ladi Garba]. When we put her in, we saw that she ... everything about her was just right, so then we wrote her down for Gimbiya, she would do the role of Gimbiya.

It is the same for someone else, for an **alhaji** it's like that, or for a **sous-préfet**, we will try a lot of people out and we'll see which one can do it right, then that's it, we'll put him in.

As for the role of Alhaji Shagali, at first I wasn't going to do it. Even though I gave this theme, I wanted someone else to take the role. Then everyone tried it, but I didn't see the pleasure in it that I wanted. So I tried the role; when I did it, people said, "Oh! You are the one to do it!" ... So I stayed as Alhaji Shagali, that's how it was.(45)

Elaborating on the qualities of appropriateness and inappropriateness for certain roles, actor Mahamadou Lido used himself as an example. He said that there are three people in the troupe who could play the part of the **sous-préfet**; in the end, he was best, not because he was more educated or wiser, but because he had the most facility in Hausa (**na hi k'arya harshe na Hausa**). For the Mainé Soroa troupe, Hausa is not their first language, but apparently a person of authority must

Troupes and Rehearsals

speak well in the context of the play--here, in Hausa for the national festival audience. Mahamadou continued his description:

> Daga halin mutum ne aka ba shi rôle.
> (It is by the character of a person that his role is given.)(46)

Some people cannot take a role of authority (**iko**) because they do not have a "calm body" (**sanyin jiki**). In his own estimation, Mahamadou cannot play a role of deference or respect (**ladabi**), because he cannot speak slowly. For this reason he is not an appropriate actor for the role of a **malam**, he would spoil it (**'bata**). He can, however, take the role of a soldier or a **sous-préfet** or a **sarki** instantly, because those are suited to his nature. The troupe looks at a person in a role and if it suits him, they give it to him without argument.(47)

Many of these automatic decisions seem to be the sort of typecasting common to conventional western theatre--beautiful actresses play beautiful women, actors play roles of their own age and physical type. A Nigerien **sous-préfet** or **sarki** will generally be a commanding figure, an established middle-aged man, although sometimes a young actor will play the role of a **sous-préfet** if he can speak French more formally than the older men in the troupe. Yet the sense of an actor's personality, his nature in real life, influences the choices considerably, for local audiences know these actors well; they constantly are aware of and react to the fact that a familiar person is acting a particular role. An illustration of the effect of this familiarity appears in Mahamadou Lido's contrast of two personalities in the Mainé troupe in terms of the comedy they inspire. When asked whether the same actors always play comic roles, Mahamadou replied:

> That depends. For instance take Alhaji [Zoubeirou], when he is on stage he can cause laughter but when you are with him you see that he isn't always funny. For instance, if he comes and it's

comic ... there's one actor here, Wakil, whose every word is like that. If he came here and said, "Good morning," to people, they'd laugh. It's just his nature. Whatever he does makes people laugh. Whether it's a humorous thing or not, you'll laugh.
     But as for Alhaji, when he goes on stage with his ideas or his skills in speaking, then when they come, the chief makes people laugh. But when he's not in the theatre ... that is, if you see him you'll laugh--it's not like that, that's not it. It's not his nature. What I mean to say is, it's God's gift that he can do that when he goes on stage.(48)

According to Alhaji Zoubeirou, everyone in the troupe likes to play the comic roles, but they are careful to put the best comedians in the scenes where they intend people to laugh.(49)

The Role of the Director

     As in the early stages of the production--the selection of a theme, arrangement of scenes, and distribution of roles--the director's authority in rehearsals rests on the group's consensus. Each director has his own personal style; some intervene more often and more imperatively than others. However, group discussion rather than direction from above seems to be the central process in most rehearsals.(50)
     For the Mainé Soroa troupe, Mahamadou Lido praised Alhaji Zoubeirou's abilities as a director in addition to his comic gifts as an actor. Mahamadou said that he himself has difficulty telling an actor what he is doing wrong; the actors ignore him because of his hot temper (**zahin rai**). But if Alhaji Zoubeirou demonstrates something to them, they agree to it, because he does it calmly (**da hankalin kwance**). In Mahamadou's words:

> If you have a director who is able to have patience, to speak slowly, then people follow him. But in my case, there is difficulty following me because I can't talk slowly.(51)

In turn, Alhaji Zoubeirou emphasized the group's participation in rehearsals. He tells everyone from the beginning to pay attention to the scene, so that when they finish, they can discuss their opinions and ideas. Each actor can suggest changes at any time and they will see which version is best. An actor may critique his own role and so may anyone else watching him; the group listens to the explanation of each idea, and if it is good (**ya yi kyau**), they will add it into the play. According to Alhaji Zoubeirou, everyone enters into these discussions, both men and women.(52)

I was not able to visit Mainé Soroa at a time when they were preparing a play, but my experience of rehearsals in Zinder showed me two distinct directing styles. During the time I was in Zinder (March to September 1981), I was privileged to observe a variety of rehearsal work by the Troupe Amadou 'Dan Bassa of the **Maison des Jeunes** and by the Radio Club Troupe.

In March, the Troupe Amadou 'Dan Bassa had extensive final rehearsals for their festival play, TALALA MAI KAMAN SAKE, before the national event in April, and in August they rehearsed the same play for a week-long tour of performances in three other towns. As director, Yazi Dogo scheduled these rehearsals in consultation with other members of the troupe; he made the announcements about rehearsal times, travel and production arrangements, and other administrative matters. But during the actual rehearsals, he was a quiet presence, observing, listening, only rarely interrupting an ongoing scene or any of the actors' comments afterwards. When he did speak, everyone listened and acquiesced to his judgment.

Several other members of the troupe--the core group who arranged the scenes and made major decisions with Yazi on the troupe's work--took more active initiative in suggesting changes to the actors and showing them how to do certain bits of action. These leading actors--Oumarou Nainou (who has since become director of the troupe, after Yazi

moved to Niamey), Abdou Louché, and Kailou Bako--
demonstrated specific actions and even entire
scenes for the other actors both when Yazi was
present and when he was out of town. At one
rehearsal just before the Diffa Festival, when they
were adding a minor role for one of the actresses,
Oumarou acted out the new part with two men from
the troupe playing the other women's roles. The
men caricatured the female characters to the
extreme with falsetto voices, mincing steps, and
gestures such as hiding their faces in false
modesty behind pieces of cloth. The impromptu
performance brought gales of laughter from the
entire troupe, and the new actress required no
further instruction.(53)

The women of the troupe were given such
instruction far more often than any of the men,
although partly this was due to the need to train
new actresses in both series of rehearsals. The
actresses would discuss their own roles when called
upon but almost never offered any comment in the
general discussions.

In an interview, Yazi Dogo and Abdou Louché
described their work as leaders with the troupe.
Both emphasized that the troupe has many seasoned
actors who need no direction; some need not attend
the rehearsals at all and can still perform well.
Yazi stated that some of the actors, given a
brief description or demonstration of a role, can
then do it to everyone's satisfaction. But others
need more help, which Yazi described as follows:

> For instance, some of them
> have no idea about what they
> should do. But we only tell
> him, "So-and-So, look, here is
> the role that you should play."
> Also we explain a little about
> what he should do. Then if they
> say, "But I don't know what to
> say," then we look among us,
> either Abdoua [Louché], or
> Oumarou [Nainou], or me, we'll
> say, "Okay, we'll show you." So
> we show him what is necessary.
> But not everything. "Now see,
> here's how it is done." We give
> him a plan, just a little bit,
> that's all. "Now you keep on

with it, think about it, and fix
it up so that it's right for
you."
Because if I show you how I
walk, that's not how you walk.
How I find my words, that's not
how you find them. But here are
just the essentials, that's all.
We do steps one, two, three. You
do it, we show you, you do it, we
tell you to change it, we add on
to it. That's how it is.(54)

Abdou Louché described three sorts of actors: the ones who are adequate (**sun isa a ciki**), the ones that have to be replaced (**sakiya**), and the new ones (**sabbi**). When the actors are only beginning, the leaders show them what to do. Some actors can watch and become accustomed (**saba**) to the group's work. Others need instruction continually; if they fail to get a part, then they are replaced. When asked about such decisions, what advice the director gives, Abdou replied:

The director? Who is it? It
could be Yazi or Kailou or
Oumarou Nainou or me. We are the
head of the troupe.(55)

The work that I saw bears witness to Abdou's assessment. When Yazi and Abdou left town for a week in March, rehearsals went on as usual under the other leaders. Few major changes were made (although the actress's role was added, as described above); most of the work was the practice of substitutes in various roles. After Yazi's return, the final polishing touches were added to the play with full consensus restored. Similarly, in August when the troupe considered planning a new production, Yazi was reluctant to do so without Oumarou Nainou.

The group dynamics of the Troupe Amadou 'Dan Bassa present a complex, ongoing interaction, combining the experience of leading actors with an apprentice induction of new members into the troupe. Yazi Dogo's quiet but well-respected presence, his experience as both an actor and as a school administrator, his humor, and the ineffable qualities of a true diplomat, kept this balance of power working as a highly successful creative unit, the troupe.

The work of Zinder's Radio Club Troupe appeared rather different. I observed one week of their rehearsals before a performance in June (the final one of three weeks of rehearsal); a month of rehearsals in September for the same play while they were lengthening it for a television serial production; and the re-working of a second play they had performed in the past, also for a future videotape. The troupe's director, Alhaji Abdousalam Adam, always took charge of the proceedings--whether acting, discussions, or administrative arrangements; he even directed me where to sit to watch. In the early stages of a scene, he would block out the action, telling the actors where to enter, when to sit down, how to move. Often he gave them exact lines to repeat in the scene, something I observed only once at the other troupe's rehearsals when an actress was having particular trouble with a speech.

In an interview, Alhaji Abdousalam explained that he himself chooses the themes for the Radio Club plays and arranges the scenes. He said that during rehearsals people learn by imitating until they have mastered it. When he asked what I had observed in their rehearsals, I replied that he seemed to put the humor in and to correct the small bits of action; he agreed that he did, seeming pleased that I had noticed. But he added that if an actor has a suggestion, the troupe may put that in as well.(56)

When Alhaji Abdousalam could not come to a rehearsal, usually because he was out of town on business, Mamane Manzo, an actor in the troupe and an **animateur** in one of the **samariyas**, took charge in his place. Usually on those days, the troupe would rehearse scenes which had already been fairly well established, and discussion and changes were minimal. On one such day, however, the troupe mapped out part of a scene they had never worked on before. At the next rehearsal after his return, Alhaji Abdousalam rearranged most of their work in light of his own larger plan. Mamane Manzo explained to me that they cannot change anything (**gyara**) without Alhaji Abdousalam.(57)

This troupe engaged in lively discussions before and during as well as after the acting of a scene. Everyone contributed ideas, teased and corrected fellow actors, asked questions about their own roles, and suggested where the story might go in the case of the new scenes for the television production. The women, particularly the older ones, participated in these discussions much more often and more forcefully than the actresses of the MJC troupe but less often than the men in either troupe. Yet Alhaji Abdousalam's opinions usually prevailed. He himself played only a small role in one of the final scenes of the first play and did not practice a role in the second, although he may well have had a role in the original production of the play. As director, he seems to work from a vision of the entire production, retaining essentially sole responsibility and control much like western directors but unlike the group dynamics of the Troupe Amadou 'Dan Bassa or the Mainé Soroa Troupe.

Actor Training in Rehearsal

Nigerien actors learn their craft by joining a troupe and acting. There is no formal training. Since the troupes are self-selected and unpaid, people with interest in acting and natural ability stay with the troupe, while those who cannot meet the troupe's criteria for performing ably will drop out on their own or through lack of assigned roles. I neither witnessed nor was told of any special acting exercises or preparations.

Rehearsals tend to be informal social gatherings and often start late. The actors share food, news and gossip until enough people have arrived to begin. Absences occur frequently for a variety of reasons--illness, travel, business, events such as weddings or naming ceremonies that troupe members are attending, and the like. If not enough troupe members appear at the scheduled time or if key actors are missing, the rehearsal will be cancelled; during the rainy season, frequent storms also cause cancellations. Twice while I was in Zinder, the stage at the **Maison des Jeunes** was being set up for evening concerts and the troupe's rehearsals were consequently postponed. Visitors may attend rehearsals, but they are usually friends of the troupe or invited guests; rarely did more than two or three non-actors, myself included, observe rehearsals. The troupes invite prospective actors to attend rehearsals and will offer them parts as they arise, either the role of an absent actor just for the day or a new part being added to a scene in ongoing work.

In Maradi, the director informed me that new actors are always welcome to join their troupe. They give no training (**formation**), but the novice actor watches what they do and then tries it. When a new role appears, they try two or three people out in it. Everyone performs it for the group and they then select the best one; if the new actor tries harder, they will let him continue in the role.(58) During the same interview, an actor in the troupe added that there is no training because every one of them is an actor; each of them takes pleasure in working in the theatre.(59)

In similar fashion, the Troupe of Mainé Soroa trains people on stage (**sur place**). According to actor Mahamadou Lido, training is a gradual process of letting the new actor become accustomed to playing a role. They give him a role and the scenes he is to do and then observe what he does and critique him afterwards. Gradually (**yau da gobe**) he will learn what is expected of him. In contrast, the experienced actor (**tsohon acteur**: the "old" actor) takes difficult roles and just performs them, needing no instruction. He can also help the young actor know what to do by his example. Mahamadou described the experienced actor in terms of this proverb:

> Tsohuwar k'ura mai rida da kwance.
> ("The old hyena seizing while lying down," i.e., it is no effort for an old hyena to catch its food).(60)

When asked what sort of advice troupe members might give new actors, Mahamadou replied:

> There's only one sort of advice--you who are directing this year, you come and sketch for him what it is necessary for him to do. When you come and do it, he watches, then you give it

to him and tell him to do it as
you've indicated. If he does it
and you see that it's right, you
say, "Okay, that's how you should
do it." But if he makes a mistake, you show him again without
tiring.(61)

One of the instances in which an actor's
experience becomes crucial occurs when someone
forgets his role. Mahamadou Lido felt that the
ability to extemporize in an unexpected situation
cannot be taught; it is a skill learned gradually.
He described Kadi, a former actress with the Mainé
troupe, a true "old hyena" (**tsohuwar k'ura**), who
could always help the other actors by finding a
subtle way of reminding them of their parts.
However, if no actor like that is on stage at the
time, the scene could be ruined.(62)

Mahamadou noted that Ladi Garba, the young
actress who played the prostitute Gimbiya in ALHAJI
SHAGALI, already had demonstrated this ability to
salvage a mistake. Alhaji Zoubeirou elaborated one
example of her skill (**dubara**). During their
performance for the regional competitions before
the Diffa Festival, Ladi started to laugh with the
audience when he (as Alhaji Shagali) began drinking
the whiskey she had poured for him instead of the
soft drink he had requested. He asked her why she
was laughing at him, and she improvised a
reply: "Alhaji, it's because you've come and I'm
so happy to see you." Thus she re-captured her
lost character and the audience never knew; it was
all within the play.(63) Whether natural presence
or a skill she had already learned, Ladi earned her
key role in the eyes of the troupe through this
inspiration.

For the MJC Troupe in Zinder, Yazi Dogo wards
against such character lapses through the structuring of their scenes. Every scene has its key word
(**mot clef**), the essential kernel of the action.
Yazi and his co-directors impress upon every actor
that he must remember that one phrase, he may
forget all the rest but not that. Forgetting the
other parts of the scene is not a serious fault,
but the important points are emphasized repeatedly
in rehearsal, Yazi stated, so that the actor will
not be confused when he goes into a performance.
If the actor should be distracted by the audience,

then it remains for the skill of the others on stage to remind him that he has forgotten, to slip him the key word unobtrusively in a sort of game with words (**jeu de mots**).(64)

The transfer from rehearsal to performance, or from a local performance before a familiar audience to a larger staging before thousands of strangers, can be devastating for any actor. As one actor in the Mainé troupe described the move from their early rehearsals out in the bush (intentionally so as to have no audience whatsoever) to their later rehearsals at Mainé's **Maison des Jeunes**, it gave them a little trouble (**wahala k'adan**) to work on a platform. But when they took their production to the Festival at Diffa, everything changed: the stage was much larger, the lights made a lot of heat [Mainé has no electricity and Diffa's stage had huge floodlights], and there were thousands of people on all sides. It was a tremendous change, but, he remarked, "Everyone got used to it ... didn't we win second prize?"(65)

A more pervasive problem among all the troupes than changes in the acting space is that of **kunya**, a Hausa concept which carries the meaning of shame as well as propriety, modesty, or appropriate conduct. Particularly among the women, for whom acting of any sort is not considered respectable behavior, feelings of shame, fear, and inhibition commonly hinder their portrayals on the stage. I was surprised to see several of the actresses in both of the Zinder troupes change, almost instantaneously, from carefree, joking, flirtatious behavior before a rehearsal began to frozen attitudes, timid voices, and faces hidden behind headscarves once they began to act--for roles which did not call for such modest behavior (a young girl who disobeys her father and sneaks off to a disco dance, and a prostitute brought by a pimp to visit a rich man). These shy gestures were portraits of **kunya** by women who had escaped its dictates in real life; however, public performance--or the realization of future performance in a rehearsal--brought back society's standards of propriety.

Ladi Garba of the Mainé troupe, whose character Gimbiya seducing and robbing Alhaji Shagali was the least respectable role of any I witnessed, told me that she had been afraid at first (**'daurin kai**), but she cast her fear aside (na hidda shi). She described acting for a beginner as follows:

> Work in the theatre is difficult for someone who is not used to it.... The problem in it, if you're not accustomed to it, is that when you come and enter [the stage], you must see the problems of it, you feel shame (kunya) to play in front of people. You do this thing, you do it like this, you truly feel the shame of it in front of people--that's the problem with it, if you aren't used to it.(66)

She admitted she would rather play a respectable wife than a role like Gimbiya but denied that she felt any shame in her performance at the Diffa Festival.(67) Nor was any apparent to me. Her lack of inhibitions on the stage kept the audience in fits of boisterous laughter.

Commenting on the troupe's difficulty in finding someone to play Gimbiya, Mahamadou Lido noted that they had tried eleven young girls (budurwa) in the role. The others could not play the role to the troupe's satisfaction. He credited this to fear ('daurin kai) and shame (kunya). When they demonstrated the scene they had arranged, the girls were ashamed to do it even with only the members of the troupe present. For this reason, in training actresses, the troupe continually brings observers to rehearsals so that the women will be accustomed to performing in front of people.(68)

In a discussion of kunya, Yazi Dogo contrasted the consciousness of the men to that of the women in the MJC Troupe: the men volunteer to come but women are not enlightened (kansu bai waye ba). The women, in his estimation, cannot separate their daily life from the work in the theatre. He believes it is necessary to leave everything in normal life outside; within the troupe everyone is the same, there should be no fighting or turmoil. But the women cannot do that as the men do; they bring the disagreements of real life into rehearsals.(69) Yazi added that neither can the women ignore the audience; they feel shame and cover their heads (**ruhe kai**) or close their mouths (**ruhe baki**). Gradually the troupe raises their consciousness (**jawon hankalinsu**) and they become accustomed to acting.(70)

    Men may also feel **kunya** in certain roles, but there are generally enough actors to replace those who feel inhibitions in playing a role. Abdou Louché described one of their plays in which he and Yazi Dogo took the roles of butchers, cutting, roasting, and selling meat on the stage. Butchers have an extremely low status in traditional Hausa society; many members of the troupe did not care to be associated with characters of that caste. However, Abdou said, it did not prevent him from putting on a robe the next day to play an important man or a **malam**. "A play's a play" (**Duk wasa wasa ne**).(71)

    A conscious separation of reality from the world of the theatre seems to be the major factor in these descriptions of **kunya**. Mahamadou Lido carried this point further, describing audience members in Mainé Soroa (a rural town of 1600 people as opposed to Zinder's 40-50,000) who curse the actors for their evil deeds on stage.(72) Not everyone, he said, could withstand such reaction to a role like that of Alhaji Shagali:

> You see, not everyone is able to take this role, he'll say, "No!" because what happens when people watch, you'll see it on stage when you are playing your role, someone out there will come and curse you out. "You! You bastard! Why are you doing that?" or [to a woman] "You! You bastard! You bitch! Why are you behaving like that?" Not everyone can feel confident with that going on. Some will run, they can't agree to do it like that, because it looks too much like reality to them. But really, it's a play, something to imitate people, to raise people's consciousness.(73)

The problem appears to be that even when the actors are not ashamed to play a role knowing it is only a play, the audience can be very distracting or even threatening. Theatrical conventions separating actors and acting from real life are still being established and defined in this genre.

Within Hausa culture, part of this ambiguity in theatrical roles may stem from the widespread practice of **bori**, the cult in which initiated members, usually women, become possessed by a variety of different spirits, good and evil. Spectators and participants at **bori** ceremonies distinguish between genuine possession, usually for healing, and the **bori** dances widely performed for entertainment. They also distinguish between the everyday personality of the adept and the spirit's inhabiting of her body during possession, when she becomes that spirit. Nonetheless, initiation into the cult separates a woman somewhat from the community, changing her ordinary status by this association with the supernatural even when she is not possessed.(74) While the troupes see their work as quite distinct from the world of **bori** manifestations, their audiences may still unconsciously associate the playing of roles with possession, becoming another being. Edris Makward notes that this is true for many other parts of Africa as well; acting has not been distinct from theatrical representation as a transformation of identity.(75)

The Rehearsal Process

Through their rehearsal work together, the troupes develop characterization, refine and add detail to the scenic framework, and establish the **score** of the play: the series of characters, actions, key words and gestures which tell a particular story and remain essentially unchanged from one performance to the next.(76) The work brought by these actors to create a play may be called improvisation; some of the troupes' members were content with the term while others objected to it. I would separate their work into two types of improvisation: the first occurs in rehearsals to create the score, where suggestions and ideas are explored through freely acting them out and then either accepted or rejected by the group; the second type provides the spark of "new" interaction in performance within the limits of the established score. Some troupes and some plays allow more of this latter improvisation within their scores than do others. The festival plays in particular seem to have a thoroughly established plan for each action and speech on the stage, partly due to the prescribed time limit. Certainly the troupes devote more time to rehearsing their festival productions (generally about six months) than for informal performances for local events (which may be organized in as little as a week or two, but rarely for more than a month). The quick productions, however, depend on a past history of working together, of knowing the other members of the troupe and their abilities quite well. Most of this ensemble work today arises from the festival preparations, the major production for nearly all of the troupes each year.

I was not able to observe a festival production from its inception, but the process described by the different troupes I interviewed follows a definite pattern. The heart of the play's score lies in its theme, which encompasses the troupe's message, the purpose of the play (**amfani**) as they see it. As described above, either one person or a group from within the troupe develops the theme into an outline of scenes and a set of basic characters. This rough plan is brought before the troupe and roles are discussed and assigned. Subsequent rehearsals with the full troupe refine, develop, and establish the score through acting it out. Improvisation forms a crucial part of this process, but the extent of what is "set," determined, or arranged, and what is "free" to change, when, and by whom, depends on the dynamics of the group's relationships--their talents, inspirations, mutual trust and respect, and their working methods. Some of this diversity appears in the rehearsal descriptions from four troupes which follow.

The Mainé Soroa Troupe

For the **samariya** theatrical troupe of Mainé Soroa, director Alhaji Zoubeirou Lawal gave the following account of their rehearsals:

> Rehearsals? What do we do? At the time we begin preparations for the Festival, when we have our theme, we go and talk to

the **sous-préfet**, we tell him that we've found a theme. Also that we want to work on it out in the bush. Then the **sous-préfet** gives us a truck and we leave town, we go out about ten kilometers and find a good spot. That's where we'll go to do our rehearsals-- out in the bush. When everyone is able to do [his role], then we can show it in town for the townspeople to see, then, for instance here at the **Maison des Jeunes**, we'll close the doors and just among ourselves we'll be able to work on it. But at first we go out in the bush. In the bush ... where there is no one at all [to watch]....

At first when we stage a play, we will do all the scenes at once. When we do it all through, everyone knows his role. There are some scenes that are difficult, some scenes that aren't difficult....

When we've done each scene, we look at the clock and see how much time it takes.(77) That's how it is. But at first we stage one after another so that every- one gets his part, then we go back and do one scene a day, or two or three ... like that. Little by little everyone is able [to do his role]. Then we'll do all the scenes together again until it's finished....

When we begin, everyone observes what we do in each scene. After we've finished, then we gather in a circle and sit. Everyone who has an opinion about this theme raises his hand and speaks. Everyone talks, whether a woman or a man, he'll say, "Oh! In this scene I saw ..." [or] "Oh! In the **sous- préfet's** speech, this is what I

> heard ..." [or] "Oh! What I
> understood in Alhaji's speech
> was...." Everyone speaks like
> that. Everyone speaks, then
> we'll keep improving it. That's
> it.(78)

Mahamadou Lido concurred with Alhaji Zoubeirou's description of their troupe's working methods. He added that the rehearsals in the bush went on for about ten days, and that when they were on the right track (**mun kama hanya**), they tried it out before some of the important people of the town: the leaders (**manya**), the elders (**dattijai**), and the government people (**'yan bariki**). These observers gave their opinions about the appropriateness of the work for the festival, what they believed should be added or taken out, and then the troupe continued its private rehearsals.(79) This incorporation of official opinion marks the importance of the troupe's performance at the national festival as representing the town of Mainé Soroa and also (after the preliminary competition) the Département of Diffa. The troupes' performances for local audiences do not usually require such an official stamp of approval.

The Maradi Troupe

In discussing their work, the Maradi Troupe emphasized the set arrangement of their plays. They alone of all the troupes I encountered write their plays down. In interviews before and after their festival performance (January and April 1981), members of the troupe adamantly insisted that they do not improvise. As actor Chaibou Begu expressed it:

> We have no improvisation.
> We write every play that we
> do, whether it is in Hausa or
> in French.(80)

However, the director of the troupe described the process of developing the play in a manner similar to the rehearsals of other troupes, with the exception that his actors write down the important things that relate to their parts. When an actor goes on stage, everyone in the Maradi troupe helps him to improve what he does and says, finding what is most suitable for each moment (**lokaci**).(81) The written version of the play comes out of this process; it is not a text presented to the actors beforehand to memorize. According to Chaibou Begu, the purpose of the written play is to insure that they will not forget what they have done and to help everyone to learn the other roles in case anything should happen that they would need to substitute for them.(82)

The written text of 'DAN KWANGILA, Maradi's 1981 Festival play, copies of which the troupe distributed to members of the jury in Diffa, is a twenty page text of the key lines. No gestures, costumes, scene locations, props or other performance elements appear in it, and the dialogue is not the lengthy elaborated version found in a complete transcription of what was said on stage (90 pages). Rather, the written play provides a bare outline of what I have called the score: the number of scenes, the characters on stage, who played each role, the central lines of their interaction. Much of what the actors know about the play--the conventions of their theatre and the rehearsed oral text of the play--does not appear; the written text remains a framework.

What requires several pages of transcription for the dialogue from the performance--such as a series of greetings when a new character enters-- may not appear at all in the text or may be reduced to one line. For example: "Bonjour, Mademoiselle, il est là votre patron?" (Good morning, Miss, is your boss in?) in the written play represents several minutes of flirtation in performance. The young man enters, greets the secretary, remarks how beautiful she looks today, asks if she is going to the party that evening. She replies that she would like to go but that she needs a new dress; he asks how much it would cost and gives her the money for it. She then says that her **mobylette** is out of gas and she cannot use it; he gives her the rest of his government gas coupons, and she agrees to meet him at eight o'clock. He then asks if her boss is in and she directs him to go inside the office (Scene 5, 'DAN KWANGILA).(83) The written line in French apparently recorded for the troupe the sense of this brief interaction: two educated people in an office (who both speak French), the bit of business to carry the scene further ("Is your boss in?"

being the young man's reason for appearing). Yet equally a part of the scene, although unwritten, was the joking rapport between the young people, the coy requests of the secretary and the man's compliance, which earns him immediate access to her employer. The mixture of Hausa and French in the actual performance of this scene came naturally to these actors, a probably unconscious portrayal of conventions in real life (when and where Hausa is appropriate in an office, what signals a joking relationship/flirtation, etc.). Their precise lines in this dialogue most likely varied from one performance to another, despite the troupe's insistence that they do not improvise, but the key points of action and speech would remain the same (in that sense it is a "set" text).

The Maradi Troupe writes more of its score than many of the other troupes, but the development of that score remains an oral process. Their knowledge of the play retains far more details than their written reminder. Nor does having a text freeze the process of change. Between the time of the written version of 'DAN KWANGILA and the troupe's performance at the National Festival in Diffa, a major character's name was changed from Alhaji Bakwai (seven) to Alhaji Gimshik'i (supporting pillar), a clearer indication of his relationship to 'Dan Kwangila (the contractor).

The Troupe Amadou 'Dan Bassa of the Maison des Jeunes, Zinder

The rehearsals I observed by Zinder's Troupe Amadou 'Dan Bassa in March 1981 were in the final stages of preparation for the National Festival in April. They had been rehearsing their play, TALALA MAI KAMAN SAKE,(84) for about two months previous to their March 9th performance at the regional competitions in Tanout, where they were chosen to represent the Zinder Département at the national event. I observed one performance in Zinder before the preliminary competitions, two performances in Tanout, and their final performance for the National Festival in Diffa, as well as rehearsals between these performances.

In this final month of preparations, more elaborate costumes were made, two cloth backdrops were painted, and a flat was built with a functional door for Talala's fancy house. None of these, however, was brought to or used in rehearsals. Many of the rehearsals had actors substituting in others' roles both because of frequent absences and in order to make everyone familiar with other roles should substitutes be needed. This indeed happened: the actor playing the judge in the final scene was unable to travel to Diffa for the festival and a replacement had to be found three days before the troupe left Zinder.

Some of the changes introduced during these last weeks of rehearsal included the following:(85)

> --The name for Talala's orphaned niece was changed from Salamatu to Rabi [both are common Hausa women's names], because the actress's mother, whose name was Salamatu, had died and she did not wish to be called by her late mother's name, even in a play.(86)
> --Talala's scene (3) at home with his two wives was clarified at several points. The troupe discussed his entrance, what he should bring his wife, what time of day it was. They decided he should bring his first wife a leg of lamb and not money, and that she should be crocheting as he entered. Alternatively, they discussed having her wash dishes, but decided against that because the scene was to be in the living room (where dishes were not appropriate) and his wife was of a status that she should not be seen washing dishes. Crocheting was felt to be most appropriate to the wife's character and it is something that the actress does well. Six or seven men in the troupe participated in this discussion, including Yazi Dogo who played Talala. The women were not present at the rehearsal at the time; they arrived later but were not consulted.(3/18/81)

--The young wife, Sululu, who leaves for her parents' house during this scene (3) because Talala has neglected her, had been critiqued by the jury at the regional competition; Yazi Dogo reported that they felt it should be clearer why she was leaving. Subsequently, over several days, the troupe rehearsed a longer dialogue between the two wives before Talala's entrance, and the first wife added a longer explanation to Talala about why the younger one had gone off.(3/30 and 3/31/81)

--The jury at Tanout had also docked points from the troupe's total for being over the ninety minute time limit. Consequently the troupe timed all the scenes carefully without interruption, but it was generally agreed that the first scene was the one that had to be cut. The essentials of the scene were delineated as settling the fight between Musa and Zangina [which brings out a discussion of **wasan nangi**, the joking relationships between different groups of people, a point about national unity], and the explanations to the visitors from abroad about the functions of Niger's **samariyas**. The number of visitors was reduced from four to three, and their series of questions distilled into three basic ones.(3/18/81)

--One of the older members of the troupe was given instructions to face the audience, to slow down his speech and to gesture more expansively. Kailou Bako demonstrated for him what they wanted him to do. At another rehearsal, his lines were stressed as one of the

the key points of the Funeral scene (2).(3/26/81)

--A woman's role was added to the scene (6) in which the destitute widows decide they must sell their dowries because Talala has failed to give them their due share of the inheritance. Instead of the widows talking over the need to sell their marriage goods, as they had in the Tanout performances, the character Alhajiya was introduced to bargain for them. This required a means of calling her; respectable widows would not be able to leave the house. So they called their son into the scene to fetch Alhajiya. While waiting for her arrival, the widows continued their dialogue about needing money, then greeted Alhajiya and asked her if she would buy the blankets and pots they showed her.

The new actress as Alhajiya, after one attempt at acting out the scene from the description, was given instructions by Oumarou Nainou in how she was to bargain; she must be polite, even friendly, but unwilling to buy anything except at a very low price. The **animateur** of the **Maison des Jeunes**, who did not act in this play, then demonstrated the role for her in caricature to the amusement of the troupe. The women repeated their scene. Then Oumarou took Alhajiya's role, with the **animateur** and another young man as the two widows. As the men imitated women in gross caricature, the humor softened the critique of the new actress yet it made their point clear. At the same time it strengthened the troupe's sense of solidarity through mutual laughter, a shared joke.(3/30/81)

--Later in the same scene (6), when Talala visits the widows, his niece Rabi's refusal to speak to him was emphasized. In the March performances, she left as soon as the women heard him arrive outside. In the rehearsal changes, her exit was delayed until he came all the way into the room where the women were sitting and had begun to greet him. [This emphasized her rudeness in not speaking to him].(3/31/81)

--Several of the actresses were critiqued repeatedly for mumbling, looking at the floor while speaking, covering their faces, fidgeting; on different occasions the men satirized this overly modest behavior (**kunya**) by imitating it.(3/30, 3/31 and 4/1/81).

--Just before the troupe's departure for the Diffa Festival and just after Yazi Dogo returned from a week's absence in Niamey, the troupe discussed the important points of the play and the problem of the time limit. They all agreed that the first two scenes, the longest in the play, needed to be shortened. Yazi, Kailou, and Abdou Louché outlined the key points, with a few comments by the others, as follows:

Scene 1: The **nangi** relationships between the different peoples, [the chain of ethnic groups linked in these traditional relationships strengthens national unity].

The purpose of the **samariyas** [as explained to the foreign visitors].

[Both of these instructive points are contained in the speeches of Mai Samari, played by Kailou].

Scene 2: The old **malam** refusing to give an appropriate **sadaka** (offering) at the Funeral. The three questions posed by Talala's friend [played by Abdou Louché]: negligence, corruption, and lack of conscience [by those officials people trust].

[The discussion passed over the next four scenes which portray the corruptions of Talala after being entrusted with his dead brother's fortune].

Scene 7: The **malam's** pronouncement of Talala's moral failings at court.(4/1/81)

These points form the core of the play, the purpose and background message against which the story of Talala neglecting his brother's family for his own aggrandizement plays itself out.

Because the score of this play had already been developed when I saw these rehearsals, the emphasis was placed on clarifying the action, bringing it to focus on the important points of the scenes. At times the scenes were acted quite quickly, the key lines spoken with no elaboration and little expressiveness. The troupe seemed very much in agreement as to what constituted this particular play: its theme, message, and essential elements--its score.

Five months later, I was fortunate to be able to see the troupe rehearse TALALA again, this time for a tour to three other cities, although I witnessed only one of their performances (in Maradi). The rehearsals in August for this tour were intended to re-create the play as they had performed it in April. I was surprised when members of the troupe asked me to bring my tapes of the play to the rehearsals. It seemed that the tapes were the simplest way to remember what they had done--a technological innovation to the oral tradition. While listening to their April performance, members of the troupe would anticipate favorite lines, usually the comic ones, and chime in with the tape or repeat the lines afterwards. Occasionally they would comment approvingly on someone's performance but rarely did they critique anyone on the tape. The tapes were used in only four rehearsals and each scene was reviewed only once or twice.(87)

Most of the scheduled rehearsals in the two weeks before the tour were either cancelled or became discussions of administrative matters such as the dates of performance and travel plans. Attendance was sparse; the actors seemed to feel they knew the play and did not need to rehearse. One major change was the replacement of the actress playing Rabi, Talala's niece; the original actress had left town. The woman who had been added as Alhajiya in April was re-trained for the larger role of Rabi, and the Alhajiya scene reverted back to a discussion about selling the widows' dowry rather than action portraying it.(Scene 6) Two of the minor male roles were also performed by substitutes, but neither of these parts was rehearsed before the troupe left Zinder. These rehearsals worked toward recalling their earlier score and reproducing their April play.(88)

Once rehearsed and set as a score in people's memories, even without the aid of a written text, a recording, or even rehearsals, a play may be performed months or even years after its original creation. Shortly after their tour, the Troupe Amadou 'Dan Bassa staged GADO K'ARHIN ALLA in Zinder with no prior rehearsal. They were asked one day to perform the same evening for visiting guests from Kano, and the leaders spent most of the afternoon locating actors and costumes. The most famous of the troupe's plays, GADO K'ARHIN ALLA was Niger's drama contribution to FESTAC in Lagos in 1977, and one of the first plays to be videotaped for Nigerien television in 1979. Although the play is well known to the troupe and to their home audience in Zinder, this impromptu performance in September 1981 took place with several key actors missing and new performers put in their roles. Yet despite the lapse in time, lack of rehearsal, and the changes in the cast, the performance sparkled and thoroughly delighted the spectators.(89) This play belongs to the troupe in a special way; like a treasured possession, they bring it out periodically, dust it off, and enjoy it anew.

The Radio Club Troupe of Zinder

The Radio Club Troupe also reproduced one of their past plays, ALHAJI SHAIDAR MATA (Alhaji Witness of Woman), during the time I was attending their rehearsals in Zinder. Alhaji Abdousalam Adam had written a one-page list of the scenes in the play, which they had performed at the **Maison des Jeunes** in Zinder quite some time earlier (no one could give me an exact date). There was no other written or recorded version of the play. At their first session of new rehearsals, Alhaji Abdousalam asked everyone what they remembered about it. In the discussion which followed, he supplied much of the overview of the play, where the actions of each scene were leading. Actor Mamane Manzo brought out many of the details of the action; the rest of the troupe, two of the women in particular, remembered characters' names and who played each role. The troupe then played through the scenes much more slowly than in their other rehearsals with continual commentary, unlike most sessions where one or more scenes would be completed before discussion of them. The process of recalling and re-creating a play that they clearly enjoyed was lively and loud; actors were rearranged on stage, lines and jokes added, actions revised and repeated until they suited the group's memory of what was to happen. At one point, the group argued over who had played a role; the actor involved could not remember whether he had done it or not. Evidently, with rotation of roles in rehearsal and the strong memory of all the characters as a part of the score, an individual sense of possessing or having accomplished a role is less important than the entire group's work.(90) Once the troupe revived their sense of the play's score, subsequent rehearsals followed their normal procedure with scenes acted and then discussed.

These rehearsals were re-creating ALHAJI SHAIDAR MATA for future videotaping by the national television station (ORTN). The arrival of television in Niger has not only encouraged dramatic activity as in this case by promoting the revival of former plays, but it has also changed its focus. Alhaji Zoubeirou explained to me that the Mainé Soroa Troupe used to perform some of the other troupes' plays in Mainé after the festivals so that local audiences could see them; with the arrival of television, they no longer do so.(91) In Zinder, Alhaji Abdousalam noted that the town's traditional **Wasan Kara** had never needed rehearsals in the past, but now since it is televised, they do rehearse because the entire country will watch them.(92) The play which the Radio Club Troupe organized as the evening's entertainment for the visiting "dignitaries" of the **Wasan Kara** (thus a play within a play), DARAJAR K'ASA AL'ADARTA, was later expanded for a television serial and subsequently instilled with broader national themes for the new audiences.

    This lengthening of an established score was the only rehearsal work I observed in its initial stages. The original play, DARAJAR K'ASA AL'ADARTA (The Value of a Country is in its Customs), follows the choices made by two young girls and their mothers, co-wives of Alhaji Na Alla (Alhaji of God). The first daughter, Taxi, disobeys her father by going off to a "modern" party with drinking, sex, drugs, and resulting arrest by the police; the second daughter stays home and agrees to marry the man of her father's choice. Alhaji Na Alla repudiates Taxi, along with her mother who condones her wild behavior, when he learns that Taxi is pregnant. The two women then seek out a **malam** for an illegal abortion, but find only arrest by the authorities.(93)

    In the second series of rehearsals to produce this play for television, a minor character's visit to the **malam** after the women arrive became an episode of itself. The visitor introduces himself as Malam JaGaba (guide), bringing a new religion from **arewa can arewa** (the distant North). In the original performance this part of the scene was brief: the local **malam** arranges with his assistant for the charlatan's arrest. This arrest creates the dramatic irony of repetition; after seeing Taxi's fate, the audience knows what happens when the **malam** sends his assistant off to bring back a "friend" to help. The troupe's expanded version included a fuller report of JaGaba's activities in town--the type of religion he preaches and his attempt to bribe local **malams** to help in his proselytizing efforts. Two new scenes were developed to follow this one, the first showing the **préfet's** office and the extent of the national threat represented by JaGaba, and the second revealing the arrest of JaGaba. This incident referred to real political events: to the Kano cultleader, Mai Tatsine, who had gathered a following of thousands for his unorthodox brand of Islam and was killed in the riots in Kano in December 1980, and also to the growing Nigerien resentment of Libya ("the distant North") during 1980 and 1981. What had been a play chastizing the loose morality of young people became a topical, political statement as well, given the prospect of national television coverage.

The first rehearsal of this expanded theme began with the scene as it had been played in the **Wasan Kara** performance. A new actor played the role of Malam Zargewa (arresting), the local **malam** who initiates the arrests, which had been Director Alhaji Abdousalam's role. Alhaji Abdousalam and Mamane Manzo described the role to this new actor and interrupted the progress of the scene in order to correct, explain, and reorder the ongoing actions. When the new actor and everyone else had a sense of the scene, Alhaji Abdousalam outlined the changes they would make for the television. Some involved increased technology, for instance adding telephone calls to the **gendarmes** to make the arrest and a taperecorder as evidence of JaGaba's heresy. The entire troupe entered into this discussion offering ideas, particularly for a place and method by which JaGaba should be arrested; these suggestions included a prostitute's house and a hotel (as a stranger in the town, he had to be staying somewhere), or a return to the **malam's** compound. They also discussed who would play the role of the **préfet**, thinking of men outside the troupe they could ask to join them. The troupe has no **fonctionnaire** members and very few of them speak French; the role of a **préfet**, one of the most highly placed government officials, requires not only authority and dignity but exceptional French.

In addition, a possible new role, a prostitute Hajiya Maduga (a created feminine form of **madugu**, a caravan leader), was suggested as someone who could bring JaGaba to introduce him to the **malam**; the later arrest could then be at her house. Concurrent with the idea of this role came discussion of which of the women could play it. The group considered both the conflict with existing roles each actress had (how easily they could double parts) and the requirements of the role: a certain age and experience, and the ability to speak Hausa well (one actress who volunteered for the role was teased for not knowing enough Hausa). These discussions were lengthy and the troupe did not rehearse any of the new ideas on that first day.(94)

The following rehearsal developed the new scene at the **préfecture**. It was apparent that Alhaji Abdousalam had thought over the ideas brought out by the previous discussion and had arranged the over-all action of the scene before this rehearsal began. First he set up the physical boundaries of the stage office--chairs, a bench, and a desk where the **préfet's** inner office was to be; he then assigned the roles of the **préfet**, a guard, and two Women's Association leaders, keeping the secret agent (**Agent Secret**) from the original play. The troupe discussed the normal procedures of a **préfecture**; very few of the actors had ever been to the Zinder building, although one had worked there as a **manoeuvre**. Several of the actors were concerned about needing to speak French; Alhaji Abdousalam told them that it was a Hausa play, if they addressed him as "Monsieur le Préfet" and then changed to Hausa, it would be quite suitable. They talked over the need for a secretary-general in the outer office; everyone agreed there would be a military guard but no one was sure where the secretaries would work. One actor used the example of the Maradi Troupe's arrangement in their recent play; he was ignored. Another actor suggested that they change it to a **sous-préfecture**; Alhaji Abdousalam rejected that location as not of the proper importance. Several members of the troupe then argued about what authority the **préfet** needed for making the arrest, which ministry was the most appropriate. Alhaji Abdousalam settled the heated discussion by declaring that the **préfet** would inform the Minister of the Interior in Niamey, by telephone.

I realized during all this discussion that a major educative function of the plays in the

Troupes and Rehearsals   109

community is to show what occurs in governmental
offices, both the normal, everyday procedures and
the divisions of administration. These actors,
like most ordinary townspeople, had little first-
hand experience of working with government officials and they seemed rather hesitant to act roles
in this unfamiliar territory.
   Once the physical space and procedural hierarchy were determined, the actual rehearsing of the
scene began. Two young actresses were to portray
the leaders of the Women's Association (**Association
des Femmes du Niger**), visiting the **préfet** on
routine business before the secret agent (the
malam's assistant) came to report on JaGaba.
Alhaji Abdousalam showed the young women what
to do, demonstrated the roles, and criticized their
giggling by mimicking them. He told them to shake
hands with the **préfet** but not to bow over in
respect (as traditionally women would do when
meeting an important man). The secret agent was
then guided through his role. Alhaji Abdousalam
directed him in telling his story about the stranger (Malam JaGaba), and several other actors
corrected him in his actions, one in particular
chastizing him for saying, "Ka gane?" (Do you
understand?) to the **préfet**. Alhaji Abdousalam
then instructed the actor playing the **préfet**
about his speech over the telephone to the minister
and his call to the **gendarmerie** to order the
arrest.
   This working through of the sequence of
actions in the scene remained open to interruption,
comment, and change throughout. When the group
decided the **gendarme** should appear on stage, an
actor leaped up to volunteer for the role. Towards
the end of the scene, the troupe decided that the
agent secret would be more appropriate as **l'Inspecteur de la Sûreté** (a National Security Inspector),
and they settled the details of the cassette
recording--who should send it to which authority as
evidence of JaGaba's crime and intentions. The
troupe agreed in the end that they did need a
secretary-general in the outer office to handle
the cassette business, as the **préfet** would not do
work of that nature himself.
   During the rehearsal, criticism was frank and
open but tempered by the group's good-natured
joking. At one point, after demonstrating the
secret agent's role and emphasizing strongly that

he do it exactly as he had been directed, Alhaji Abdousalam broke the intensity of his critique by jumping off the stage on one foot. The actor then repeated the scene as instructed and with a straight face also hopped off; the troupe burst into laughter. After more than an hour and a half's work on this one scene, Alhaji Abdousalam announced that it was good (**da kyau**), to everyone's agreement.(95)

The changes developed by this newly added scene called for re-adjustments in the earlier scene at Malam Zargewa's house. Instead of the **malam** listening to JaGaba's account of the new religion and sending for an arresting officer, a taperecording of the story was required. Because Malam Zargewa would not logically record a visitor's first conversation with him, a dramatic means of making JaGaba repeat his story was devised, allowing the audience to see the taperecorder being hidden under the **malam's** robes.(96) The troupe took great pleasure in solving problems like this one, refining the scenes to mesh together in every detail. Much like the process by which a storytelling artist can weave different episodes of a narrative together, the theatrical troupe expanded their original story paralleling the young girl's sins against Islam with the broader societal heresy of the false **malam**. This structural expansion will be discussed further in Chapter III.

The rehearsal process by which this expanded story was developed by the members of the Radio Club Troupe incorporated the continual interaction of discussion and acting, a working improvisation. Actors suggested ideas to one another to perform. In the critiques which followed, the ideas might be retained, revised, or eliminated. There seemed to me a high level of general agreement in these decisions, but even when disagreements were not resolved, the actors conceded to the group's opinion or to Alhaji Abdousalam's judgment. Through this process, typical of those described by other troupes for their rehearsal work, the Radio Club Troupe established the score of the play.

Improvisation in Performance

From the work which I observed both in rehearsal and in performance, improvisation before

Troupes and Rehearsals   111

an audience appears to have highly structured limits and it remains the preserve of experienced actors. The message of a play does not permit much variation or addition once the group feels that it is set. Movements on the stage and groupings of actors for a scene will change in rehearsal but not in performance; an actor may not decide to enter a scene unexpectedly in a performance with an inspired speech or a joke. The dialogue is never static since actors rarely memorize exact lines, but it follows a set pattern. Greetings may be shortened or expanded from those practiced in rehearsal, but they follow the boundaries of real-life conventions. Key lines also follow a certain order, the rehearsed pattern: the actors know what to expect next and who will say it (as demonstrated by Maradi's written outline of 'DAN KWANGILA).

   Within this framework, there is room for a certain degree of improvisation--if the audience does not seem to understand something, a speech may be repeated or elaborated; if a joke is particularly successful, it may be drawn out. Or, as Yazi Dogo pointed out in an interview, the languages used may change from performances in one town to the next. His Zinder troupe can perform in French or in different dialects of Hausa depending on the audience.(97)   Usually, however, any new material in a performance is introduced only by the most experienced actors, the leaders of the troupe who hold the major roles. The troupes appreciate new comic material, as do their audiences, but new didactic material is rare in performance.

   During my year of research, I witnessed only one totally improvised performance, a **saynète** (short play) by the Troupe Amadou 'Dan Bassa of Zinder. They had performed the play, GIRMAN KAI RAWANIN TSIYA (A Swelled Head is the Turban of Indigence)(98) only one other time, on their tour in Niamey two weeks before their performance in Zinder. They repeated it because of its success but on neither occasion did they rehearse it beforehand. The play is comedy, its purpose sheer entertainment. Its story is typical of the oral narrative tradition, the tale of a prodigal son whose father dies and entrusts his inheritance to an old friend to retain until the son proves himself responsible. Relying on the troupe's strengths, the comic role of the drunken son was

taken by Yazi Dogo, his foils--the conservative
elders--by Oumarou Nainou and Kailou Bako. The
rest of the troupe filled in as the son's drinking
companions and later as the father's neighbors and
friends at his funeral.
    The structure of the piece is simple, center-
ing in the repetition of drinking scenes, the first
as the father dies, the second as the friend
entrusted with the inheritance also dies. The son
is too busy in both instances to do his duty and
attend to them. Thus he arrives at the bedside of
his father's friend too late to learn where the
money is hidden. The major secondary comic action
takes place at the father's funeral (Scene 3)
between the bar scenes. There, amidst the solemn
grieving by the neighbors seated in prayer, the son
solemnly swears that the first person to stand up
will be the next one to die. As chaos erupts with
all the men telling each other to stand up, arguing, and finally crawling off the stage, the son
laughs at his own joke. But the joke recoils on
him when it is his father's friend who dies,
without revealing where his money is buried.
Within this bare frame, the troupe played with the
play and their audience howled in appreciation.(99)
    This performance seems a classic example of
what Yazi Dogo described as the plays the troupe
performed in its early days, sheer exuberant
fun.(100) In recent years, the troupe more consciously concerns itself with conveying a central
instructive message, but their talent for humor is
still very much a part of their plays. The sort of
immediate improvisation of GIRMAN KAI RAWANIN TSIYA
is now the exception rather than the rule in their
performances, but it nonetheless informs all of the
work that they do however predetermined its score.
    The rehearsal work of both of the Zinder
troupes concentrates on the message and structure
of the work, allowing the comic elements to have a
fresh quality in performance from not being over-
rehearsed. As quoted earlier in some of the
interviews on actors playing certain roles, the
comedy is generally entrusted to a few actors. The
comic parts are structured within the score, but
their details belong to the actors' inspiration.
For example, in TALALA MAI KAMAN SAKE, a pimp is
invited to Talala's fancy house to discuss what
women he should bring for Talala to entertain
there. In rehearsal, Dodo Abdou Nagondja (as Savon

Robb) merely walked on stage and discussed the business with Yazi Dogo (Talala) and Abdou Louché (Talala's friend). In performance, Dodo affected an exaggeratedly effeminate walk and voice causing shrieks of laughter through the audience. Later during one rehearsal of the same scene, Yazi (as Talala) rose to show the young woman into the bedroom, with an added gesture--nervously scratching his crotch. The entire troupe, who had seen the scene dozens of times before, burst into laughter.(101) Yazi repeated the gesture in certain performances thereafter, but not for the television cameras at the National Festival.

The experience and judgment of these actors and their obvious pleasure in performing animate their work in front of an audience, bringing it to full, comic life. As Oumarou Nainou told me at one of the troupe's cancelled rehearsals, they do not really rehearse what they do, as in western drama; their work is improvised, everything is in the performance.(102)

A veteran comedian of the Mainé Soroa Troupe, Alhaji Zoubeirou Lawal was chosen as the best actor in the 1981 Festival. He expressed the importance of comedy and of performance in this way:

> In my opinion, you have to have comedy, the comic roles, in a play. For myself, I can understand things with humor better. When I'm in a play, the comedy, the thing which I do when I go on stage, as Mamadou just told you ... it is when I go on the stage that I find my skill.

He continued, explaining that people will not listen to preaching from the stage but will get up and leave the theatre. However, if a play is funny, then people will stay and watch, as they did for their troupe's play at the Diffa Festival.

> Why? It's because of the comedy. Comedy holds people. For this reason, if a person wants to create a play and to put some message in it for the people of this country, then he

> should also put in something so that people will laugh. Every time you are preaching, there's someone sleeping in the audience. As soon as you do something funny--Woooo! he wakes up and sees what is going on. That's why I think comedy is more important than instruction.(103)

Mahamadou Lido, who highly praised Alhaji Zoubeirou's acting skill as a comedian (see above), chose to disagree with his emphasis on comic elements. In Mahamadou's view, the instructive themes are the most important; the comedy arises naturally as when people see Alhaji Zoubeirou playing a drunken man. The troupe did it for the message but people will laugh. He agreed that people need the comic elements in order to pay attention to the instruction, but he reiterated that the message is the focal point.(104) Clearly, both comedy and message are integral parts of the process, whichever may come first in people's minds.

Among troupes throughout the country, directors and actors stressed the importance of both comedy (**ban dariya**) and serious messages (**ban ilimi, jawon hankali**) in their plays. The tension between message and comedy reflects the dual purposes inherent in their work: to educate and to entertain. It also reflects, in part, the dynamic relationship between the score and improvisation, between the conscious, rehearsed structuring of the play and the vital communication that occurs between actors and audience in performance. The following chapters will focus on the development of specific plays' scores from two perspectives--that of structure and that of characterization--and then return to the question of performance.

ENDNOTES: CHAPTER TWO

1. The Nigerien category of fonctionnaires/civil servants includes nearly everyone with a secondary education, as major industries and communications as well as education, health care and administration are under government control.
2. Interview with Malam Boubé and members of the **Samariya** of Dogondoutchi, Niger, 12 December 1980.
3. See Jacqueline Nicolas, "LES JUMENTS DES DIEUX": Rites de possession et condition féminine en pays Hausa (ETUDES NIGÉRIENNES No 21, IFAN-CNRS, République du Niger, n.d.).
4. Interview with Abdoullahi Bagoudou, conducted by Aboubacar Mahamane, Gaya, Niger, 10 December 1980. His original statement:

> 'Yam mata nan 'yam mata muke sawa, saboda ba mu sa mata ... don ba mu so mu yi aiki da matan mutane haka, e, ko ko ya zamanto mata wanda, wani mace wanda a zauna a bi'da kanta, ba mu so mu yi aiki da ita, don tana 'bata mana haraka. Saboda mun zo ta ga wurin kwa'dayinta, ga abin da muke so ta yi, ta kuma ga inda zuciyata yin ta ba shi yiwuwa. Ya saboda hakanan da 'yam mata muke aiki. 'Yam matan kuma saboda hakanan ne mun hita ba mu bari su tahi ko'ina, su na amana ne a hannunmu. E.

5. Interview with members of the **Samariya** of Matameye, Niger, 17 January 1981.
6. Nicolas, pp. 17, 97ff.
7. Victor Turner discusses the distinctive creativity of outsiders and marginal groups of a society in "Passages, Margins and Poverty: Religious Symbols of Communitas," Chapter 6 of DRAMAS, FIELDS AND METAPHORS: SYMBOLIC ACTION IN HUMAN SOCIETY (Ithaca: Cornell University Press, 1974).
8. Interview with Abdou Louché and Yazi Dogo, Zinder, Niger, 22 April 1981.

9. Babacar L. Mariko, LE SAHEL, 14-15 février 1981, p. 3. The original French:

> Mais, le Festival national de la jeunesse, en tant que fête, est aussi un moment privilégié d'expression et de communication totales par le jeu de l'Art, du sport et du contact entre les hommes physiquement, intellectuellement et spirituellement. Il en résulte que le Festival national de la Jeunesse se définit comme une occasion essentielle de réflexion collective, d'échanges multiples et de fraternisation réelle.

10. Interview with Alhaji Zoubeirou Lawal and members of the Troupe Théâtrale de Mainé Soroa, conducted by Aboubacar Mahamane, Mainé Soroa, Niger, 18 April 1981.
11. Alhaji Zoubeirou Lawal, 18 April 1981.
12. Interview with members of the Troupe Théâtrale de Maradi, conducted by Aboubacar Mahamane, Maradi, Niger, 27 April 1981.
13. Yazi Dogo, 22 April 1981.
14. Kélitigui A Mariko, "Le Cinquième Festival National de la Jeunesse--1980--Essai d'examen critique des prestations des Troupes engagées--observations et suggestions pour l'avenir" (unpublished paper, Niamey, 9 May 1980), p. 3.

> La pièce de Zinder, en partant d'un fait banal a essayé de faire ressortir la nécessité et l'obligation pour tous, riches et pauvres, de respecter la loi. Du comportement de Maman Arrivé, qui ne traite qu'avec les banques et la Chambre de Commerce, plusieurs problèmes font simultanément irruption: Relations maîtres-parents d'élèves, relations au sein même d'une famille, au sein de l'école,

entre les enseignants, etc....
A chaque étape de la pièce,de nouveaux sujets viennent se greffer au tronc principal....
   Avec la finesse et l'expérience qui leur sont reconnues, les acteurs de la troupe, sans acrimonie, plutôt avec malice, ont abordé de nombreux problèmes à la façon de l'homme de la rue.

15. Interview with Yazi Dogo, Zinder, Niger, 14 August 1981. His statement:

   Lokacin da muka hwara shirin wannan wasan kwaikwayo wanda munka ba suna BA GA IRINTA BA, mun zamna su da yawa, muna tambaya kowa ya kawo thèmes saboda muna tsarawa shirin zuwa Festival. To, muka zamna, kowa yana kawowa nashi, a duba a ce, "A, wannan ya yi, wannan bai yi ba."
   Can! Sai muka tuna muka ce, "Kai! Akwai abu guda wanda ya dame mu, mu duka, har manyanmu, har gwamnati, shi ne sha'anin yara 'yan makaranta, da malaman makaranta, da uban nan yara." Sai muka ce, "I, lalle wannan ya dace, wannan thème mai kyau ne."
   Sai muka shiga da'da binciki muna ta nema. Da yake cikin troupe 'dinmu akwai malaman makaranta da yawa. Sai suka shiga binciki, kowa ya kawo wa'dannan irin nashi ra'ayi, muka samu, muna tsarawa, muna ka duka abun da yake damuwan malaman makaranta, abun da yake damun uban nan yara, abun da yake damun su ma yara da kansu. I. To. Sai muka ce, "Lalle, wannan ya kamata mu tsara mu yi wani abu bisa gare shi, saboda amhwani

ne na mu duka--uban nan yara su
gane, malaman makaranta su
gane, manyanmu su ma su gane
sha'anin makaranta." To haka
nan ne.

16. Abdoullahi Bagoudou, 10 December 1980.
His statement:

Harakan jama'a sai jama'a.
Duk abun da na samu in za
ni sai in tara su duka. Wani
bi kuma sai mu yi kamar ban
san komi ba, ni tambaye su....
Ni ce, "To, da bana mi ya
kamata mu yi bisa kan mi za a
yi?" ... Sai kowa ya kawo
ra'ayinsa. To. Na ga ra'ayin-
su ya dace, sai in gaya musu,
in kuma bai dace ba, da sannu
sannu sai in kyauto, "Kai, ka
gani bisa kan abin da ka ce ka
gani ga abin da zai hana
mu." ... "Yanzu sai ku shirya
mu yi bisa kan abu **kaza**! Amma
kuma ku duba ku gani tukuna,
abunda kunka gani in daidai ne
ku gaya mini, in ba daidai ba
ne kuma ku gaya mini." To, shi
ke nan, sai mu shirya mu kama
aiki.

17. Interview with Alhaji Abdousalam Adam,
conducted by Aboubacar Mahamane, Zinder, Niger, 13
January 1981. His statement:

Wannan **recherche** kin
th**é**mes, ai, wannan bai ya da
wuya. Saboda su **animateurs**
kin da za su ha'du, kowane yana
da irin ra'ayinshi, abun da
yake gani ya kamata a yiwo
mutane wasa bisa abu kaza don a
jawon hankalinshi.
To. In lokacin da muka
je, in kamar mun yi kamar wata
teyatur ta kusa k'arewa, ko ko
ran da muka k'are ta kamar hin

mako mai zuwa, sai mu ce, "To, kowane ya zo da ra'ayinshi na sabon thême wanda za mu hwara wasa a kanshi."

A lokacin aka zo mutum 'dai ko biyu ko uku, sai ya kawo thême, kuma sai mu ga wanda ya hi dacewa tsakaninmu, sai a ci gaba da shi a lokacinmu.

18. Personal communication from Malam Sani Na'Awa, Director of the Troupe Théâtrale ORTN of Zinder, 17 August 1981.
19. BABBAN RUMBU MATARSHI TUKUNYA, by the Troupe Théâtrale ORTN of Zinder. Five episodes produced and broadcast for national radio, August-September 1981.
20. Maradi Troupe, 27 April 1981.
21. Maradi Troupe, 27 April 1981. The scene summaries are my paraphrases in translation; most are consolidations of two or three actors' statements.
22. Yazi Dogo, 22 April 1981. His statement:

Ke nan bayan mun yi komi da komi sai mu rubuta ta. Amma ba mu yi rubuta ta mu zo mu ce, "A yi ta." Saboda sauyawa ga ta yi kan a k'are ta ta yi sauya bwi ko uku ma. I.

23. Yazi Dogo, 22 April 1981.
24. Interview with Alhaji Zoubeirou Lawal, conducted by Aboubacar Mahamane, Mainé Soroa, Niger, 17 April 1981. His statement:

Amma don ni na rubuta, ba na ceya, ba na tsaya bisa abin da na yi. Ba haka ba ne. In mu yi, sa'annan sai mu k'ira mutane, "To, ku zo ku gani yanda mun yi." To. Ko ya gani, yana kawo idée kinshi, yana kawo ra'ayinshi, to, sa'annan sai mu aiki da shi. A bisa haka ne, mun samu mun fudda tableaux nan guda uku. Ya zamanto, ta, a yi shidda.

25. Alhaji Zoubeirou Lawal, 17 April 1981.
26. Mahamadou Lido, 18 April 1981. His statement:

> Ga shi yanzu, wannan thême, Alhaji shi ya kawo shi, Alhaji Zoubeirou, wannan pièce wanda muka yi présenter. To. Shi rôle guda na yana ciki. Mutum nawa a bisa chantier? Mutum nawa a cikin scène kin? Ke nan in ba da su ba, ba ya yiwuwa.
> [General agreement from several others in the troupe:] Ba ya yiwuwa.
> To ni, sai ni ga dan mutum ka samo thême, in anka yi shi ya yi kyau, a ce, "Na Wane ne." Wannan ba da suna ne kam, banza da wohi, don mutum guda ba shi iya yi komi. Ba ya yiwuwa.

27. I did not pursue this question of what "is not shown," and why **tatsuniya**/stories are not appropriate theatre subjects with the Mainé Troupe; it remains a fascinating subject for future inquiry. Several members of other troupes claimed that they did create plays from traditional stories; others denied that they did so. The prevailing attitude seemed to be that plays should portray real human situations, either current or historical ones, and not the realm of fantasy.

28. Mahamadou Lido, 18 April 1981.
29. Alhaji Zoubeirou Lawal, 17 April 1981.
30. Alhaji Zoubeirou Lawal, 17 April 1981.
31. ALHAJI SHAGALI, by the Troupe Théâtrale de Mainé Soroa, performed at the National Festival in Diffa, Niger, 12 April 1981.
32. Speech by Dioudé Laya, President of the Jury for the National Festival in Diffa, Niger, 14 April 1981.
33. An actor in the Maradi Troupe, 27 April 1981.
34. Alhaji Zoubeirou Lawal, 17 April 1981.
35. See the reference to **Kalankuwa** cited in Chapter I, from Ibrahim Yaro Yahaya's paper,

"Nazarin kan Yanayin Wasan Kwaikwayon Hausa" (Kano, Nigeria: Center for the Study of Nigerian Languages, Bayero University College, 1978).
36. Interview with Alhaji Abdousalam Adam, Zinder, Niger, 30 June 1981.
37. WASAN KARA, Zinder, Niger, 21 June 1981.
38. Yazi Dogo, 22 April 1981. His statement:

> Mu duba muke tsakamu, Wane ya kamata? Wane ya kamata ya yi rôle kaza? Saboda duba muka yi, mu dubi huskar acteur, mu dubi abin da za shi yi.

39. Yazi Dogo, 22 April 1981.
40. Yazi Dogo, 22 April 1981.
41. Interview with Chaibou Begu and administrators of the Troupe Théâtrale of Maradi, Niger, 8 January 1981.
42. Director of the Maradi Troupe, 27 April 1981. His statement:

> Ka san akwai rôle wanda ya armen mutum. Da an gan shi an sa aka ce, "Wanga rôle shi, za yi daidai da shi." To haka nan muke rarraba, za a ce, "Wanga da ... wanga zai yi muna da kyau."

43. Chaibou Begu, 27 April 1981.
44. Ladi Garba was such a success in the role of Gimbiya that in this interview only a few days after the performance, the troupe affectionately referred to her by her character's name. She was present during the interview.
45. Alhaji Zoubeirou Lawal, 17 April 1981. His statement:

> Kamar lokacin da mun soma shirye-shirye na Festival, kamar préparations na Festival haka ... sa'annan mun k'ira samari da 'yam mata na acteurs a cikin troupe kinmu. To, ga shi, mun samu thême. Kuma yaya za mu yi? Kowa ya 'dauka rôle kinshi wanda ya yi daidai da shi, wanda yana iya ya yi ko

ko tana iya ta yi. Sa'annan mu, in mun yi monter sa'annan ni ko in 'dauka **rôle** kin wani alhaji ko ko wani malam. Sai in gani kowa ya 'dauka.

Kamar lokacin da Gimbiya mun sa ta a cikin **rôle** kin Gimbiya. Akwai wata wanda mun sa ta, tana yi tana yi, mun gani ba ta iya ta yi, ko ta yi dai, ba ta daceya. Sai mun sa wata kuma haka nan ne, bai yiwuwa, sai munka sa ta. In muna sa ta, ita mun gani, halaman tana yi daidai, sa'annan Gimbiya ga shi cene(?) tana yi.

Kuma wani, alhaji ma haka nan ne, ko wani **sous-préfet** ne sai mu yi **essayer** mutane da yawa mun gani, wanda mun gani wanda zai yi daidai, shi ke nan, sai mu sa shi.

Kamar **rôle** kin Alhaji Shagali, da ba na ba da **thème** kin, so nike kowa ya 'dauka **rôle**. Sa'annan kowa ya yi ya yi, ba na ... ba na gani da'dinshi kamar yadda nike so. Sai na ta'ba **rôle** kin, kuma da na 'dauka, mutane suka ce, "Ah! Kai ne za ka yi." ... Na tsaya kuma Alhaji Shagali, haka ne.

46. Mahamadou Lido, 18 April 1981.
47. Mahamadou Lido, 18 April 1981.
48. Mahamadou Lido, 18 April 1981. His statement:

Ça dépend. Kamar shi ne, Alhaji, bisa **scène** ne yake iya ba da dariya amma ba, don kuna tare ba kun ga kullum dan ... abun dariya. Kamar in ya zo kamar abun dariya yana ... akwai **acteur** nan ne na guda, e, Wakil, wanda ko magana

> ya yi hakanga shigo nan da ya
> ce mutane, "Ina kwana?" sai a
> yi dariya. Donc, shi **nature**
> kinshi ce. Komi ya yi sai a ba
> mutum dariya. Ko na ban dariya
> yana ko ba na ban dariya ba sai
> ka yi dariya....
> Shi Alhaji, sai ya hau **sur
> scène** nan na wa'dannan,
> dubarori ko ko martabobi
> zanceya, sa'annan na suka zo
> Maina ya ba mutum dariya. Amma
> ba wai, in babu shi cikin
> teyatur wai ta ... in ka gan
> shi ka yi dariya, ba haka nan
> ba ne, ba dai ba ne. Ba **nature**
> kinshi ba ce. Wato baiwa ce
> dai ta Alla in ya hau **scène** ya
> samu yana hakanan.

49. Alhaji Zoubeirou Lawal, 17 April 1981.
50. Connie Stephens notes that this group process is characteristic of Nigerien decision-making in other spheres as well. It is the expressed ideal of the Development Society program, which stresses dialogue (**concertation**) and **participation** among citizens. (Personal communication, June 1983).
51. Mahamadou Lido, 18 April 1981. His statement:

> In **metteur en scène** an
> samu mai iya hak'uri ya fa'di
> kalma sannu sannu, sai mutane
> su bi. Amma kamar mu akwai
> wuyar bi tunda ba mu iya magana
> sannu.

52. Alhaji Zoubeirou Lawal, 17 April 1981.
53. Rehearsal notes, Maison des Jeunes (MJC), Zinder, 30 March 1981.
54. Yazi Dogo, 22 April 1981. His statement:

> Kamar wa'danda ba su da
> **idée** kin abun da za su yi.
> Amma dai a ce, "Wane, Kai ga
> **rôle** kin da za ka yi." Kuma an
> hwa'da ma taimakin ga shi dai
> yake yi. To sai su ce, "Ni,

ban san abin da zan hwa'di ba." Sai mu nemi cikinmu ko Abdoua ko ni ko Oumarou Nainou, sai a ce, "To. Za a gwada ma." Sai a gwada ma abin da ya kamata. Amma ba duka ba ne. "Yanzu dai ka ga yadda ake yi." An yi ma 'dan **plan**, 'dan ka'dan haka ne ma. "Yanzu sai ka rik'a kuma ka yi tunani, ka gyara shi daidai da kai." Tunda ni in na nuna ma yadda nike tahiya ba kake tahiya ba. Yadda nike samu maganganuna, kai yadda ba kake samu, amma dai ga yake kamata, shi ke nan. An yi mataki 'daya, biyu, uku. Kana yi, ana gwada ma, kana yi, ana ce a saki, ana k'arawa. Akwai haka nan.

55. Abdou Louché, 22 April 1981. His statement:

Wa ne ne **metteur en scène**? Ya iya zamanto ko Yazi ne, ko Kailou, ko Oumarou Nainou, ko ni. A cikinmu dai mu ne dai kan **troupe** 'din.

56. Alhaji Abousalam Adam, 30 June 1981.
57. Personal communication, Zinder, 15 September 1981.
58. Director of the Maradi Troupe, 27 April 1981.
59. An actor in the Maradi Troupe, 27 April 1981.
60. Mahamadou Lido, 18 April 1981. I am grateful to Neil Skinner for this analysis of the proverb.
61. Mahamadou Lido, 18 April 1981. His statement:

Jawon hankalinshi guda ne--kai da ka gaya bana ka zo ka kwatantama yanda ya kamata ya yi. In ka zo ka yi ya gani, sai a maida shi a ce yanda wanda ... yanda aka kwatamta maka. To in ya kwata in ya yi anka ga ya yi shi daidai sai a ce, "To haka ya kamata ka yi." Ko kuma ya yi kuskure a sake kwatamtama ba gajiya ake nan.

62. Mahamadou Lido, 18 April 1981.
63. Alhaji Zoubeirou Lawal, 18 April 1981.
64. Yazi Dogo, 22 April 1981.
65. An actor in the Mainé Soroa Troupe, 18 April 1981.
66. Ladi Garba, 18 April 1981. Her statement:

Aikin teyatur kam yana da wuya a wanda bai saba ba.... Wahalashi, kamar in ba ka saba yi ba, in ka zo ka shiga, dole sai ka gani wahalashi ne, kana jin kunya ka yi gaban mutane. Ka yi wannan abun, ka yi wannan abun haka, kunyashi kake ji k'warai ka yi gaban mutane, shi ne wahalashi, in ba ka saba ba.

67. Ladi Garba, 18 April 1981.
68. Mahamadou Lido, 18 April 1981.
69. Yazi Dogo, 22 April 1981.
70. Yazi Dogo, 22 April 1981.
71. Abdou Louché, 22 April 1981.
72. Population figures are from Samuel Decalo, HISTORICAL DICTIONARY OF NIGER (Metuchen, N.J.: Scarecrow Press, 1979), pp. 154; 240.
73. Mahamadou Lido, 18 April 1981. His statement:

Ka ga ba duk kowa ke iya 'dauko wannan rôle ba, dan sai a ce, "Kai! Wannan shege! Don mi ka yi haka?" ko "Ke! Shegiya! 'Yar banza! Don mi kike haka?" To, ba kowa ke iya amincewa da hakanan ba. Wasu za su gudu, ba su yarda su yi hakanan, sai su dibi kamar abun gaskiya ne. Shi ko, wasa

ce aka ce, a kwatamtama mutane,
ta jawon hankalin mutane.

74. Nicolas, pp. 5-6. See also A.V. King, "A Bòorìi Liturgy from Katsina," AFRICAN LANGUAGE STUDIES, VII (1967), pp. 105-25; and Fremont E. Besmer, "Bòorìi: Structure and Process in Performance," FOLIO ORIENTALIA, XVI (1975), pp. 101-30.

75. Personal communication, October 1983.

76. My sense of the term **score** is derived from Phillip Zarrilli's definition: "A performance score consists of all the created and/or received conventions which collectively constitute the complete composition performed." (From "A Microanalysis of Performance Structure and Time in Kathakali Dance-Drama," in his THE KATHAKALI COMPLEX: ACTOR, PERFORMANCE, STRUCTURE, New Delhi: Abhinav, 1983).

This use of **score** is similar to Richard Schechner's definition of **script**: "all that can be transmitted from time to time and place to place; the basic code of the event" (p. 39), or "the interior map of a particular production" (p. 44). He distinguishes **script** from **drama**, "a written narrative text, score, scenario, instruction, plan or map" (p. 39), "what the writer writes" (p. 44), and both of these from **theatre** and **performance**. See "Drama, Script, Theatre and Performance," in his ESSAYS ON PEFORMANCE THEORY, 1970-1976 (New York: Drama Book Specialists, 1977). I prefer **score** to **script** because of the strong connotations of a written document in the English word **script** and in the western drama tradition.

77. Alhaji Zoubeirou's concern with the timing of each scene reflects the importance of the time limit for festival performances; plays over an hour and a half automatically lose points in the competition. Time was not a concern for other types of performance as far as I could determine.

78. Alhaji Zoubeirou Lawal, 17 April 1981. His statement:

> Répétitions? Inda za mu yi? Lokacin da mun soma préparations na Festival, sai in mun samu théme kin, sai mu tahi mu gaya ma **sous-préfet**, sa'annan ga shi mun samu

thème. Ta taka so muke mu yi shi a can daji! Sa'annan **sous-préfet** sai ya ba mu mota, sai mu bar gari, mun ... **kilomètres** goma haka, mu samu wuri na kirki, sa'annan a can za mu tahi mu yi **répétitions** kinmu a cikin daji. Lokacin da kowa ya iya, sa'annan in kaman mu gwada a cikin gari mutane na gari sun gani, sa'annan kamar nan **Maison des Jeunes** sai mu rufe k'oha a cikinmu muna iya mu yi. Amma da fari a daji ne za mu yi. A daji. Inda babu kowa....

Da fari inda za mu yi **monter** teyatur, gaba 'daya za mu yi **tableau** duka. In mu yi gaba 'daya kowa ya san **rôle** kinshi kuma akwai **tableau** mai wuya, akwai **tableau** wanda bai ya da wuya. To....

Kowani **tableau** in mun yi sai mu gani **montre**, mu ga lokacin da ya 'dauka. Haka nan ne. Amma da fari sai mu yi **monter** gaba 'daya, kowa ya samu **rôle** kinshi, sa'annan sai mu koma ko **tableau** guda ne rana guda za mu yi, ko ko biyu ko uku ne ... haka nan ne. Da ka'dan ka'dan ne sai kowa ya iya, kuma sa'annan kullum muna yin shi har gaba 'daya **tableau** kin ya k'are....

In mun fara, kowa kallon abin da muke yi **tableau-tableau** yake yi. Bayan mun k'are ta, sai mu yi **centre**(?) haka mu zauna, to, duk wanda ya ga ra'ayi a cikin wannan **thème** kin sai ya da'da hannu ya yi magana. Kowa ya yi magana, ko mace ko namiji sai ya ce, "Ap! Ni ga cikin **tableau** ka da'da abin da na gani..." "Ap! Cikin maganan **sous-préfet** ga abin da na ji." "Ap! Ni cikin magana na Alhaji ga abin da na

gani." Kowa yana fa'di haka. Kowa ya fa'di sa'annan sai mu gyaggyara kuma. Haka ne.
(The ? marks a word I could not distinguish on the tape.)

79. Mahamadou Lido, 18 April 1981.
80. Chaibou Begu, 8 January 1981. His statement:

Ba mu **improvisation**. Duk piéce 'din da muke yi da Hausa ne ko da Faranshi kuma sai mu rubuta ta.

81. Director of the Maradi Troupe, 27 April 1981.
82. Chaibou Begu, 8 January 1981.
83. 'DAN KWANGILAA, mimeographed text by the Maradi Theatrical Troupe, 1981, Scene 5 (shaahii na biyar), p. 12. (The line is in French in the original, with "Mademoiselle" abbreviated "Mlle"). The performance description is from an audio tape of the troupe's performance in Diffa, Niger, 9 April 1981, transcribed by Aboubacar Mahamane. The dialogue in performance is a mixture of Hausa and French.
84. The title, TALALA MAI KAMAN SAKE, is a proverb, literally "tethering (with a long rope) like release." R.C. Abraham translates the proverb: "It's a case of giving him a rope to hang himself with!" (DICTIONARY OF THE HAUSA LANGUAGE, London: University of London Press, 1962), p. 845.

In his Introduction to the performance of the play at the Diffa Festival, the **Inspecteur de la Jeunesse** for the **Département** of Zinder made the following explanation of the title:

La chèvre qu'on attache au bout d'une longue corde se croit à liberté jusqu'au moment où tenter de dépasser son ère de pâturage elle se sent retenue. Telle est dans sa traduction la plus simple le sense de "Talala Mai Kaman Sake." Notre personnage est à l'image de cette chèvre.

> Devant la confiance de la famille du défunt, Talala s'est octroyé une certaine liberté qui va jusqu'à l'abus du détriment. Mais comme nous l'avons dit plus haut: chaque liberté a sa fin. La réaction des victimes à bout de patience ne suffit pas attendre. C'est alors seulement que notre personnage compris, mais un peu tard, toute la signification du proverbe, "Talala Mai Kaman Sake."

85. The dates after each paragraph refer to my rehearsal notes for these changes, some of which occurred over several days, but I have tried to note the most important points of change. These rehearsals took place between the Zinder regional competitions in Tanout, 5-11 March, and the National Festival in Diffa, 6-14 April 1981.

86. Personal communication from Yazi Dogo, Zinder, 10 September 1981.

87. Rehearsal notes, MJC, Zinder, 17, 18, 21 and 23 August 1981.

88. Rehearsal notes, MJC, Zinder, 17-26 August 1981.

89. GADO K'ARHIN ALLA, performance by the Troupe Amadou 'Dan Bassa at the MJC, Zinder, Niger, 13 September 1981.

90. Rehearsal notes, the Radio Club, Zinder, 16, 22 and 23 September 1981.

91. Alhaji Zoubeirou Lawal, 17 April 1981.

92. Alhaji Abdousalam Adam, 30 June 1981.

93. DARAJAR K'ASA AL'ADARTA, performance by the Radio Club Troupe as part of the WASAN KARA, at the MJC, Zinder, Niger, (9:00 p.m.) 21 June 1981.

94. Rehearsal notes, the Radio Club, Zinder, 5 September 1981.

95. Rehearsal notes, the Radio Club, Zinder, 8 September 1981.

96. Rehearsal notes, the Radio Club, Zinder, 12 September 1981.

97. Yazi Dogo, 14 August 1981.

98. R.C. Abraham records a similar proverb, "Girman kai rawanin k'yasuwa," translating it, "Pride comes before a fall," (DICTIONARY OF THE HAUSA LANGUAGE, p. 728).

99. GIRMAN KAI RAWANIN TSIYA, performance by the Troupe Amadou 'Dan Bassa at the MJC, Zinder, Niger, 12 September 1981.
100. Yazi Dogo, 14 August 1981. (See quotation at the end of Chapter I).
101. Rehearsal notes, MJC, Zinder, 1 April 1981.
102. Personal communication from Oumarou Nainou, Zinder, 26 August 1981.
103. Alhaji Zoubeirou Lawal, 18 April 1981. His statement:

> To, ni a ganina, rôle kin ban dariya nan, ban dariya nan dole ne a yi shi cikin teyatur. Ni na hi ganeya da ban dariya nan. Ban dariya, lokacin da ina teyatur kin nan, ni kaina wani abu, sai na hau bisa **scène** ne kamar yanda Mamadou da ya gaya maka dazu, sai na hau bisa **scène** ne, zan samu fasa....
> Ban dariya ya rik'e mutanen. Saboda wannan, in mutum yana so ya shirya teyatur, ya sa abun jawon hankalin mutanen k'asa, sa'annan ya sa kuma abun da mutane su samu su yi dariya. Kowani lokacin ana jawon hankalin nan wani yana barci a cikin masu kallo, lokacin da an yi dariya gaba 'daya a woooo ... kina ... sai ya hwalka kuma ya ga abun da ake yi. Saboda wannan ne, ni a ganina, na ban dariya, ya hi na ilimi.

104. Mahamadou Lido, 18 April 1981.

CHAPTER III
PLAY STRUCTURE

The troupes begin their work with a theme, a general idea, and then plan scenes to develop it, adding and selecting actions, revising it continually to suit the group's sense of what is appropriate. Yet from the broader perspective of their theatrical tradition and in comparison to the works of other Nigerien troupes, the plays show patterns of structure more fundamental than their topical themes. Each play is a new work of art but built with familiar themes, characters and scenes. Nigerien audiences take delight in the sense of the familiar and in the suspense of seeing how the troupe will work with its chosen character types and stock scenes, how they will arrange them, improvise from them and render them anew. In this sense, the current plays retain strong ties to the oral narrative tradition in which storytellers create spontaneous, original performances from well-known tales. Their structural patterns may or may not be consciously planned for they are as familiar to the teller and audience as the characters, songs and stories themselves. The plays reflect similar traditional patterns; they also project the troupes' efforts to portray current reality, to outline social problems and their solutions. For this, the plays take on a more typically western form from theatrical realism: settings from daily life, scene units based on changes of time and location, human beings as the only characters--eliminating the fantastic realm of narrative. In their ongoing work, the troupes use patterns and forms that seem to best fit their present purposes, combining elements new and old, foreign and familiar.

In analyzing oral narrative performance, Harold Scheub notes the importance of the traditional repertoire of images for both the performer (the storyteller) and her audience; the audience experiences meaning through the performance itself, not through the revelation of new information in the story.(1)

> If a key emotion-evoking device in narrative is the image, the major shaping tool is repetition, patterning of various kinds that includes anticipation and predictability as essential aesthetic adjuncts....
> The performer works with an audience that has the same repertory of images that she has, and this provides a necessary common experience. There is, moreover, aesthetic satisfaction in the predictability of the narrative....
> The images are known, the patterns are familiar. The precise organization of the images and the arrangement of the patterns are not necessarily known for the specific performance, and this unknown factor introduces a tension which contributes to yet another reservoir of emotions....(2)

Like narrative, each performance of a folk drama plays with this tension between the predictable/familiar and the unexpected. Comedy as well depends on repetition and audience expectations to produce its full effect.

Where Scheub posits **images** as the basic units of narrative, Bernard Beckerman defines **activity** as the basic medium of the theatre, the means by which ideas can be projected.(3) The segments of a play, the types of activities, become its building blocks. "Just as there are character types which recur in play after play, so there are segmental types which run throughout dramatic history."(4) He cites persuasion, confession, messages and farewells as some of these recurring types of segments. Further, Beckerman states that each age fosters its own archetypal dramatic activities, citing the debates of Greek drama or the conversations of nineteenth century realism as examples.(5) Each age finds certain activities particularly satisfying, and these develop as sources for new plays. "In drama each individual creative choice is made within a frame of socio-aesthetic practice so that the theater artist naturally selects his materials from a context of expectations."(6) Beckerman's work suggests that an activity which recurs in many plays demonstrates an effective choice within the tradition, one with strong appeal to audiences and a significant ability to convey the performer/creator's ideas.

Recurrent activities in the Hausa plays begin with formal settings drawn from real life. Scenes most typically take place at the **sarki's** court, the **sous-préfecture**, the offices of government officials, or the compounds of important men in the community. These are public places, the realms of official activity but not of chance meetings. Rarely if ever do the troupes set scenes in marketplaces, **autogares**, on the street, or in a mosque. The plays contain plans, meetings and intrigue, but not the coincidence of passers-by. The characters are known to one another, either invited or having business at the location; thus many of these scenes have a ceremonial, planned quality about them.

Such formal scenes dominate nearly every play, but they appear at different points in the action. For example, a meeting at the **sous-préfet's** office may begin the play, as in ALHAJI SHAGALI where the **sous-préfet** awards Shagali the construction project, initiating the central story line.(7) Or, as in KOWA YA BUGI RUWA IDONAY, the scene at the **sous-préfecture** may mark the point of resolution of the conflict; here, the **sarki** informs the **sous-préfet** of the new doctor's conspiracy with Mai Gari (the village headman) to sell medicines, and the **sous-préfet** takes steps to curtail their crime. (Scene 4)(8) Whereas in ALHAJI SHAGALI the scenes at the **sous-préfecture** frame the entire play, awarding the contract in Scene 1 and punishing Shagali in the final scene, Filingué's play uses a similar formal meeting at the **sous-préfecture** as a dramatic, climactic scene instead. The Filingué Troupe frames KOWA YA BUGI RUWA IDONAY and this meeting at the **sous-préfecture** with two village meetings at Mai Gari's compound, another official setting. The first scene introduces the new doctor and the final one presents the **sous-préfet** announcing his removal from that post for his corrupt activities.(Scene 5)

The Troupe from Agadez mixed similar scenes in yet another combination in their 1981 Festival play, WALWALE.(9) The play centers its story in a town's decision to build a pump at their primary school; Walwale's reluctance to participate runs counter to the cooperation needed for the success of the project. Opening with a meeting of leading citizens in which the school's principal explains the problems due to the lack of water at the school and the elders decide to build a pump, the play moves to a town meeting in which everyone agrees to the project and pledges financial assistance except Walwale.(Scene 2) The troupe included a subsequent scene at the **sous-préfecture** to demonstrate the concrete reality of the project: the **sous-préfet** presides over the choice of a contractor after the town leaders have collected the money. (Scene 5) Unlike the conflict-generating scene of Mainé Soroa's ALHAJI SHAGALI or the climactic resolution of Filingué's KOWA YA BUGI RUWA IDONAY, this scene at the **sous-préfecture** advances the action from the planning stage to actual construction with an official stamp of approval. In this way it prepares for the following scene, a second town meeting, in which the pump is formally opened. It is this meeting which becomes the climactic focus of the play, a public celebration over the successful community effort.(Scene 6) The performance in Diffa highlighted this moment with a stage effect rare for Nigerien productions--real water flowing out of the pump.(10)

In contrast to these public forums, Walwale's repentance in the final two scenes takes place privately at home, and then he apologizes to the town's leaders at Mai Gari's compound.(Scenes 7 and 8) Through this structuring of their scenes, the Agadez Troupe emphasized the importance of the community over one man's lack of cooperation. The town can successfully build the pump without Walwale, but his participation is valuable. This message carries a different thrust from that of Maradi's 'DAN KWANGILA or Mainé Soroa's ALHAJI

SHAGALI whose major characters bear lone responsibility for the failure of their projects.

Another typical scene, somewhat less formal than the above meetings, is the gathering of men to gossip at an important man's house. These scenes accurately represent village life where Hausa men pass a lot of their time discussing business, news and local affairs with their peers in the marketplace, in the outer reception room (*zaure*) of someone's compound, or under a shady tree. Again, the troupes transpose this typical scene, familiar to their audiences in everyday life, and incorporate it into their plots in diverse ways. In 'DAN KWANGILA, the congenial group at Alhaji Gimshik'i's compound in the first scene discusses the national development efforts, teases Rangama for his forgetfulness, and learns of the government's construction plans by means of a radio announcement.(11) This scene introduces both the character of Rangama and the conflict caused by his decision to venture into construction. Another early expository scene, the second one in ALHAJI SHAGALI, presents a group of townsmen discussing Shagali's inept handling of his contract, a condemnation his actions later justify. In WALWALE, the arrival of several important men to visit Walwale in Scene 3 allows him to explain why he remains skeptical of the plans for the school pump.

A more dramatically intense placement of a similar gossip scene occurs in BA GA IRINTA BA.(12) In this scene, Langa Langa hosts Mamman Arrivé's friends and neighbors at his house, and their talk turns from sugar cane and a lost truck to Mamman's troubles at the school. When Mamman himself appears to report the events of the meeting at the mayor's office, his friends convince him of the seriousness of his unruly behavior and advise him to seek reconciliation with the authorities.(Scene 5) It is with this scene that Mamman's spiraling series of abuses stop and he begins the process of repentance.

In all of the Hausa plays I observed in Niger, the troupes carried nearly all of the action forward through such discussions and meetings. Rarely were there scenes of violent action. I saw only one play in which a character stabbed another in a fight; this highly sensational action amazed and amused its audience.(13) Much more typical and versatile in this theatre are the ritual gatherings of people in office or compound, reflections of common activities in Nigerien life. Despite the comic elements which often occur within them, the formal settings underline the serious referents of the plays' themes, portraying the reality of government and business affairs--the realm of national development efforts, regional projects, plans for the future, and the maintenance of social order in a changing society.

In contrast to the formal settings, domestic scenes stand out in high relief. There are usually only one or two in a given play, while the official and other meetings take up five or six scenes; some plays, such as KOWA YA BUGI RUWA IDONAY have no domestic scenes at all. Yet even at a character's home, the action usually revolves around visits to the master of the house (**mai gida**), representing the public face of the household (the **zaure**) rather than the inner, women's space (**cikin gida**). Thus, in TALALA MAI KAMAN SAKE, Talala receives a series of visitors--the contractor Musa, Malam, 'Dan Hulani, and his nephew--before he confronts his young wife.(Scene 3)(14) Alhaji Shagali entertains his foreman at home and conspires with Boka Mai Burgami before he calls his wives to come out so that he can tell them of his travel plans. (Scene 4) In the subsequent scenes of both plays, as Talala invites young women to his new house and Shagali visits Gimbiya, the comedy intensifies for the very reason that the characters trespass beyond the formal, proper (public) visiting space toward an acutely personal one. Such scandalous settings were used by both troupes to arouse and sustain comic expectations in the scenes while highlighting their stories of personal corruption.

Comparatively few domestic scenes appear in the festival plays, partly due to the scarcity of actresses in many troupes and partly because of the nationalistic themes the plays portray.(15) Government affairs and development projects remain largely masculine prerogatives although more efforts are being made to involve the nation's women in them. Local plays more frequently incorporate family issues than do the festival entries. The student play I observed in Tchin Tabaraden concerned the (fictional) first woman customs official and the conflicts between her family and

her job.(16) The Zinder Radio Club Troupe's first
production of DARAJAR K'ASA AL'ADARTA focussed on
the family problems posed by two young daughters
wanting to join the "modern" lifestyle of dances,
alcohol, drugs and sex. The majority of scenes in
this play occurred in different domestic settings--
four in the home of the family of main characters
(**Gidan Alhaji Na Alla**), one in a girlfriend's
house, and the party scene in the home of a decadent young man.(17)

At times, the troupes explore domestic issues
even in their festival plays, but usually the
domestic aspect is subsumed by its political
significance. When the Zinder Troupe presented
the problem of Mamman Arrivé's delinquent son in BA
GA IRINTA BA, they emphasized its public ramifications within the school system and in the town; the
only two domestic scenes in the play were the
opening and closing ones at Mamman's home. Another
of the Zinder Troupe's plays, TALALA MAI KAMAN
SAKE, examined the betrayal of trust within a
family over their inheritance, also a problem with
wide social implications. Four of the seven scenes
in this play were set in the characters' homes and
women played a larger role in the action. As
actresses gain acceptance in the troupes, on the
stage, and in the public activities of society,
doubtless more of their concerns will begin to
appear in the plays, increasing the number of
scenes set within their traditional sphere of
activity, the family.

Within these broad scenic frameworks, whose
major activities could usually be described as
meetings or visits, the troupes make use of a
variety of specific actions and devices. The
popular recurrence of these devices is rapidly
establishing conventions for this theatre. One
such convention, the official pronouncement,
commonly introduces new action or a topic of
conflict, as in the **sous-préfet's** bestowing the
clinic contract on Alhaji Shagali (Scene 1), or the
president of the commission concluding their debate
by announcing the offer of a contract to 'Dan
Kwangila.(Scene 3) In GADO KARHIN ALLA, the
Zinder Troupe transforms this type of announcement
into the first resolution of the play's conflict,
the choice of the new **sarki** from among the eligible
princes. Indeed, the troupe expanded this an-

nouncement into a series of speeches by the **sous-préfet**, the **préfet**, the region's **député**, and the **sarki** himself (Scene 5), marking the importance of this moment in the play through the repetition and solemnity.(18)

Variations on these announcements by officials often use a radio as the vehicle for the new information. By this means, the Zinder Troupe channelled a discussion of the purposes of Niger's **samariyas** into the main story of TALALA MAI KAMAN SAKE with a radio obituary for Talala's brother, a member of the **samariya**.(Scene 1) Similarly, the Maradi Troupe revealed 'Dan Kwangila's interest in construction through a radio announcement of the competition for contracts.(Scene 1) A more traditional type of public announcer, the town drummer/crier, was employed by the Agadez Troupe in WALWALE to call people to the opening ceremony for the pump (Scene 6), and by the ORTN (Radio) Troupe to broadcast news of a town meeting in BABBAN RUMBU MATARSHI TUKUNYA.(19) In these different guises, the dramatic device of an announcement has become a standard, efficient convention within the tradition. It works well in conjunction with the formal scenes to advance the action and to focus on the central issues of discussion.

Effective comic bits also continually reappear in new contexts. Telephones rarely reach the proper party on the first attempt; servants and wives often will not come when they are called; ethnic characters and sometimes deaf or crippled ones employ distorted speech; secretaries flirt with visitors to their bosses. The strong association of certain types of characters with such comic actions will be discussed in the next chapter.

In their characteristic style, the Zinder Troupe refined one of these jokes from the topical slogan, **masu yanzu yanzu** (literally, possessors of immediacy--what I have translated as "instant action"). A member of the troupe threw this phrase into the general greetings for K'arawrawa, the gossip monger in BA GA IRINTA BA (Scene 5), and the troupe chose to accentuate it in their next play as a cogent characterization for Savon Robb, the pimp in TALALA MAI KAMAN SAKE.(20)

Along with conventional and comic devices, the troupes mine the rich lore of tradition for material to enrich their plays. They draw from a wide

Play Structure

range of traditional practices including weddings, naming ceremonies, and funerals, to include as dramatic activities within their scenes. Or ritual events may form the background theme for an entire play, as in GADO K'ARHIN ALLA with its portrayal of the death of a **sarki** (Scene 1), the election of his successor (Scenes 2-4), the installation ceremony (Scene 5), and the **durbar** salute to the new **sarki**.(Scene 8)(21) Plays may even contain other dramatic performances within them, as did ANA SARA ANA DIBIN BAKIN GATARI by the Troupe of Madaoua with its incorporation of a **bori** possession dance.(22)

All of these recurrent activities as well as the actors' experience of performances form a potential pool of material for any new production. The troupes shape their plot using these stock settings and actions, with some new ones. They work largely by instinct, by what seems suitable to the group. Yet part of this instinct derives from their innate knowledge of the oral narrative tradition and its patterns.

Narrative Patterns

Internal repetition forms a central element of oral literature and these plays are no exception. Repetitions of actions, of segments, and even of entire scenes within a play emphasize and reaffirm the troupe's intended message.

Repetition most often underscores the faults of the central characters, a major theme in most plays. Mamman Arrivé yells at his wife and son (Scene 1), continues to abuse the teachers and the director at the school (Scene 2), and then verbally assaults the assembled townspeople and officials at the mayor's office.(Scene 4) The new doctor Saluhu in KOWA YA BUGI RUWA IDONAY treats one patient after another, giving no one any help (Scene 2), while Prince Shaho sends for three different charlatans to help him win the election in GADO K'ARHIN ALLA.(Scene 4) Talala receives a series of visitors, gradually revealing the depths of his deception (Scenes 3, 4 and 5), while 'Dan Kwangila makes a series of visits--to Alhaji Gimshik'i, to the commission member, to the bank, to the city planning office, to his work site--all the while forgetting things, misunderstanding the other characters, and neglecting his responsibilities.(Scenes 1, 2, 4, 5 and 6)(23) These repetitions focus and develop the problems at the center of each play emphasizing the troupes' themes through satire.

This is the type of repetition that the Mainé Soroa Troupe removed from ALHAJI SHAGALI, feeling that a few detailed scenes would better serve their story. As their director stated, however, they used to include a greater number of scenes in their plays, but they no longer find this necessary.(24) Apparently, the character types and plots have become so familiar to audiences that they no longer need the repetition, or it may be merely implied as in the hearsay discussions of Shagali's actions by his peers in Scene 2. The Mainé Troupe now prefers to concentrate on one aspect of a familiar story once they have sketched its course.

Repeated settings within a play usually draw attention to the changes that have taken place in the course of the action. Plays often begin and end at the same site creating a cyclical feeling, but the repetition often is more central than just the physical location of the scenes. Mamman Arrivé's home forms the setting in the opening and closing scenes of his play; in both, his son appears crying and complaining that someone has hit him. Mamman reacts angrily both times but modifies his impulses the second time and demands an explanation. As his brother then comments to him:

>   Yaya: You're beginning to understand. Really, you're beginning to understand.
>   (Ka hwara ganewa. Ashe ka hwara ganewa).
>   (BA GA IRINTA BA, Scene 8)

Nonetheless, it is the action rather than the comment that impresses itself most forcefully on the audience, who has seen the change in Mamman Arrivé's behavior between the two scenes. Even more powerful are the almost identical opening and closing scenes at the **sous-préfecture** in ALHAJI SHAGALI. Both portray the **sous-préfet** gathering the same group of people, first to grant Shagali the contract, and finally to strip him not only of the project but of his freedom.(Scenes 1 and 6)(25)

Repetition in the first and last scenes is only one of many possibilities, however. Other scenes may be repeated to show a shift in the flow of the action. Scenes 6 and 7 of 'DAN KWANGILA reiterate the discontent of Rangama's workers, but in Scene 7 the consecutive inspections by the employees' welfare officer and the city planning director turn the tide of complaints against Rangama. In BA GA IRINTA BA, the troupe employed two teachers' meetings at the school to demonstrate the turn in Mamman Arrivé's tactics. Both scenes begin with the teachers discussing school affairs and Mamman interrupting. In the first meeting, he demands to see Madame and curses everyone on the school staff (Scene 2); in contrast, in the later scene he asks to see Madame to obtain her pardon. (Scene 6)

These repeated scenes and portions of scenes function like the narrative models Harold Scheub has termed patterned image-sets:

> Patterned image-sets consist of two similar sets of images ... brought together one immediately following the other; the second image-set differs only slightly from the first, and it is in that difference ... that the point of the narrative is made.(26)

This basic structuring technique of narrative is well known to actors and audiences close to the oral tradition. It appears equally effective in structuring the action of their plays.

A more complex narrative pattern, but no less common, Scheub terms parallel image-sets. Where patterned image-sets are similar, parallel image-sets juxtapose two dissimilar sets of narrative images, whose differences reveal the theme of the performance.(27) Scheub cites a classic example of contrasting parallel image-sets in the widespread story of two sisters, the good girl and the bad girl. Each has a series of adventures but they react in opposing ways: the good sister is kind, helps the characters and creatures that she meets, and receives a reward (a husband, riches, etc.), while her greedy sister hurries along, ignoring or abusing those she meets, and receives her due reward (a beating, disease and pestilence, or the like).(28) This narrative model has proved particularly useful, although probably unconsciously so, to the Hausa troupes developing their themes into plays.

A striking example of this pattern appears in the Zinder Radio Club Troupe's first production of DARAJAR K'ASA AL'ADARTA.(29) This play uses not only the model but also the story of the good and bad sisters, in modern guise. The troupe intended the play to focus on the problems of current western culture's attraction to Nigerien youth ('**yan yaran zamani**) through the importation of disco music, drugs and alcohol.(30) They centered their story around the family of Alhaji Na Alla (Alhaji of God), his two wives, and their two teen-aged daughters, Taxi and Cha-cha-cha. A fashionably decadent young man, Monsieur Mazari (a greedy man), invites the girls to a disco party at his house; their father forbids them to attend and warns his wives to keep them at home. The elder wife wants her daughter Taxi to catch a "modern" husband and allows her to go to the party secretly, while the younger wife obeys her husband and orders Cha-cha-cha to stay home.(Scene 1)

Taxi subsequently attends the party, where everyone is arrested by the police for drug possession and indecent behavior.(Scene 3) As Alhaji Na Alla is arranging for husbands for both girls, following traditional custom, his discussion is interrupted by the announcement that his daughter is being held at the police station. He calls for his wives and daughters, only to find that Cha-cha-cha is at home but Taxi is not.(Scene 4) After obtaining Taxi's release from custody and learning that she is pregnant (Scene 5), Na Alla repudiates both Taxi and her mother (Scene 6) and then hosts a wedding.(Scene 8) In typically ironic Hausa fashion, not only does Cha-cha-cha receive a husband in this final scene, but her father remarries as well, replacing his divorced wife. In sharp contrast, Taxi and her mother earn a second arrest by the authorities when they seek an illegal abortion.(Scene 7)

In this play, the negative set of actions receives greater elaboration than the positive model, but the parallel contrast remains clear. As in most of the plays, the portrayal of the evil side of a social problem is given prominence, both as an indictment by the troupe and because the wicked generally have greater comic potential than do law-abiding citizens. Through their use of a well-known story pattern, the Radio Club Troupe successfully fused a serious community concern about the growing corruption of youth with comic material, particularly in the party scene which was replete with visual and verbal humor.(Scene 3) Traditional values of right and wrong so permeate these models and the familiar story of the two sisters that the troupe could rely on their audience's expectations from the pattern as they created an entertaining new version of the story for the stage.

In KUSKURE KARATU NE (A Mistake is a Lesson),(31) the Tahoua Troupe developed a nationalistic theme through the same model of divergent sets of actions. The play follows two groups of pilgrims to Mecca, one of which uses the official Nigerien procedures and successfully completes the trip, while the others attempt to cut corners and expense and subsequently find themselves victimized by an unscrupulous foreigner. This dual model was clearly indicated by the troupe in their program listing the scenes of the play for the Diffa performance:

> KUSKUREE KARATU NEE: EXPERIENCE IS A SCHOOL is the story of a peasant, Madugu, who wants to go to Mecca, like a large number of his peers. This desire is strengthened by the outcome of an abundant harvest.
> To be African is to work together and communal decisions are the secret of unity. That is why in Madugu's village all the future pilgrims meet to decide how they will settle their expenses. Thus arise two camps:
> 1) For Madugu and his companions,there is no question of buying their tickets in Niger when it is possible to get a lower fare abroad.
> 2) For Arzika, buying a ticket abroad dis-

> plays a lack of public spirit and nationalism, something he cannot condone. Because he believes "the road of peace is never too long," he will travel from Niamey via Air Niger.
>
> And it is with this disagreement that our brothers part company, nonetheless firmly convinced that they will meet each other in Mecca.
>
> Will they meet there? Without further ado, let's wish them Bon Voyage and a Happy Pilgrimage.(32)

Again, as in DARAJAR K'ASA AL'ADARTA, the scenes for the group following the proper, national channels are fewer and less detailed the scenes portraying Madugu (a caravan leader) who hopes to find cheaper air fares abroad, but the troupe explicitly depicts the contrast. Arzika's nationalistic group listens to the Nigerien regulations and learns what papers and vaccinations they are required to have (Scene 2); they line up to leave on the plane for Mecca (Scene 5); and they return from the pilgrimage in white robes with expensive gifts and radios.(Scene 10) The airport scene was particularly popular in the Diffa performance because of the large, painted Air Niger plane which was rolled out on stage and the recorded sound effects of take-off at the end of the scene; the audience burst into applause.(33) Such elaborate scenery and sound effects are rare enough in Nigerien productions that they dramatically emphasize any scene in which they appear.

Madugu's experiences on the other hand, detail the mistakes predicted by the play's title. Madugu fails to heed the advice of Arzika in the first scene of the play:

> Arzika: Madugu, where are we going to go and pay our money for the journey east except in our own

> country where we pay our money and go?
> ... Look Madugu, follow God's advice, whenever God gives you advice, that is the advice a man must give himself, Madugu. Whose town will satisfy you if your own town doesn't satisfy you? Whose house will satisfy you if your own house doesn't satisfy you? Madugu, listen to what I am telling you. (Scene 1)(34)

Instead, Madugu entrusts his savings and those of his group to an unknown agent, 'Dan Kamasho (son of commission). Even his friends suspiciously ask about the extremely low fares and what preparations they must make for the trip, but Madugu apologizes for their questions and turns their money over to 'Dan Kamasho on his assurance that he will take care of everything for them.(Scene 3) The successful departure of Arzika's group on Air Niger (Scene 5) immediately precedes Madugu's arrival at the foreign airport where his name does not appear on the passenger list and a report arrives that 'Dan Kamasho has fled to Cairo.(Scene 6) Reiterating and deepening Madugu's chagrin in the following scene, the customs officials at the border nearly arrest him for arriving at the same time as a young man smuggling drugs.(Scene 7) This highly comic scene shows Madugu's ignorance and gullibility once again: he has foolishly taken the young man's pills for a headache.

The two scenes (4 and 8) at Madugu's home before and after his trip accentuate his shame in not completing the pilgrimage. Scene 4 portrays a series of Madugu's friends and relatives coming to bid him farewell and to request gifts from Mecca; these visits recall the solemnity of the pilgrimage as well as its economic significance--the **hajj** is a major life event in Hausa communities. Later, following the airport scenes and Madugu's adventures at the border, he returns home to the shocked disbelief of his wife, children and friends. The same characters who joyfully sent him off now must hear the account of his failure.(Scene 8) Other villagers then learn the gossip in Scene 9, including a report of Arzika's return from Mecca. In the final scene at Arzika's compound, the village elders greet Alhaji Arzika, hear his account of his travels, and receive their gifts. In turn, Madugu receives a lecture from Arzika on his mistakes and he publicly repents:

>Madugu: Oh, because of this affair, I, Madugu, have two causes for shame....
>   The great shame is that when I got wealth from our country, from the suffering and cultivating that I did to get the money for the journey east, I refused to follow the arrangements of our country. I went and gave it all to a worthless vagrant, not knowing what he would do....
>   This thing that has happened to me, Madugu, let it be a warning to our citizens.
>(Scene 10)(35)

This verbal confession summarizes in a concise conclusion what the action has already shown: Madugu's failure. His defeat carries a strong feeling of predestination from the beginning, largely due to the troupe's use of the contrasting models in the play.

With plays such as 'DAN KWANGILA and ALHAJI SHAGALI, similar contrastive models are still at work but they are no longer explicitly portrayed. The role of the good contractor appears implicitly in the background--in the advice the **sous-préfet** gives Shagali as he announces the contract (Scene 1), in the commission's debate over the qualities needed by their contractor in 'DAN KWANGILA (Scene 3), in Shagali's neighbors' criticism of his work (Scene 2), or in the counsel Rangama repeatedly receives on how best to complete his project. (Scenes 2, 4, and 5)

Beyond the specific references in these plays to the exemplary contractor lies the national image of the model citizen of the Development Society, promoted through government campaigns, projects, and the media; such a citizen is honest, hardworking, cooperative, loyal to community and country. In the festival performances surrounding the plays, the songs in particular and many of the **ballets** as well exhort the duties and responsibilities of Niger's citizens; nationalism pervades the festival context of these plays. Thus, the troupes need not always develop parallel plots at length to call forth these ideal models; they may choose to concentrate instead on the more insightful--and comic--tales of going astray. The familiar contrastive pattern used in both the narrative tradition and in other plays allows them to invoke an immediate image of the good prototype, in many cases a nationalistic one, and then to delve into the details of the evil aberration.

In BA GA IRINTA BA, the Zinder Troupe employed contrasting sets of action in two ways, first to develop Mamman Arrivé's opposition to his community and then to demonstrate his change of heart. In the first series, the troupe set Mamman's actions against those of Langa Langa, Bartelemi, and the other parents. Where Langa Langa joins the community organizations, Mamman scorns them; where Langa Langa counsels discussion of Sanussi's problems, Mamman takes off in the heat of the moment to blame the teacher.(Scene 1) Bartelemi expresses concern for his son's progress, tells his teacher to punish the boy to keep him working, and explains his recent absence due to illness. Conversely, Mamman does not know that his son has skipped class for seven days, and he curses his teacher for punishing him.(Scene 2) Then, in the later scene at the mayor's office, the troupe again opposes Mamman's actions to those of other parents. The mayor listens to each of the three fathers who explain why they made angry visits to the school--a drunken teacher who never came to class, the requirement that the girls wear (indecent) short pants and jump around, and so on. All the parents present their complaints and listen with deference as the mayor and other officials respond, while Mamman Arrivé disrupts the parents' recitals and the officials' explanations with his loud, abusive comments.(Scene 4) Finally, Mamman confronts his neighbors who are gathered at Langa Langa's house to discuss his impending punishment. Once again, Mamman's plan of action--to bribe the police commissioner--runs counter to the ideas of his friends who urge him to ask pardon for his outbursts.(Scene 5)

In this first set of scenes detailing the play's conflict, the troupe establishes a dominant opposition between Mamman's actions and those of all the other parents. In each scene, Mamman's actions remain the same: arrogant, rude, aggressive confrontations. The other characters replace one another in a series representing the community at large. Although their actions are not precisely identical, their collective opposition to Mamman Arrivé progressively unites them and creates a broader meaning through the values that both sides come to represent. Mamman's isolation becomes more and more complete, and he is forced to humble himself and ask for pardon, to accede to the community's code of ethics.

Subsequently, the second set of scenes reverses Mamman's actions in abbreviated form. These final scenes are shorter and play through rapidly, relying on the model established earlier. Mamman returns to the school to seek Madame's pardon (Scene 6); then he and the school officials go to the police station to clear his name with the town authorities.(Scene 7) The final scene returns to Mamman's home where his older brother points out that Mamman has been spoiling his son, not attending to his familial duties. Sanussi's reappearance in tears subsequently generates a new response from his father.(Scene 8)

The structural repetition of settings and characters accentuates Mamman's new humility, although he retains his feisty retorts even as he begs for mercy:

    Madame: But, Mr. Director, I don't forgive him.
    Mamman Arrive: Come, come, Madame! ... Don't you see the town elders have come. Really!
    Mai Samari: Consider our position, young lady. Don't consider Mamman, but consider our position....

> Mamman
> Arrive: Don't follow my character.
> Director: Look at the importance of this one the [President of the Parents Association] and Mai Samari.
> Mamman
> Arrive: That's right! (Scene 6)(36)

Mamman may reform his actions out of necessity, but he will never truly reform in spirit. The comic tension created by his reversal, playing both the bad and the good roles, heightens audience interest in Mamman as a central character and in the play's larger theme of community.

In the narrative tradition, more complex stories using parallel image sets often are quite long, compounding image sequences one after another to interact on many levels of meaning. I observed only one play which was evolving similarly complex sequences, but the process appeared very much the same as that which Scheub describes for narrative: models are established and details within one image set may become a bridge into a new set.(37) The play in which this occurred, DARAJAR K'ASA AL'ADARTA, was first performed as the evening's entertainment for Zinder's **Wasan Kara** in June 1981. The Radio Club Troupe rehearsed additional scenes for the play in September of that year to expand it into a television serial; unfortunately, I had to leave Zinder before the final videotaping, if indeed it took place.(38) Nonetheless, the troupe's rehearsals showed the process of creating complex new themes as well as lengthening the single evening's performance into a series of episodes.

As discussed above, the original performance of DARAJAR K'ASA AL'ADARTA developed the divergent paths of two sisters attracted to the decadence of modern youthful pursuits. Taxi finds pregnancy and arrest on her route, while her sister who stays at home is married in customary fashion. In their later rehearsals, the troupe opened up the ending to this first version of the play in order to explore a second, more political, theme. In the original Scene 7, in which Taxi and her mother visit Malam Zargewa to try to obtain an abortion, their appearance was followed by another **malam's** visit, a follower of a charlatan prophet from the "distant North" whom Malam Zargewa arrests. This brief visit repeated the pattern of arrest which Taxi and her mother encounter: Malam Zargewa in both cases sends his student to fetch another **malam**, a disguised police officer, who then listens to the incriminating stories and handcuffs first the women and later the false **malam**.(39)

The false preacher, JaGaba (guide), formed the starting point for the second story which the troupe developed within the play. In their rehearsed rough drafts, JaGaba's account of his new religion was expanded so that not only was he preaching a heretical form of Islam but he explained his plan to bribe the local **malams** to help him in his work. Malam Zargewa feigned interest to draw out the details of JaGaba's heresy; in one rehearsed version, Zargewa then sent JaGaba off with one of his Qu'ranic students, while he relayed the facts of the situation to the police agent. When JaGaba was brought back, the secret agent posed as another interested **malam** and tape-recorded the repetition of JaGaba's preaching.(40)

Just as Taxi's attendance at the party and her pregnancy become public knowledge when her father is summoned to the police station (Scene 5), so is JaGaba's private proselytizing brought to official attention in the subsequent scene at the **préfecture**. With the taperecording as proof of his intentions, the **préfet** arranges with the **gendarmes** for JaGaba's arrest and notifies the higher authorities in Niamey of his activities.(41) As the troupe expanded these scenes, Taxi's arrest was taken out of the earlier scene at Malam Zargewa's compound (Scene 7), to be joined with JaGaba's arrest in the end (Scene 9), although I never saw this scene rehearsed.

On the surface, the two stories joined in this re-working of the play seem very different. A teen-aged girl's illegitimate pregnancy normally would have little to do with a stranger coming into the community to preach a new religion. Yet the play's structural juxtaposition of the two sequences draws out a broader theme. Both Taxi and JaGaba make personal decisions which hold serious social implications; both become part of movements from outside the community which threaten its stability. Taxi is lured by the fast life of disco music, sexual license and drugs; JaGaba has been converted to an unorthodox cult of Islam, one based on wealth and personal persuasion rather than the rigors of prayer and fasting. Each character sins against the established religious and social norms and further threatens the community with the possible conversion of others. Their dual exposure by Malam Zargewa, on behalf of both the religious community and the state, equates the two as outcasts and brings both to trial by the authorities. Through these parallel stories, the Radio Club Troupe demonstrates the resilience of the community and its values as it condemns the corruption of young people and the insidious influence of false religion.

At the same time, the addition of the JaGaba sequence suggests a nationalistic view. While JaGaba's religious movement is specifically noted as coming from the distant North, a topical reference to Qaddafi's expansionist policies in Libya, the youthful drug culture that seduces Taxi has obvious western origins. Nigerien national values become tied to the events of the plot--Taxi's first arrest is a local one, but JaGaba's capture involves a growing number of government officials, from the **gendarmes** to the **préfet** to the minister they telephone in Niamey. Through the union of the two sets of action, local and national, the troupe has created a drama with intricate social, moral, religious, and political facets to its themes.

Although the majority of theatrical performances do not have the time to develop more than one story sequence, the Radio Club Troupe's serial work demonstrates the potential within the tradition to create complex structures and themes. Using forms and devices familiar from the narrative tradition, the troupes can create manifold possibilities in future productions.

Social Drama Form

While narrative patterns emerge in the troupes' plays unconsciously for the most part, the troupes profess an active concern in portraying the social problems of contemporary life. This adds a second structuring dimension to their plays, that of realism. The specific western dramatic movement known as realism has doubtless had an impact on Nigerien theatre through the scattered influences of western education, literature, stage drama, television, and films, but it would be extremely difficult to document the extent of that impact on village troupes having few educated members and rare glimpses of western theatre. Nigerien troupes have inherited a model for theatre auditoriums separating spectators from actors on a raised stage, and a convention of evening performances lasting only several hours with breaks between the scenes of a play. This physical structuring affects the form of the plays on a very basic level, likening them to the western theatre which developed such a stage and scenic framework. But on a deeper level, the Hausa plays show affinities to western theatre and other world theatre traditions in structural patterns which Victor Turner has termed social dramas.

Turner describes social dramas in four distinct phases:

> I hold that the social drama form occurs on all levels of social organization from state to family. A social drama is initiated when the peaceful tenor of regular, norm-governed social life is interrupted by the **breach** of a rule controlling one of its salient relationships. This leads swiftly or slowly to a state of **crisis**, which, if not soon sealed off, may split the community into contending factions and coalitions. To prevent this, **redressive** means are taken by those who consider themselves or are considered the most legitimate or authoritative representatives of the relevant community. Redress usually involves ritualized action, whether legal (in formal or informal courts), religious (involving beliefs in the retributive action of powerful supernatural entities, and often involving an act of sacrifice), or military (for example, feuding, headhunting, or engaging in

> organized warfare). If the situation does not regress to **crisis** ... the next phase of social drama comes into play, which involves alternative solutions to the problem. The first is **reconciliation** of the conflicting parties following judicial, ritual, or military processes; the second, **consensual recognition of irremediable breach**, usually followed by the spatial separation of the parties.(42)

Turner suggests that the roots of theatre, and of other cultural genres as well, lie in this process of social drama.

> The third stage, modes of redress, which always contained at least the germ of self-reflexivity, a public way of assessing our social behavior, has moved out of the domains of law and religion and into those of the various arts.... By means of such genres as theatre, including puppetry and shadow theatre, dance drama, and professional story-telling, performances are presented which probe a community's weaknesses, call its leaders to account, desacralize its most cherished values and beliefs, portray its characteristic conflicts and suggest remedies for them, and generally take stock of its current situation in the known "world."(43)

For Turner, the social dramas of real life are a part of everyone's experience in any culture at any time, and cultural performances reflect that experience. The content of these performances may come from the breach, crisis, and final outcomes of social dramas, while the redressive procedures affect their form.(44)

Richard Schechner applies Turner's model of social drama to dramatic structures and finds that it fits them all. "This suggests a universal dramatic structure parallel to social process: drama is that art whose subject, structure and action is social process."(45) Schechner then posits a model of interaction between social drama and aesthetic drama as a figure eight, where the social and political actions of real conflicts feed into the themes of artistic drama, and the theatrical techniques of the stage in turn affect the form of social action.(46) Turner himself critiques Schechner's model as "equilibrist," but notes the importance of bringing out the dynamic relation between social drama and expressive cultural genres.(47) Indeed, the circular movement of this social drama model itself--which Turner developed from (Aristotelian) dramatic theory and applied to observed social reality, while Schechner has brought Turner's model back to gain new insight into drama--reflects its usefulness in relating dramatic and social processes.

The spare framework of the Filingué Troupe's KOWA YA BUGI RUWA IDONAY provides a classic example of Turner's social drama model at work within a play. After the opening scene setting the situation of the play--the arrival of a new doctor to the village clinic--the play devotes one scene to each of Turner's phases. In the second scene, the doctor appears at work in the clinic mistreating his patients--a breach of his duties. The crisis spreads in the following scene as the doctor allies himself with the village headman to sell the medicines provided gratis by the government.(Scene 3) Redressive action follows as the region's **sarki** and **sous-préfet** confer on solutions to the problem (Scene 4), and the final scene portrays the doctor's and Mai Gari's dismisssal from their positions of power, establishing Turner's irreconcilable breach or schism.(Scene 5) The play's form stresses first the opposition between the corrupt doctor and the community, and then the process by which that conflict becomes resolved.

In more elaborate detail, the Zinder Troupe's production of BA GA IRINTA BA also clearly demonstrates the full social drama paradigm. The breach of social norms occurs when Mamman Arrivé abuses the teachers at the primary school.(Scene 2) The reverberations of this action through the town become the crisis; it is not an isolated incident but a recurring problem, which the school director must bring before the inspector's attention (Scene 3), and ultimately before the mayor and the community leaders.(Scene 4) The town meeting displays the redressive actions by the authorities who demand Mamman Arrivé's silence as they hear the cases of the other parents and resolve their complaints. The commissioner orders Mamman to appear at the police station the next day for his punishment (Scene 4), a direct show of authoritative force. The final scenes of the play then detail Mamman's reintegration into the community. (Scenes 5-8)

In Yazi Dogo's explanations of the troupe's work on this play, he emphasized their intention to demonstrate how problems within the school system affect everyone in the town.(48) In trying to realistically present the progression of Mamman Arrivé's problem through the system, the troupe followed the established administrative complaint process: from the school director to the inspector to the mayor, in consultation with the traditional leaders.

For any of the Zinder troupe's plays, the actors review the chosen theme, looking at it from beginning to end so that they can chart a scenic plan that seems necessary (**ya kamata**), right (**daidai**), and suitable (**abin da ya dace**) to everyone in the group.(49) What the troupe finds appropriate usually strikes a responsive chord in their audiences. The spectators recognize the social processes portrayed through the plot and they relate the troupe's message (**amfani**), along with their own responses, to their social reality. The troupe believes that the dramatic story of Mamman Arrivé will shed light on the complex problems in the existing school system and help people to work together on future solutions. Their replication of the form of a social drama creates an effective forum for comparison between the fiction of the play and current reality; what happens after the performance will depend on the audience.

Other plays emphasize one or another phase of the process Turner outlines. Maradi's 'DAN KWANGI-LA uses multiple scenes to develop the breach of Alhaji Rangama's methods of fulfilling his contract obligations: his bribing the commission member

(Scene 2), his unorthodox loan from the bank (Scene 4), his impatience with official forms and regulations.(Scene 5) The crisis brought on by his style of business does not appear until Scene 6 when the troupe presents the work site, Rangama's discontented workers, and his slipshod standards for the building. Yet this scene makes dramatically clear the wide ramifications of Rangama's incompetence. Redressive action quickly follows as the employees' welfare officer and the building inspector appear in the next scene to condemn Rangama's work.(Scene 7) Unlike the emphasis placed on Mamman Arrivé's reintegration into the community, the Maradi Troupe presents Rangama in the final scene descending into insanity, a fate that effectively cuts him off from his community. (Scene 8)

The structure of TALALA MAI KAMAN SAKE intertwines Talala's breach of his role as guardian and the crisis it causes in his late brother's family. The first two scenes of the play establish Talala as executor for his brother's estate, and his deception is only gradually revealed in the following four scenes. Talala's sale of his brother's cattle and his use of the estate's money to build a new house for himself contrast with his refusal to pay his nephew's modest school fees in Scene 3. Scene 4 develops Talala's extravagance and immorality at the new house, while Scenes 5 and 6 portray the plight of his niece, whose house is robbed, and the deprivation of his widowed sisters-in-law, who resolve to sell their dowry goods to buy food. In this way, the Zinder Troupe juxtaposes Talala's negligence (a breach of the community's values) and his family's mounting crisis (representing a grave danger to the social structure). At the end of the play, his niece and the widows take the case to court where the judges rule against Talala.(Scene 7) This scene emphasizes Turner's redressive action phase (in the form of an explicit judicial process) over the final outcome. It is left for the audience to assume that Talala will pay his fines and rejoin the community. That justice ultimately prevails seems more important in the troupe's presentation of the play than whatever Talala's individual fate might be.

Turner's social drama form appears particularly striking in the festival plays whose nationalistic themes frequently concern the conflicts of actual Nigerien communities: criticism of the schools, corruption among contractors and other government employees, the moral irresponsibility of certain men in power. These staged plays quite naturally follow the process of real political events. Yet, as Turner argues, the model applies equally well to any social unit, and the Zinder Radio Club's work on DARAJAR K'ASA AL'ADARTA provides an apt example. The play's initial focus on a single family still shows the social drama pattern: Taxi disobeys her father by going to the party (the breach); her arrest requires her father to bail her out at the police station (the crisis); he repudiates Taxi and her mother (redressive action); and he remarries (establishing a new social unit), while the two women seek solutions on their own (schism).

As the troupe expanded the story to include Malam JaGaba's heresy, the pattern was repeated in the wider, national arena. JaGaba preaches a new form of Islam (the breach); he proposes to initiate new members into his cult through the local **malams** (crisis); his recorded statements lead to his arrest (redressive action) and punishment (presumably imprisonment or banishment). As suggested above, the comparative placement of the family's conflict with the national threat of a foreign cult-leader provokes the audience to examine multiple messages within the play.

Turner's concept of social drama corresponds to what the Nigerien troupe members refer to as theme, and the form he defines for social drama structures their framework of scenes. Troupe members may name their themes as "enterprise" or "problems within the schools," but as they work through their scenes, the connections come from a sense of social process. In the Maradi Troupe's outline of the scenes of 'DAN KWANGILA, they spoke of the necessary steps in a contract.(50) Zinder's BA GA IRINTA BA similarly followed the complaint process through the hierarchy of the administration. Such over-all thematic structures relate the plays to actual experience--the current manifestations of real social dramas. Within these large frameworks, the troupes use patterns of repetition and action that will specifically and concretely develop their themes. The patterns from the oral narrative tradition intuitively known to both actors and audiences serve well to communicate the plot of the play and the underlying meanings of its story.

    The theatre, as Turner and Schechner emphasize, provides a reflection of social life. In a developing country in the midst of ongoing, radical social change, this opportunity for reflexivity, for self-assessment as a nation, remains crucial. Niger's theatre has been successful in presenting current issues both from the authorities' viewpoint of what their programs are intended to accomplish and from the perspective of villagers concerned with local problems. The plays are intended to be educational and entertaining; their popularity attests to a compelling blend of both purposes. By using familiar, conventional scenes and characters, the troupes draw their audiences into the fictional world of the plays, one that seems similar to their own. The actors convey thematic messages by means of narrative patterns they share with their audience from the oral tradition, and through the familiar form of social dramas which they share from everyday experience. Using these forms, the troupes involve the audience in the play, requiring a new look at past and present reality and demanding a future response.

ENDNOTES CHAPTER III

1. Harold Scheub, "Oral Narrative Process and the Use of Models," NEW LITERARY HISTORY, VI (1975), p. 360; Harold Scheub, "Performance of Oral Narrative," FRONTIERS OF FOLKLORE, ed. William Bascom (Boulder, Colorado: Westview Press, 1977), pp. 54-5.
2. Scheub, "Performance of Oral Narrative," pp. 54-5.
3. Bernard Beckerman, DYNAMICS OF DRAMA: THEORY AND METHOD OF ANALYSIS (New York: Alfred A. Knopf, 1970), p. 13.
4. Beckerman, p. 69.
5. Beckerman, pp. 120-4.
6. Beckerman, p. 23.
7. ALHAJI SHAGALI, by the Troupe Théâtrale de Mainé Soroa, performed at the National Festival in Diffa, Niger, 12 April 1981. Synopses of this play and those following appear in the Appendix.
8. KOWA YA BUGI RUWA IDONAY, by the Troupe Théâtrale de Filingué, performed at the National Festival in Diffa, Niger, 13 April 1981.
9. WALWALE, by the Troupe Théâtrale d'Agadez, performed at the National Festival in Diffa, Niger, 7 April 1981.
10. Performance notes, WALWALE, MJC, Diffa, 7 April 1981.
11. 'DAN KWANGILA, by the Troupe Théâtrale de Maradi, performed at the National Festival in Diffa, Niger, 9 April 1981.
12. BA GA IRINTA BA, by the Troupe Amadou 'Dan Bassa of Zinder, performed at the National Festival in Niamey, Niger, April 1980.
13. COHABITATION ENTRE ELEVEURS ET CULTIVATEURS, by the Troupe Théâtrale de Matameye, performed at the Eliminatoires for the Département of Zinder in Tanout, Niger, 7 March 1981.
14. TALALA MAI KAMAN SAKE, by the Troupe Amadou 'Dan Bassa of Zinder, performed at the National Festival in Diffa, Niger, 8 April 1981.
15. This contrasts with the published Hausa plays from Nigeria, many of which portray familial issues--conflicts between husbands and wives, between married couples and their in-laws, between parents and children. The festival competition in Niger and civic sponsorship of the samariya troupes is probably the major cause of this difference.

16. MADAME SIDIKOU, by the CEG Student Troupe, Tchin Tabaraden, Niger, 17 December 1980.
17. DARAJAR K'ASA AL'ADARTA, by the Radio Club Troupe of Zinder, Niger, 21 June 1981.
18. GAADOO K'ARHIN ALLAA (Waasan Kwaykoyoo na Zinder a 1973), transcribed by Abuubakar Mahamman, (Niamey: CELHTO, 1977), Scene 5, pp. 34-40.
19. BABBAN RUMBU MATARSHI TUKUNYA, a radio performance by the ORTN Troupe of Zinder, Episode 4, recorded 31 August 1981.
20. I believe the phrase to be an advertizing slogan from Nigeria, but I did not learn its precise origin.
21. GADO K'ARHIN ALLA, by the Troupe Amadou 'Dan Bassa of Zinder, videotaped by ORTN (Niamey, 1979); see also the published text, GAADOO K'ARHIN ALLAA.
22. ANA SARA ANA DIBIN BAKIN GATARI (While Chopping, One Looks at the Edge of the Axe), by the Troupe Théâtrale de Madaoua, videotaped by ORTN (Niamey, 1980).
23. See further discussion of these scenes in Chapter IV.
24. Interview with Alhaji Zoubeirou Lawal, Mainé Soroa, Niger, 17 April 1981.
25. See further discussion of these scenes in Chapter IV.
26. Harold Scheub, "Parallel Image-Sets in African Oral Narrative Performances," REVIEW OF NATIONAL LITERATURES, 2 (1971), p. 222.
27. Scheub, "Parallel Image-Sets," p. 207.
28. Scheub, "Parallel Image-Sets," pp. 206-7. For Nigerien Hausa examples of the good girl/bad girl narrative, see Connie L. Stephens, "The Relationship of Social Symbols and Narrative Metaphor: A Study of Fantasy and Disguise in the Hausa Tatsuniya of Niger," (Diss. University of Wisconsin-Madison, 1981), performances 605 and 606, pp. 1043-1107.
29. DARAJAR K'ASA AL'ADARTA, performance by the Radio Club Troupe of Zinder as part of the Wasan Kara, MJC, Zinder, 21 June 1981.
30. Interview with Alhaji Abdousalam Adam, Zinder, Niger, 30 June 1980.
31. KUSKURE KARATU NE, by the Troupe Théâtrale de Tahoua, performed at the National Festival in Diffa, Niger, 10 April 1981.

Play Structure

32. Program for KUSKUREE KARATU NEE, distributed by the Inspection Départementale de la Jeunesse des Sports de Tahoua at the Diffa performance, 10 April 1981.
33. Performance notes, KUSKURE KARATU NE, Diffa, 10 April 1981.
34. Kuskure Karatu Ne, Scene 1. The transcription of this play is by Aboubacar Mahamane; the English translation is mine. The original Hausa:

> Arzika: Madugu ina za mu tahiya mu zuba ku'dinmu na zuwa gabas ille mu tsaya na nan ga k'asammu mu zuba kudinmu mu tahi....
> Diba Madugu, bidi nasihwa ga Alla, inda duk Alla ya maka nasihwa to dole na mutun shi ma nasihwa Madugu. Da garin wani ya k'oshi gara garinku ya k'oshi, da gidan wani ya k'oshi gara gidanku ya k'oshi Madugu, ka ji abunda na gaya maka.

35. KUSKURE KARATU NE, Scene 10.

> Madugu: An, wanga abu ni Madugu da ya zame mini kumya biyu....
> Babban kumya ta da na samu arzikina cikin k'asanmu na wahala ga nomana na samu, ku'dina na zuwa gabas, na k'i yarda da al'amarin k'asanmu na tahi na zo na kai ma wani 'dan iska su na rasa inda yaka yi ba....
> Wanga abu da ya hwaru bisa gare ni Madugu ya zama galga'di ga 'yan k'asa.

36. BA GA IRINTA BA, Scene 6. The transcription of this play is mine with help gratefully acknowledged from Aboubacar Mahamane and Yazi Dogo; the English translation is mine. The original Hausa:

Madame:	Kai, Directeur. Ni ba na yahe mishi ba.
Mamman Arrivé:	Haba, Madame! ... Ba ki ga manya garin nan suka zo. Haba!
Mai Samari:	Ki diba darajammu, yarinya! Ba Mamman za ki diba ba, darajammu za ki diba....
Mamman Arrivé:	Ni ka a bi halina.
Directeur:	Ki dubi yauni wannan da Mai Samari.
Mamman Arrivé:	Yauwa!

37. Harold Scheub, "Oral Narrative Process," pp. 353-77; Harold Scheub, "The Technique of the Expansible Image in Xhosa Ntsomi Performances," RESEARCH IN AFRICAN LITERATURES, I, no. 2 (1970), pp. 119-46.

38. See discussion of these rehearsals in Chapter II, "Radio Club Troupe of Zinder." After two weeks of rehearsals for this play, the troupe began work on a second one. Director Alhaji Abdousalam Adam told me that they were preparing three plays from their repertoire for possible videotaping. I left the country in November before any final arrangements with ORTN for videotaping had been made.

39. Rehearsal notes, Radio Club, Zinder, Niger, September 1981.

40. Rehearsal notes, Radio Club, Zinder, Niger, 12 September 1981.

41. Rehearsal notes, Radio Club, Zinder, Niger, 8 and 9 September 1981.

42. Victor Turner, FROM RITUAL TO THEATRE: THE HUMAN SERIOUSNESS OF PLAY (New York: Performing Arts Journal Publications, 1982), p. 92; see also his DRAMAS, FIELDS, AND METAPHORS: SYMBOLIC ACTION IN HUMAN SOCIETY (Ithaca: Cornell University Press, 1974), pp. 38-41.

43. Turner, FROM RITUAL TO THEATRE, p. 11.

44. Turner, FROM RITUAL TO THEATRE, p. 78.

45. Richard Schechner, ESSAYS ON PERFORMANCE THEORY, 1970-1976 (New York: Drama Book Specialists, 1977), p. 121.

46. Schechner, pp. 140-44.

47. Turner, FROM RITUAL TO THEATRE, p. 74.

48. See quotation and discussion in Chapter II, "Development of a Theme," (Interview with Yazi Dogo, Zinder, Niger, 14 August 1981).

49. Interview with Yazi Dogo and Abdou Louché, conducted by Aboubacar Mahamane, Zinder, Niger, 22 April 1981.

50. See Chapter II, "The Arrangement of Scenes," (Interview with the Maradi Troupe, 27 April 1981).

CHAPTER IV
CHARACTERS IN ACTION

Once the Hausa troupes have set out the broad scenic framework for their chosen theme, they begin to assign actors to roles within that structure. Characters in this sense remain subordinate to the action, and they are easily recognized as stock types. In a discussion of comedy, Northrop Frye finds this functional emphasis true of all drama:

> In drama, characterization depends on function; what a character is follows from what he has to do in the play. Dramatic function in its turn depends on the structure of the play; the character has certain things to do because the play has such and such a shape. The structure of the play in its turn depends on the category of the play; if it is comedy, its structure will require a comic resolution and a prevailing comic mood.(1)

Frye decries the notion of lifelike characters being the antithesis of stock types as a "vulgar error"; rather, he finds a stock type as necessary to the character as a skeleton to the actor who plays it.(2) This view of the centrality of function parallels V. Propp's analysis of folktales, where different characters may perform the same functions in a story. Propp posits function as: "an act of a character, defined from the point of view of its significance for the course of the action."(3) As in oral narratives, the individual identities of characters in plays remain secondary to the actions they perform.

Within the Hausa plays, the functions of various characters generally serve one of the troupes' two major purposes: they work to convey instructional messages or to provide comic entertainment. Most of the many roles in a play will thus be either serious or comic types. Unifying these diverse tendencies are the more complex central characters, who are usually comic types but whose deeds and misdeeds carry the main thematic message through the course of the play.

As noted in Chapter II, certain actors in the troupes have become associated with certain types of roles. Several actors and directors discussed the ability of individual performers to play roles of authority or comic roles, with different natural abilities complementing each type. With this incipient specialization and the added experience of each new performance, individual actors are developing their own repertoires of skills. Using these skills, they create characters in performance.

Like the **Commedia dell'Arte** performers of the sixteenth and seventeenth centuries in Europe, the Nigerien troupes draw their material from a broad range of sources but continually recycle things that have worked well in past plays. As Kenneth McKee writes of the **Commedia** tradition:

> It inherited a fragmentary legacy from many sources: from the **commedia erudita** of the Renaissance; from the clowns and variety artists who entertained at the festivities of the nobles; from the king's jesters; from the minstrels and jongleurs and medicine shows which in Medieval days attracted crowds of spectators on populous streets; from the comedies of Terence and Plautus; from Atellan farces in Rome; and even from Asiatic mimes.
> Although all these elements contributed to the formation of the **commedia dell'arte**, the influence of each was completely

Characters in Action 167

submerged and scarcely recognizable when the genre reached maturity in the hands of the notable player companies which started to form after 1550.(4)

From these eclectic models and from their own inspirations, the **commedia** actors developed personal repertoires of techniques, monologues, jokes and **lazzi** (turn, trick, jest), sometimes writing these down and passing them on to the next generation.(5) Actors frequently played the same character for many years; some passed the roles themselves on to their children.(6) Each **commedia** performance was improvised from a brief scenario of the major plot actions, incorporating the actors' store of dialogues and comic jests. The group's cohesion and long experience working together were essential to this ability to improvise.(7)

The present-day Hausa troupes in Niger have rather different antecedents from European comedy, although they include some knowledge of the **commedia dell'arte** itself by way of the French educational system and the popularity of French comedy, particularly that of Molière. Nonetheless, their methods of developing a play are not very different from the Italian troupes. Through their apprenticeship into the work of a troupe, Nigerien actors develop the skills, actions and ideas that they bring to each new production, fleshing out its score (an unwritten scenario) in rehearsals and in later performances. Actors gather potential material from each other, from observation of other troupes' performances, and from everyday life, trying out new ideas in rehearsals and polishing them through interaction and discussion with other members of the troupe. Their audiences, far from demanding constant novelty, enjoy the repetition of character types and stock actions, anticipating the familiar comedy much as European audiences must have enjoyed the **commedia dell'arte** performances freshly built on old characters and tricks.

Characters are defined by their functions, their actions in the over-all design of the play, but they are brought to life by the improvisation and creativity of the performers within the limits of that design. Unlike the **commedia** tradition, Nigerien actors do not play the same roles year after year, but the stock character types work in

much the same way. Harlequin or Pulcinella may not
appear in each new play, but the Hausa characters
are nonetheless utterly familiar as soon as they
walk on the stage. Often their titles or the
meanings of their names immediately label their
types and set the tone--serious or comic--for the
subsequent activity of the scene.

Many characters never have individual names at
all but are called only by their titles: **Sarki**
(chief), **Mai Samari** (head of the **samariya**),
Sous-Préfet, Director, Mayor. This usage echoes
the French custom of addressing important people by
their titles ("Monsieur le Directeur"). It also
follows the Hausa tradition of address through
titles and epithets; a **sarki** is never spoken to by
name but as "Sarki," "Toron Giwa" (bull elephant),
or another praise name. In the Hausa oral narrative tradition as well, characters rarely are
given personal names, as Neil Skinner and H.A.S.
Johnston each note in their anthologies of Hausa
stories.(8)

The titles emphasize the official functions of
the roles, parallels to their duties in actual
life. A **sarki** or a **sous-préfet** as local officials
of the highest rank will be portrayed as figures of
authority, serious voices in the community. Such
rulers will make pronouncements; an inspector
will investigate situations within his jurisdiction; a director will organize the course of events
in his realm. Satire and criticism in the plays
rarely touch these higher levels of authority out
of respect for their counterparts in real life. As
a result, titled roles tend to be straightforward,
serious roles, forming a solid reference to reality
against which the comic roles contrast.

In BA GA IRINTA BA, the Troupe Amadou 'Dan
Bassa of Zinder portrayed a variety of such functional roles in both the traditional and the
administrative hierarchies. The majority of
the characters in the play never needed given
names. When Mamman Arrivé's delinquent son claims
that his teacher has hit him, Mamman descends in
fury on the teachers' meeting cursing Madame
(his son's teacher), the director, and one **monsieur**
after another who rise to defend her. The actors
referred to one another as "Directeur," "Monsieur,"
and "Madame," only occasionally slipping into the
actors' real names or nicknames (Yazi, or 'Dan
K'arami, "little one/junior").(Scene 2)

The director of the school takes the complaint to his supervisor, the school inspector, who also refers it to higher levels of authority, the mayor and the police commissioner. These characters act on the model of their real-life counterparts listening to the complaints and working to solve the problems. When the mayor calls for a town meeting, local representatives of the people--Mai Samari and the President of the Parents' Association (called "Président")--also attend. These titled characters play the functional roles of traditional elders, working for a peaceful reconciliation between Mamman Arrivé and the governmental authorities.

Individual characteristics given to any of these roles serve to underline the action, not the personality of the character. For example, the mayor forgets things (past requests by the school director), and the police commissioner's son is failing at school because of his father's frequent transfers from one town to another. Yet although these facets add sympathy and individuality to these characters, their central purpose is to raise new issues in the complex problems of the school system, the theme of the play.(9)

Common Hausa names generally mark characters who have no titles and who may require names for reference, but who are not central figures in the play. Ordinary names suggest ordinary people. The troupe may, in these cases, even refer to the character by the actor's own name. In TALALA MAI KAMAN SAKE by the Troupe Amadou 'Dan Bassa, Talala's nephew was named Sule in a rehearsal which occurred after several performances of the play. Formerly, the character had had no given name; he was merely the nephew schoolboy (**Samari**/ young man). The troupe decided that Talala would surely address him by name, so they gave the character a common form of the actor's real name, Suleman.(10) In the same play, as noted in Chapter II, the niece's name was changed in deference to the actress's wishes; at the festival performance, her own name, Tsaibatu, was used.(11)

In BA GA IRINTA BA, the common names appear among the neighbors and townspeople and in Mamman Arrivé's family. His wife Gimbiya, his son Sanussi, his sister Jatu, and his brother Yaya (which means older brother) all have ordinary names. Sanussi appears like any other spoiled child; his mischievous behavior is not unique or unusual. Mamman himself should be like other people in the town, with his common first name, except that his money has given him pretensions that he has "arrived." As his brother reminds him in the final scene, Mamman has lost his good sense; he is spoiling his son with his new wealth.

> Yaya: Think about when we were kids, did anyone at our house ever treat us like that?
> Mamman: How could they?
> Yaya: Or if we went and fought, and someone beat us, and we went home crying, Papa would beat us, too.
> Mamman: For sure!
> Yaya: So you get yourself some money and go and spoil your kid, eh?
> (Scene 8)(12)

Yaya emphasizes in his speech what the family's names have implied from the outset: these are ordinary people, neighbors, relatives--like anybody in the audience.

Metaphorical names for characters signal their importance and give an immediate glimpse of their type. Major characters' names and usually minor comic characters' names as well are chosen carefully. Maradi's 'Dan Kwangila (the contractor) is referred to not only by his title but also by his given name, Alhaji Arzika Rangama (Alhaji Wealth by Barter). Talala of TALALA MAI KAMAN SAKE quite clearly becomes the major character of the play as soon as he appears. **Talala** (a long tethering rope) is not normally a personal name; the character is, however, the object of the title's proverb, "giving someone a rope to hang himself with."(13) Zinder's Mamman Arrivé was such a popular name that both the play, BA GA IRINTA BA, and the actor, Oumarou Nainou, have since become known more commonly by their character's name than their own.(14)

Walwale's name (unravel) metaphorically contrasts with the names of the series of town leaders whose plans he opposes: President Tumka (tie together), Sassak'e (carpenter), Sinadiri (solder), and Tubalaje (bricks). At the end of the play, Walwale shows his repentance by announcing that he has changed his name:

> Walwale: Mai Gari, for God's sake, you know my name is not Walwale, my name is Muhammad, by God....
>
> Mai Gari: You have given yourself the name of Walwale because whenever you see a good thing, you undo it, you say, "What's the use of it?" You unravel it. Now if you've really left off unravelling (**walwale**), from now on your name will become Muhammad. So be it, everyone will hear it.
> (Scene 8)(15)

Walwale sheds his old name and his antisocial behavior, taking not only a common Muslim Hausa name but the leadership role the Prophet's name implies. After earlier refusing to contribute even 500 francs ($2.00) to the effort to bring piped water to the primary school, he now volunteers to personally supply all the bricks to build a wall around the school.(Scene 8)

Minor characters may also hold significant or comic names. 'Dan Kwangila's mentor as a corrupt entrepreneur is named Alhaji Gimshik'i (supporting pillar), while the foreigners who betray his enterprise by leaving the country with the project's funds are called Joseph (noteworthy because it is French) and Bienvenu (welcome), with Bienvenu the more significant of the two as the accountant. I observed several plays with bumbling servants named Dodo (a traditional evil spirit believed to live in wells, an ogre), and country bumpkins named 'Dan Hulani (literally, son of a Fulani), pointing to the character's ethnic origins although it is not an uncommon name for Hausa men. The procurer in TALALA was dubbed Savon Robb, an imported beauty cream widely sold in local markets. In BA GA IRINTA BA, the town gossip is known as K'arawrawa (the bell), with the metaphor brought directly into the dialogue:

> K'arawrawa: K'arawrawa fa yanzu za ta buga.
> (The bell is about to ring, i.e., I have some good gossip to tell you).(Scene 6)

Unusual names whose meanings are known to the audience thus call attention to a character and what he is likely to do.

Serious Characters

To introduce the serious theme of many of these plays, especially the entries in the national festival competition, the characters of the **sarki** and/or **sous-préfet** appear. Scenes at the **sarki's** court, a standard element of plays in the 1970's,(16) are still common in the **ballets** but occur less frequently in the plays I observed. The **ballet** I saw in rehearsal by the troupe from Matameye in March 1981 added such a scene at the **sarki's** court after their performance at the departmental competition and before their festival performance.(17) In this brief opening scene, the wrestlers, the main dancers in the **ballet**, informed the **sarki** of their intentions to compete and he granted permission for the festivities to occur. Similar scenes accompanied nearly all of the **ballets** in the 1981 Festival, creating an explanatory and traditional setting for the dancing.

Scenes in the plays which take place at the **sous-préfecture** serve the same function as those at the **sarki's** court and often include the **sarki** and the **sous-préfet** working in harmony with each other. A strong message of the continuity of power accompanies these local leaders joining forces, representing the power of traditional rulers allied with the present governmental hierarchy.

The troupe from Mainé Soroa used such scenes to open and close ALHAJI SHAGALI, with classic examples of the **sous-préfet** and **sarki** charac-

Characters in Action

ters.(18) In Scene 1, the **sous-préfet** calls a formal meeting to award Alhaji Shagali the contract to build a village clinic. The invited town representatives--the **sarki**, Major, and other elders--as well as Alhaji Shagali assemble in the **sous-préfet's** office to hear his announcement:

> Sous-préfet: The reason that I decided to call you in front of the Sarki and Major and the leaders of the Development Society...
> Shagali: Indeed.
> Sous-préfet: First, to thank you for what you have outlined in your plans.
> Shagali: Why, thank you!
> Sous-préfet: And second, to give you some advice.
> (Scene 1)(19)

Within the **sous-préfet's** formal announcement, he warns Alhaji Shagali of the importance of completing the project during the time period he has promised (ten months), and of contributing to their **département's** development as part of the national effort (the Development Society). The **sarki** says little during this speech, but his presence at the meeting signifies his accord.

The **sous-préfet** as the vehicle for these announcements sets the play in motion. His injunctions, as the audience expects, become the very things Shagali fails to do as the action unfolds.(20) At the end of the play, the **sous-préfet** reappears in an almost identical scene to pronounce judgment on Shagali's mismanagement of the project. After the same group of important townspeople re-assembles in his office, the **sous-préfet** sends for Alhaji Shagali, refuses to listen to his fabricated story about losing the money in a traffic accident, and has his guard haul Shagali off to prison. Yet the story does not quite end there, because the clinic must still be built; the community's development takes precedence over one man's failure. The **sous-préfet** asks the town elders to choose another contractor and then makes a final pronouncement:

> Brothers, members of the community, I want to call your attention to one thing: today our country will progress only if every man, woman, and child will stand up and proclaim that he will help the country's development. As I see it, if what Alhaji Shagali has done continues, the country will never, ever, move forward. Why is that? Because it is a structure of lies.
>
> Everyone knew that Alhaji Shagali did not have the character for this work, but I was a stranger to the town and didn't know anything about him. He, however, was familiar with the important people, he knew the intricacies of affairs, he had friends in high places, he came when they had a meeting and they supported his bid for the construction. And where did it get you?
>
> So--I want to inform you all in this district, that from now on, if I have anything to do with it, there will be no more "help" to anyone. Even if a person has strong backing, I will dismiss him; if he wants the work, he can do it in accordance with his abilities.(Scene 6)(21)

Here, as in the first scene, the **sous-préfet** stands as a spokesman for authority and for the didactic message of the play.

This union of traditional and current rulers appears even more sharply in KOWA YA BUGI RUWA IDONAY, the 1981 Festival play by the Filingué Troupe.(22) The first scene takes place at the village headman Mai Gari's compound, where the **chef médical** arrives to introduce the new doctor to the village community. As the play progresses, the corrupt doctor conspires with Mai Gari to cheat the villagers by selling the medicines which he is supposed to provide free of charge as part of the government's health program. It is the region's **sarki** who finally reports the situation to the **sous-préfet** (Scene 4), thus uniting officials at a higher level in order to curtail the corruption of those within their jurisdiction. The traditional and administrative conspirators at the village level meet their match in the coordinated efforts of the regional authorities. In this way, the play places the dichotomy of just and unjust authority not between the old and the new, but between higher and lower officials; the region's superiors are truly superior characters. The play's final scene returns to the village where the **sous-préfet** condemns Mai Gari, fires the doctor, and installs a new headman, thus resolving the conflict with his stamp of authority.(Scene 5)

Accompanying Filingué's **sarki** is his **dogari**, a **sarki's** traditional retainer/guard, whose distinctive uniform is a bold red and green robe. Accompanying the **sous-préfet** in this play, and in many of the others, is a military guard in western-style khaki uniform and beret. Both depict real figures, visually signalling the rank and importance of the men they protect. In the plays, the guard characters rarely say more than, "Yes, sir!" although they may run errands for the **sarki** or **sous-préfet**, or formally introduce his visitors, furthering the action of the scene.

Typical of these guards is that of the **sous-préfet** in ALHAJI SHAGALI, as the first scene opens:

> Sous-préfet: Guard!
> Guard: Yes, commandant!
> Sous-préfet: At ease. Eh, the **sarki** and Major are coming along with some other people. I want to see them. When they come, don't stop them, let them come right in.
> Guard: Yes, sir! (Scene1)(23)

The **sous-préfet's** directions to the guard and the visitors' announcement of who they are provide a simple expository function. Yet the guard also becomes a concrete symbol of the power of the **sarki** or **sous-préfet** in his control over people. Physical power is a factor of importance in a society

which traditionally held a wide range of
patron-client and owner-slave relationships, later
to be conquered only by the French military forces
in colonial battles. The current military regime
in Niger continues to retain soldiers as guards for
its higher officials, many of whom are military
officers themselves. With this background in
reality, the mere presence of a guard character
in a play signals a specific realm of authority and
a range of concomitant meaning. The guard in
ALHAJI SHAGALI may act as a receptionist in the
beginning of the play, but by the end, he receives
orders to arrest Shagali.

>
> Sous-préfet: ... Oh, Guard!
> Guard: Yes, Commandant!
> Sous-préfet: Go and put Alhaji in the hands of the Commandant of the Brigade, he's to hold him until I release him.
> Guard: Yes, sir! (Scene 6)(24)

Although a very minor role as adjunct of the **sarki**
or **sous-préfet**, a **dogari** or guard signals the
serious implications of the scene's action.

GADO K'ARHIN ALLA focusses on the election of
a **sarki**, portraying the interaction of traditional
rulers with modern bureaucracy as a central
theme.(25) In the first scene, the aging **sarki**
dies, after calling on his courtiers to make his
son Baydu his heir. The courtiers then dispute the
other possible candidates until the **sous-préfet**
arrives to establish the official list of princes
for the government to choose from. As the **waziri**
informs the others:

> Waziri: Well! I hear what you are saying about Prince Shaho and Prince Mushe, but haven't you noticed that the times now are not like yours in the old days, or didn't you know that? In the old times, the court and the **sarki's** slaves met and chose the chief. But now, don't you know the world has changed? It's not the

same as it was. The **sarki** himself is a civil servant, they pay him, or didn't you know that? Will you come saying, "Prince So-and-So! Prince So-and-So!" Are **you** going to choose the chief? You and the **liman** are going to do it? Don't you know there are other people to choose the **sarki**? ...

Galadima: Waziri, if you knew all that, there's no use for you to quarrel. Just now you spoke about the **sous-préfet**, didn't you? (Scene 2)(26)

After he enters, the **sous-préfet** explains that they must wait for word from Niamey and the **préfet**, who will choose someone able to work well with the Party and the government.(27)

The government officials reappear in Scene 5 to announce the new **sarki**, Salihi (honesty). Here, the **sous-préfet** makes a speech condemning those who would try to cheat the government and then introduces the **préfet**. The **préfet**, who apologizes for his Hausa (a realistic touch since most of the nation's highest officials are Zarma), expresses his condolences to the community at the death of the old **sarki** and warns against rivalries continuing after the new one is installed (a foreshadowing of the following scene). He then announces that Prince Salihi is the successful candidate.(28)

Following these speeches by the governmental leaders, the troupe includes music and a mimed portrayal of the traditional installation ceremony for a **sarki**, including the **doka** dressing him in appropriate robes and turban and the **sarki** beating the ceremonial drum. The new **sarki** then addresses the crowd himself, thanking God, the prophets and the ancestors, the Party and the government, and calling for God's blessings on the entire community.(29) His traditional prayers are followed by a speech by the region's **député**, their representative to the National Assembly. This character dates the play before the military takeover when the National Assembly and the Party's political activities were banned (1974). However, the performance I saw in 1981 retained both the character's title and his hopes for relief from the drought, a topical reference to the early 1970's, as well as pleas for national unity and cooperation with Nigeria. (Scene 5)(30)

Together the characters in this scene present a unified, harmonious network of authority with links between traditional and post-independence officials, between local and national powers, between man and God. These characters are not meant to portray individuals but rather to represent the order of the world, the hierarchy of power as Nigeriens experience it.

What the installation ceremony and speeches resolve on a national level, Salihi as **sarki** resolves on the familial level in the final scenes of the play. In Scene 6, the other princely candidates meet to express their displeasure at the choice of Salihi; their meeting is interrupted by a summons to appear at his court. Scene 7 at the **sarki's** court shows Salihi's wise reconciliation of his rivals:

> The reason that I have called all of you together is for good news. I have always told you, if you understand me, that when they made me chief, it was not to separate me from you. This house belongs to all of us. You know well that if the house is ruined, we are all ruined, not just the one who sits in the chair of the house.(31)

He then announces in his power as **sarki** that Shaho is to have the title of **Yakudima**, Baydu that of **Yarima**, and Mushe that of **Magaji**, and he declares that he will not listen to any gossip or accusations about his brothers.(Scene 7) The final scene of the play presents the **Hawan Daba** (Durbar), the traditional salute to a **sarki** by his followers mounted on horseback, including the other princes whose good favor he has claimed. A manifestation of traditional homage, this salute resolves the conflict among the candidates in magnificent mimed spectacle--decorated (wooden) horses, music, festival robes, the **sarki** under his umbrella, and the courtiers raising their swords in tribute. (Scene 8)

In TALALA MAI KAMAN SAKE, the Troupe Amadou 'Dan Bassa incorporates other traditional, respected roles, those of the religious scholars (the **malams**) as well as the head of the **samariya** (Mai Samari) and the judge (Juju).(32) In the opening scene, Mai Samari reconciles a dispute between two members of the **samariya** who should have a joking relationship with each other (**wasan nangi**). Mai Samari draws out the example of different ethnic groups within Niger having a chain of such relationships with one another:

> Mai Samari: Haven't you got that in your head? If he curses you, it's not you he's cursing. If you notice, if you go from here in the east to the west, our country is all one and the same. Listen to me carefully now. In this country the Beriberi joke with the Fulani, right?
> Musa: Yes.
> Mai Samari: If you continue, you'll meet up with the Gwari who jokes with the man from Gobir, if you go even further, you'll meet the man from Katsina who jokes with the man from Gobir, you go even further, you'll see the man from the Arewa joking with the man from Adar....
> Look and you'll see all of our country has the same mother, the same father, if you go [anywhere] they'll tell you this people

and that one have a joking relationship.(Scene 1)(33)

This speech provides one of the central didactic points of the play, emphasizing traditional relationships as the basis of national unity and harmony. Audiences expect this sort of wise pronouncement from a community leader like Mai Samari. The actor chosen for the role, Kailou Bako, a middle-aged man with impressive public-speaking ability, performed in accordance with those expectations, lending weight to the message of his lecture.(34)

The religious officials in the second scene of TALALA MAI KAMAN SAKE--**Liman** (imam), **Ladan** (muezzin), and **Na'ibi** (deputy imam)--receive, acknowledge and distribute the funeral offerings and say the appropriate prayers. These leaders give religious sanction to Talala as caretaker for his late brother's estate, thereby establishing the social and religious expectations he will violate by his actions in the rest of the play. In the final scene of judgment against Talala, the **malams** as well as the government's appointed judge define Talala's failure. Quoting verses from the Qur'an in Arabic, the **alkali** (Muslim judge) concludes:

> I swear by God and the Prophet, all the people who abuse the wealth of orphans will be like the eye of a needle in ten countries on the Day of Resurrection. This one [Talala] will be in the fire.(Scene 7)(35)

These figures seated in judgment, dressed in the black robes of the court, and speaking solemnly in Arabic as well as in Hausa evoke the audience's respect for Islamic scholars in real court cases. The actors portray these scholarly judges with verisimilitude, focussing attention on the gravity of Talala's offenses and the warning message of the play.

Both BA GA IRINTA BA and 'DAN KWANGILA present a wider array of authoritative figures, but their functions remain basically the same as those of the **sarkis**, **sous-préfets**, and scholars of the other plays. Part of the instructive purpose in these plays is to demonstrate through scenes based on real models how various offices in the administatrive hierarchy work. As Yazi Dogo noted in an interview with reference to BA GA IRINTA BA, the troupe wanted to show that the problems at school affect everyone and that the ramifications extend through the various levels of government.(36) The troupes are thus creating new characters who are analogous to the older authoritative types (the **sarki** and his titled attendants) and to real offices within the present-day community.

In Maradi's 'DAN KWANGILA, the construction contract is not awarded directly by the **sous-préfet** as in ALHAJI SHAGALI, but by a planning commission whose members discuss the various dossiers submitted to them.(Scene 3)(37) Here, the president of the commission (**Président**) conducts the meeting mostly in French according to a standard bureaucratic model. As he enters, the committee members stand up in respect; he asks them to sit down and announces the business at hand:

> Gentlemen, members of the commission, the order of the day for the present meeting consists of only one matter. As you know, it is for the examination of the dossiers concerning the announcement of Offer number 007 of March 3, 1981, pertaining to the construction of a clinic at the village of Maigémé in the district of Dakoro.
> Before getting into the heart of the matter, I would like to direct your attention to certain points. The choice of dossier should be executed in the greatest objectivity, and since the state has enlarged the National Investment Fund, it is our task as technicians to retain a serious entrepreneur and above all, to oversee the execution of the work. For this, gentlemen, without further delay, let us go on to the perusal of the docu-

ments. Mr. Ruwa, please present the dossiers.(Scene 3)(38)

While Mainassara, the committee member Rangama bribed in the preceding scene, skews the subsequent proceedings, the president remains above reproach, a bureaucrat conducting his affairs in proper order.

Similarly, in the scene at the bank (Scene 4), it is a lower official, Hamza, who has been corrupted, rather than the bank's director. As the scene opens, Hamza and Alhaji Gimshik'i are saying goodbye to one another after arranging a business matter. Gimshik'i then recommends that Rangama also see Hamza to fix his loan. As Rangama arranges with Hamza to receive his money after business hours, two **fonctionnaires** complain of having to wait days before they can even see Hamza about their small loans. Hamza laughs at them, their anger rises, and the director overhears the fight and comes out to investigate the commotion. After listening to the complaints, the director rebukes Hamza:

> This is very serious. Hamza, how is it that you hold up the requests of civil servants for a full week? It's normal that they're making a fuss, they are the first to come and you neglect them. It's definitely your habit; moreover, this is not the first time, I know, people are always telling me this. It's not right for people to leave work, and then you come and scorn them. In fact, we must seek our clients out. Whether the clients are civil servants or merchants, you must not discriminate between them. They are all the same to you.(Scene 4)(39)

He continues by warning Hamza against any future instances of the kind and telling him that he wants to examine Alhaji Rangama's papers as well. This righteous authority of the director, in contrast to the clerk Hamza's clear corruption, repeats the opposition of characters in the previous committee

scene and reverberates in the scenes that follow.
 In Scene 5 at the Office of City Planning, the director receives two visitors, a friend from the Bureau of Topography and Rangama. Although the Maradi Troupe named the two fonctionnaires Hamidu ("Chef d'Urbanisme") and Dauda ("Monsieur de Topo"), these personal names are never used in the dialogue and the characters could easily be left with just their titles.(40) The scene opens with the flirtation between the secretary at the city planning office and the man from the topographical office described in Chapter II. Again, the petty corruption of one official, here using his government gas coupons for personal gifts rather than for work, receives a rebuke from a higher official as the director lectures him on not using government vehicles after hours. Rangama's ever greater infractions of the rules--not waiting for permission to enter the office, not waiting for proper clearance for his papers from Niamey, and in the next two scenes, his attempts to cheat his workers and to bypass the building regulations--are quelled by the director as well. Not only does he refuse to let Rangama begin the project before he receives authorization from Niamey (Scene 5), but he arrives to inspect the work site and orders it to be destroyed because the bricks have not been constructed to the standard building code.

> No, it won't do. I won't come in the name of the government and accept this building to give the government for admitting sick people. It won't do.
> (Scene 6)(41)

He also tells Rangama not to come to his house, nor to his office, clearly announcing to all that he cannot be bribed; he will not reconsider his decision to destroy the shoddy building.
 In this scene, the city planning director follows the inspector of employee welfare, who has just condemned Rangama's treatment of his workers (for inadequate wages, no over-time compensation, hiring foreign laborers before Nigerien workers, etc.). These two characters as well as the bank director and the commission's president in essence play the same role: that of the proper official, the authoritative administrator who works diligent-

ly for the good of the people and cannot be corrupted. The different characters are variant repetitions of the same type, reinforcing one another and strengthening the didactic image each and all of them portray.

Comic Characters

At the same time as these serious straight men project the nationalistic or moral messages of the plays, they become the foils for the ever-present comic types. To the homes and offices of important people come constant streams of bumbling servants, false **malams**, sick or crippled supplicants, and ethnic yokels, who both further the action and provide comic relief.

William O. Beeman describes a servant clown character as central to the humor of traditional Iranian improvisatory theatre.(42)

> The clown is nearly always in the role of a servant, although this is not a fixed requirement. The typical comic situation involves the clown in interaction with some authority figure: the master of the house, usually the **hajji**; the mistress of the house; the king, minister, or other member of court.
> In these interactions the clown continually distorts the pattern of normal linguistic and social interaction. He gives inappropriate answers, repeats directions and names incorrectly, usually changing innocent phrases into mocking, satirical or ribald commentary; or he responds to orders with taunts or insults....
> All of this inappropriate behavior is masked with a show of stupidity or ignorance. The clown distorts normal physical movement by jumping, running, flailing his arms, and twisting his body into odd shapes. He is also the chief agent in setting up physical humor....

> The overall effect is that of
> a fun-house mirror image of other
> characters in the perfor-
> mance.(43)

Beeman analyzes the humor of this clown/servant mocking authority as stemming from his stupidity and low social status: he cannot be blamed for his actions because he does them in apparent ignorance. The audience members for this rural theatre are typically of higher status than the clown but of lower status than his master; thus, they observe him defying the social order and getting away with it as they might wish to but never could do. The clown's comedy serves as a release for tensions within a rigidly hierarchical social system, Beeman concludes, like the classic role of a trickster.(44)

Unlike the clown who provides nearly all of the humor in the Iranian plays with the other characters and the story itself as his foils, the Nigerien servants hold minor roles and are but one of many types of comic characters, including the **alhajis** they often attend. Yet all of these comic types share characteristics with the Iranian clown and other tricksters; whether they play major or minor roles in a particular story, they form a universal brotherhood of fools.

In the Hausa plays, clumsy servants represent the comic counterpart to the guards of the **sarki** or **sous-préfet**, in this case demonstrating not only their master's wealth and power but also his foibles. Bumbling servants most often assist the corrupt civil servants and the rich **alhajis** in their plots and in their comedy as well. Their appearance signals the humorous turn of a scene.

These servants often cause laughter as much for what they will not or cannot do as for what they do. In 'DAN KWANGILA, the corrupt commission member, Mainassara, has a servant, Dodo, who never comes when called. In terms of the ongoing action, Dodo's function is to announce the arrival of Rangama and later to carry in all the goods he has brought as bribes for Mainassara, including a color television set. Dodo says little, but the actor emphasized his slowness and clumsiness so that Mainassara could continually yell at him to hurry up, to be careful, to try to come when called--with his commands escalating to the most important and funniest, "Don't drop that box!".(Scene 2)

In TALALA MAI KAMAN SAKE, the bumbling servant Agogo (a watch) appears when Talala's elaborate new house is completed. Talala and his friend ask Agogo to go and fetch the young woman they are interested in entertaining, graphically describing her voluptuous figure and where she lives. Agogo insists that he cannot possibly persuade her to come, a fact visually and aurally vindicated for the audience by his scruffy appearance and disjointed speech, but he suggests that they recruit Savon Robb to help them in their plan:

>   Talala: She's the one we want brought here.
>   Friend: Yes.
>   Agogo: Woooah, that one is beyond my strength.
>   Talala: Nonsense!
>   Friend: Really!
>   Agogo: By God. She...
>   Friend: Nonsense, Agogo, you're getting rusty, by God and the Prophet.
>   Agogo: That one requires Savon Robb.
>   Friend: Who?
>   Talala: Savon Robb?
>   Agogo: Yes. The one they call "Instant Action."
>   (Scene 4)(45)

Agogo develops the comic suspense of the scene through his hesitations and verbal accounts of characters who later appear. The salacious nature of the search, Agogo's inadequacy for the task, and the mention of a character with a name like Savon Robb, all promise high humor ahead.

Mamman Lawal, who acted the role of Agogo at the Diffa performance with no prior rehearsals, explained to me that it had always been his role, but that he had had to do the technical work at the Tanout competitions and was unable to perform there.(46) Agogo is typical of the roles he usually plays, slightly crazy and always humorous.

In GADO K'ARHIN ALLA, La'ba'ba (newborn) presents a similar type of messenger/servant at the beck and call of Shaho (hawk), one of the candidates competing to become the **sarki**. In the production I observed in Zinder, La'ba'ba was played by a very tall, lanky young man whose gown was too short, emphasizing his long legs and uncoordinated movements as he continually ran in and out on Shaho's errands.(47) The published text of the play records Shaho's repeated commands and admonishments to La'ba'ba:

> Shaho: Now then. La'ba'ba! La'ba'ba!
> La'ba'ba: Yes, may your wishes be fulfilled.
> Shaho: Hey, when someone calls you, don't you come? Don't you know tomorrow is the chief's coronation day? Follow Malam and go.
> (Scene 4)(48)

La'ba'ba acts primarily as a messenger physically ushering in (and out) the various charlatans Shaho engages to help him win the chief's election; La'ba'ba's clumsiness, repetitions and questions emphasize the absurdity of Shaho's frantic attempts to enlist magic aids for his candidacy.(Scene 4)

The characters La'ba'ba fetches for Shaho represent another comic type: the false **malam**. In contrast to the true Muslim scholars, exemplary members of the community, these false **malams** or **marabouts** deal in magic charms both good and evil, commercial remedies for any and all ailments. In GADO K'ARHIN ALLA, Malam Gobe da Nisa (tomorrow is far) appears with the dress and dignified bearing of a pious scholar; he even prays with Shaho before agreeing to provide a means for assuring him the title of **sarki** at the installation ceremony. But the play's joke falls on Shaho when the actual charm is brought and Malam Gobe da Nisa gives him instructions for using it. Instead of the normal amulet created from writing a few appropriate verses of the Qur'an and washing off the ink to drink, Malam Gobe da Nisa sends for a huge clay water pot, saying that he has written the names of everyone in the **sarki's** domain--rulers and peasants alike--and poured them into it. Shaho is to drink the entire contents of the pot that night before the ceremonies but without urinating. Shaho hastily sends the **malam** home and asks La'ba'ba to find another.(Scene 4)(49)

Abdou Louché's portrayal of Malam Gobe da Nisa strengthens the humor of this scene by presenting this impossible task with utter seriousness. As he and Yazi Dogo remarked in an interview, the troupe often gives Abdou roles of authority;(50) his deep voice and natural eloquence aid him in such serious roles. In GADO K'ARHIN ALLA, he displayed those same authoritative characteristics to command a foolishly absurd task, instilling the scene with the utmost irony.

Similar charlatans appear in TALALA MAI KAMAN SAKE and ALHAJI SHAGALI as conspirators with the main characters. Among Talala's visitors in Scene 3 appears a **malam**, given no other name, who is friendly with both Talala and the contractor for his new house. Malam accepts money (a gift to buy cola nuts) from the contractor, who is leaving just as he arrives at Talala's door. Their brief exchange sets the tone for Malam's subsequent conversation with Talala. After greeting Talala, Malam explains why he has come: while telling fortunes for other people, he has foreseen trouble for Talala, jealous enemies encircling him. Talala concurs that since the inheritance has been in his hands, he has needed medicine against enemies. He asks that Malam "bind up the mouths" of his brother's widows and children so that they cannot bring him trouble in the future. Malam agrees to do it, accepts Talala's money, and takes his leave, commenting on the importance of good neighbors. (Scene 3)

Like Malam Gobe da Nisa, this **malam** retains the trappings of a real scholar--a turban, prayer beads, and robes (although he wears a bright pink, not the traditional white). He also returns Talala's greetings with conventional pious modesty:

> Talala: Gafarta Malam. (God forgive us,Malam).
> Malam: Almajiri. (I'm only a pupil).
> Talala: Bismillah. (Please sit down).
> Malam: Almajiri. (I'm only a pupil).

> Talala: Bismillah. (Please sit down).
> Malam: Bismillah Allah. (In God's name) [as he sits down].(Scene 3)

However, his casting of lots, his cunning visit, and his assistance to Talala in suppressing the voices and rights of his brother's family contrast this **malam** markedly with the Islamic judges in the final scene of the play (described above), who condemn Talala's betrayal of his moral obligations. (Scene 7)

In a similar scene to that of Malam's visit to Talala, Boka Mai Burgami (the wizard with a goat-skin bag) visits Alhaji Shagali at his home in Mainé Soroa's play.(Scene 4) The **boka** is not a Muslim **malam**, but a traditional herbalist, here intended to have all the connotations of "pagan witchdoctor." Alhaji Shagali himself remarks to his foreman that the **malams** will no longer do what he wants to have done--the destruction of the engineer who continually criticizes his project and who will not accept his bribes.

> Shagali: By God, you know, in the old days, if you set the **malams** to take care of it, he wouldn't be sleeping in this town today.
> Maître: Yes, but the **malams** won't do it.
> Shagali: Now if you ask them, [they will say] the Islamic religious association forbids it, Allah doesn't like it, and so on, that's what they'll tell you.
> (Scene 4)(51)

But what the **malams** no longer do, Boka Mai Burgami will do, as Maître reminds Alhaji Shagali. He immediately sends for Mai Burgami.

Mai Burgami arrives on the scene wearing short pants, an immediate visual indication of his "pagan" status and bush origins as no dignified Muslim man would wear such garments, and he carries the leather bag full of charms for which he is named. He refuses to come all the way inside the house and sits instead on a mat, "No, Alhaji, this is enough for me here." When Shagali asks why he has not seen him in town, Mai Burgami says that a man who seeks food has to go where he must and cannot say when he will return. This brief dialogue further establishes him as an itinerant beggar, selling his medicines in distant villages. Shagali then explains his project and the differences between the old engineer, a good friend of his, and the new replacement, whom he cannot get along with. They speak in euphemisms of Mai Burgami's task:

> Shagali: You know what you should do with him.
> Mai Burgami: Yes, Alhaji.
> Shagali: Yes
> Mai Burgami: That's not difficult for us.
> Shagali: Yes.
> Mai Burgami: If we make an effort to do the thing as we see it, to do our work, now if we begin this black work, we'll finish it. (Scene 4)(52)

Yet the evil nature of Mai Burgami's work is clear, with a local audience knowing exactly what sort of concrete actions might be meant. Mai Burgami then casts lots on the ground and tells Alhaji Shagali that there will be no problem, it is as good as done. His fee will be only 80,000 francs, which Shagali gives him, after earlier in the same scene quibbling over 3,000 and 5,000 francs needed by his unpaid laborers.(53) The **boka's** visit thus demonstrates Shagali's skewed values while comically portraying a rogue from the bush.(Scene 4)

Another generally comic category of minor characters is that of sick and crippled people. In GADO K'ARHIN ALLA, they enter in a group to beg Mushe (Monsieur) for grain from the government; he refuses to help them but gives the grain to his friends and his mistress instead. The original production of the play took place during the severe drought throughout the Sahel region in the early 1970's; Mushe's job is to distribute the grain donated as part of the international relief effort. Yet, as always, this serious indictment of corrupt officials includes comedy in the figures of the beggars themselves--able actors mimicking deformed, uncoordinated, and inarticulate outcasts. The troupe's comic intent here is demonstrated in their choice of actor Ibrahim "Gliss" Tando to speak for the group. A leading comedian in the troupe, well-known for his lack of inhibitions on stage, Gliss contorts his body, grunts and groans--a hilarious caricature of multiple disabilities.(54)

Portraying disabled people as comic presents a cultural distinction from the Euro-American tendency to pity and ignore them. Hausa people are more frank about discussing such things, addressing people by their outstanding physical characteristics (**Dogo**/"tall man") or with irony (**Malam Dogo** for a dwarf).(55) Disabilities and poverty are seen as God's will but with a sense that the person somehow deserved his misfortune. The word **tsiya** (poverty) implies not only lack of money but also meanness and quarrelsomeness of character, and its opposite, **arziki** (wealth), suggests that one has God's favor.(56) This contrasts with the Christian view that poverty may be more spiritually wholesome than wealth. On the other hand, Islam institutes a role for the poor and handicapped--that of begging--and a responsibility among the rest of society to give alms. The poor and disabled thus have a more visible, matter-of-fact, and accepted--if lowly--place in society than in the West.

In his study of traditional Bamana theatre in Mali, James T. Brink notes that a large number of the plays, which are all satiric comedies, include handicapped and sick people in caricature.

> A number of [thematic ideas] address the foibles and problems of the social category Bamana designate as 'the useless ones,' i.e., the physically decrepit and 'ugly,' including sick persons, blind persons, lepers, cripples, and the mentally retarded or insane. All these persons are considered useless, since they

are socially dependent and since
they possess no social or economic means for entering into
relations and alliances with
persons beyond their own kinship
group. They are thus outside the
society's mainstream, but they
are believed to think of themselves as normal Bamana or at
least as persons who continually
aspire to become normal.(57)

Brink's analysis of the Bamana plays' various types of thematic material--"useless" people, marriage conflicts, power alignments, ethnic and Muslim stereotypes, etc.--demonstrates the cutting edge between areas of real social conflict and the satirical mockery of the dramas. For Niger's Hausa plays, the use of disabled or ethnic characters does not seem so central to their themes but does serve the same dual purpose of providing humor with a serious twist.

In Filingué's 1981 Festival play, KOWA YA BUGI RUWA IDONAY, representing the **Département** of Niamey, sick people provided a significant portion of the comedy.(58) This contrasted with the Niamey **Département's** Instrumental Ensemble for the same year, which was dedicated to the International Year of the Handicapped and portrayed all of the highly skilled musicians and singers as disabled people.(59) The second scene of the play consists almost entirely of a series of patients who visit the clinic, showing the new doctor's lack of scruples in typically comic fashion. For example, among the patients is a young woman complaining of a headache. The doctor feels her breasts before he gives her some aspirin. Then a young man describes the "itch in his pants," the curse of women--a comic reference to venereal disease, which the audience found highly amusing. Last of the diverse disease-ridden group is a Fulani man who refuses to give up his stick to be examined, insisting that he is not the sick one, it is his donkey.(Scene 2) These comic characters repeatedly portray the doctor's unprofessional work, the key critical theme of the play.

The ignorant Fulani suggests yet another comic category, that of ethnic stereotypes. Members of other ethnic groups become the object of jokes, as in most cultures, due to their unfamiliarity with the language and customs. In the Bamana theatre of Mali, Brink notes the traditional use of ethnic stereotypes for comedy.(60) HAUSA TALES AND TRADITIONS, based on Frank Edgar's collection of stories published in 1913, includes stereotyped descriptions of other Hausa people in addition to their neighbors--the Fulani (who mispronounce words, are easily fooled, and appear ignorant of the sexual facts of life), the Gwari (hard workers but pagan and stupid), the Kanuri ("masters of lies"), and so on.(61) As M.G. Smith notes in the introduction to these stories, in a highly stratified society with continual historical influx of other peoples, Hausa narratives and other folk genres reflect different social milieux and their stereotypes of other groups.(62) The more recent plays unselfconsciously take up the same sort of social stereotypes, varying with their region and time period.

Filingué's Fulani herdsman brings his sick donkey to the new **dispensaire**, not knowing the clinic is only for people. Zinder's 'Dan Hulani in TALALA MAI KAMAN SAKE refuses the chair Talala offers to him because he has never sat on one; instead, he squats on the floor with his stick. (Scene 3) The herding sticks form inseparable markers of the Fulani character type as do pointed caps, brightly colored clothing and strong accents. For example, Talala's 'Dan Hulani confuses masculine and feminine pronouns:

"Saniya wannan ya aihu."
(This cow [he] has given birth)

and he says /s/ for /sh/:

"asirin"   (**ashirin**/"twenty")
"assa!"   (**asha**!/an exclamation like "oh my!") (Scene 3)

The actor, Délégué Harouna, cultivated such an accent for the part; his normal speech does not include these traits.(63) In all of the plays, the distinctive clothing and accents are exaggerated traits taken from observations of Fulani people in real life and common Hausa stereotypes of them.

Hausa and Zarma people are less obviously distinguishable from one another by dress or behavior; ethnic jokes thus usually take linguistic form. Current politics may also be reflected in the comparatively mild Zarma caricatures, since many of the high officials in the present regime are Zarma. In Maradi's 'DAN KWANGILA, the secretary at the bank responds to Alhaji Rangama in Zarma:

> Rangama: Malmazal, sannu da aiki malmazal. (Mamzel, greetings, Mamzel/**mademoiselle**)
> Lamisi: Fofo Alhaji, ifo no ni ga ba? (Zarma)
> Rangama: In yi gaba? Yo Malmazal in na yi gaba wannan ya k'oro ni ke kin ce in yi gaba, in na yi gaba wajen wa za ni nuhwa? (I should go in? [**yi gaba**] But Mamzel, if I go by here, they'll throw me out, you say to go by, but if I go in, where should I head toward?)
> Lamisi: Alhaji na aza kina jin zabarmanci ce na ce ki yi gaba ba, ina tambaye ki ne mi kike so. (Alhaji, I thought you hear Zarma, I don't say you go on, I ask you what you want?) [Here, as indications of non-native Hausa, she mixes tenses, uses the feminine form of you--**ki**--and forgets half of the negative marker].
> (Scene 4)

Rangama's crude French triggers her response in Zarma, which he misinterprets as permission in Hausa to enter. This linguistic mélange serves more to focus on Rangama's ineptitude in comic fashion than on the Zarma secretary as a character. Actresses are rarely given comic roles or actions to perform perhaps because their acting skills are thought less reliable. In this case, the confusion rather than the character carries the humor.

A variety of ethnic characters later appears at the construction site in 'DAN KWANGILA.(Scenes 6 and 7) Rangama's Yoruba foreman, Joseph, criticizes all the workers except Bagobiri (literally, a man from Gobir); 'Dan Kwangila's response is, "So hire more people from Gobir." (Scene 6) Apparently, Bagobiri is the only laborer willing to work hard for the low wages Rangama offers. He is portrayed as an ignorant bumpkin as in the next scene when the employees' welfare inspector asks to see the workers' representative; when the others sarcastically point to him as Rangama's favorite, Bagobiri responds, "What's a representative?" (Scene 7)

The Yoruba foreman (Joseph) and accountant (Bienvenu) also appear comic in dress, manner and speech. They wear shorts, which only non-Muslims, lower class men (like the construction workers they supervise) and young boys will do in Hausa society; they curse at the workers in flawed Hausa and speak Yoruba to one another off to the side. During one fight, another worker rails at Joseph for wanting to take a large rat home to eat, a custom the Hausa worker considers indecent.(Scene 6) The audience at the Diffa performance found all the fighting, accusations, and ethnic jibes hilarious.

Yet these Yoruba characters also speak French, a sign of status, which serves to highlight Rangama's ignorance.

>Bienvenu: Akwai wata na ce ta yi **demandi**. (I said there's another who is applying). [French **demande**/application; Bienvenu also uses the Hausa feminine-**ta**--for a male worker].

Rangama: Wani ya yi demande?
(Another who is
asking for work)...
Bienvenu: **Manoeuvre qualifié**,
Alhaji. (He's a
skilled worker,
Alhaji).
Rangama: An. (Oh).
Bienvenu: **Septième catégorie**.
(The seventh category).
Rangama: Jikka bakwai in Allah
ya yarda. (Seven
thousand [francs], if
God wills).
Bienvenu: A'a ba ki gani ba
Alhaji. (No, you
don't understand,
Alhaji). [Here he
uses the feminine
you--ki].
Rangama: An. (Oh).
Bienvenu: **Septième catégorie**.
(The seventh category).
Rangama: Yo **sept** aka ce. (So
you said "seven").
Bienvenu: Ka ma in na doki
septième catégorie
manoeuvre qualifié
dofiya. (Well, if
he's in the seventh
category, he's a
skilled worker,
dofiya).
Rangama: Kai, **dofin** mi! (You,
dofin what).
(Scene 6)(64)

Rangama obviously knows little about either his business or his employees; they, quite literally, do not speak the same language.

Joseph and Bienvenu's private chats in Yoruba at the construction site only achieve their full impact later as a messenger reports to Rangama in the final scene that Bienvenu has left the country with the project's money. The fault of their treachery is not so much linked to them as Yoruba, but as foreigners, as Rangama laments:

> This pagan, this pagan cheated me, this pagan betrayed me.... The employees' officer told me to work with our countrymen, if I had hired our countrymen, do you understand? I'd have met them with this money.
> (Scene 8)(65)

Rangama learns this lesson in nationalism too late to save his project or his profits.

A more sympathetic and even more comic Yoruba character appears in Zinder's BA GA IRINTA BA in the figure of Bartelemi. Bartelemi visits the primary school during the teachers' meeting (Scene 2) to inquire about his son's progress and to inform his teacher that the boy missed class because of illness. This vignette of the model parent sets an immediate contrast to Mamman Arrivé, who comes shortly after Bartelemi and vilifies his son's teacher, the director, and anyone else who gets in his way. Not merely a flat, didactic prologue, however, Bartelemi provides a comic balance to Mamman Arrivé as well, through Ibrahim "Gliss" Tando's portrayal of the Yoruba stereotype stretched to its full comic potential. Both Bartelemi's French and his Hausa have comic flaws, and he repeatedly refers to tapioca (a food associated with the Yoruba, not eaten by the Hausa), wax cloth (imported from the coast), and his country (Benin or Nigeria), none of which has much to do with the school matters at hand. Then in his exhortations to his son's teacher to punish the boy--a direct contrast to Mamman Arrivé's subsequent complaint about his son being beaten--Bartelemi's antics reach the point of linguistic unintelligibility and comic climax.

> Ah! For us, education for us, it's not this. The child come to school, he say, hey! Ask, take notebook for you.... But not education for us, for you, papa no matter, mama no matter.... Boy she go to school, eh, you take stone, throw lizard,

                hwuh!   Get on donkey, hwuh!
                hwuh! hwuh!.... But us, never.
                (Scene 2)(66)

As Gliss turned the polite model parent into an
imitation of a donkey, the audience responded
hysterically. After his exit, the teachers comment
that Bartelemi takes care of his son and then that
"Hausa is difficult," a neat summary of the
troupe's purposes in putting Bartelemi on stage.
He is a classic example of their finesse in combining humor with a moral lesson in one character.
    Ibrahim "Gliss" Tando's most famous role, that
of the **boka** in GADO K'ARHIN ALLA, surpasses categorization as either an ethnic type or a false
malam. Although a minor role, this comic character
goes beyond any stereotype in Gliss's unique and
hilarious portrayal; nonetheless, he borrows
characteristics freely from many different types.
Boka is one of the magicians whom Shaho summons for
help in the election of the new **sarki**. He appears
with his interpreter (played by Yazi Dogo) because
he cannot understand Hausa; earlier, Shaho describes him as a Bagwari (a Gwari man), calling
up the stereotyped connotations of pagan, rural,
and stupid. Boka's spiritual powers, however,
set him above the princely Shaho, as the interpreter reminds him that he is not permitted to look at
the **boka** directly.(67)
    In the performances I observed, the costumes
of the **boka** and his interpreter reinforced Shaho's
pagan image. They consisted of black tunics,
shorts, and pointed caps decorated with cowry
shells; the **boka's** attire was far more elaborate
than his companion's. This dramatic and utterly
non-Hausa clothing immediately set them apart from
the rest of the characters.(68)
    The interpreter's role of relaying everything
that passes between Shaho and Boka intensifies the
humor by repeating both Boka's nonsense utterances
and Shaho's eagerness to hear and do whatever he is
told. Yazi Dogo, a master of comic timing, provided judicious pauses and played up the suspense
as he "translated" long and excited pronouncements
with just a few quiet words.

             Boka: Y i r t i i .   A a !   A a !
                Layyaa! Layyaa! Laysuu
                gibinaa oo Yuubaanaa,

                Yuubaanaa, Yuubaanaa,
                wurtibii wurtibii Yuu-
                baanaa, Yuubaanaa ...
                Sustubii, sustubii,
                Yaahahhaa Yaahahha Yii-
                hahhaa. Yuubaanaa.
Interpreter: Too yaa zoo, babban
                aljanin yaa zoo. (So
                he has come, the great
                spirit has come).
       Boka: Yirtilsibiiyaa turbiilaa.
Interpreter: Ka naa jin abun da ya
                cee, yaa gan ka a nan
                wurin da na'dii. (Did
                you understand what he
                said? He's seen you here
                with the [sarki's]
                turban).(Scene 4)(69)

    The comedy of the scene intensifies as Boka makes his demands for payment (a black goat, a red one and a white one, then three gourds of beer, and a black bull). He then tells Shaho that he must find a black donkey and saddle it, he must wear a black turban, mount the donkey and ride it through the crowd at the installation ceremony calling "Yuubaanaa! Yuubaanaa!" as he comes.(70) Boka, all the while speaking his mysterious and comic language, begins to jump up and down, hop on one foot, and finally careen around the stage followed by the faithful interpreter. Shaho, in his long robes, tries to imitate them in these undignified exercises, which no Hausa nobleman would ever be seen performing.(71)

    Gliss as the **boka** remains a key element of this farcical follow-the-leader act. Audiences throughout the country are familiar with his broad physical humor, and earlier within this play, he appears in the roles of the **liman** and the leader of the crippled beggars. Gliss is uninhibited and unpredictable on stage, so that much of the excitement of this scene is raised by the audience's expectations of the unexpected, their eager anticipation of the outrageous.

    This performance carries the ethnic stereotype to a comic extreme. No longer is the **boka** related to any real group of people (the Gwari reference serves more as pale foreshadowing that he is foreign); he speaks no known language and carica-

tures all languages in nonsense syllables. The
interpreter's role, an indispensable adjunct
like the helper in traditional narrative,(72)
intensifies the comedy through repetition and
suspense until the audience finds out what all the
nonsense means, precisely what indignities the
noble Shaho is being told to undergo. Moreover,
Boka's ridiculous behavior and instructions are
unlike any seen in daily life by any **malam** or
genuine **boka**. As in ALHAJI SHAGALI, where the
malams' powers are superseded by Boka Mai Burgami,
Boka in GADO K'ARHIN ALLA follows Malam Gobe da
Nisa and then takes the usual character type a step
further, pushing it to its comic limits. The
entire scene is a brilliant **tour de force** display-
ing fully the comic talents of the Zinder Troupe's
leading actors, Kailou Bako (as Shaho), Abdou
Louché (Malam Gobe da Nisa), Yazi Dogo (Interpreter) and Ibrahim "Gliss" Tando (Boka).

Central Characters

The central characters in most of these plays
defy categorization as either comic or serious
types; they are both. Usually played by the most
experienced actors, these major roles project both
the instructional message of the play and its humor
through the actor's personal charisma and skill.
Central characters usually follow a wayward path--
'Dan Kwangila and Alhaji Shagali cheat the government and their workers, Mamman Arrivé fights
the entire town with his arrogance, Talala deprives
his brother's widows and orphans of their inheri-
tance--but they are not single-minded villains.
Like the trickster figure in oral traditions
worldwide, they have comic appeal, a beguiling
charm; audiences like them, laugh at them, and
follow their dramatic careers with interest.

Alhaji Arzika Rangama, the 'Dan Kwangila of
the Maradi Troupe's title, is a novice contractor
who fails to follow the wise advice he is given
throughout the play. Part of the appeal of this
character rises from his very ineptitude in actor
Lobi Aboubacar's coy portrayal. In the first
scene of the play, Rangama arrives late to the
gathering at Alhaji Gimshik'i's house and explains
that he had left home without giving his wife money
to buy ingredients for the day's soup, so that he

had to go back again. The townsmen laugh at Rangama and tease him for his forgetfulness--a significant mark of his character as it is a man's daily duty to pay for ingredients for his family's evening meal. After this joke, the group listens to the radio news including the announcement of the clinic construction projects. Rangama does not understand the French announcements, but after someone else explains what was said, he immediately decides to apply.

> Rangama: I think I will apply, I'll try it out.
> Issa: What!
> Sale: But, Alhaji Rangama, how do you presume to apply?
> Rangama: What?
> Sale: What's come over you?
> Rangama: Hey, a rich man has to get into whatever there is to do....
> Sa'idu: Now, Alhaji Arzika, with this you are beginning your dabbling (**rangama**) again. This affair is for contractors.
> Group: Yes, that's right.
> Sa'idu: This sort of building is not selling used clothes.
> (Scene 1)(73)

This dialogue emphasizes the significance of Rangama's name, "wealth by barter"; (74) his background, trading in used clothes; and his inexperience in the kind of work involved in a major building project.(Scene 1)

Alhaji Gimshik'i sends Rangama on to Niamey to visit a friend who is a member of the commission which will award the contract. Yet even this man, who accepts a bribe to arrange the contract for Rangama, offers useful advice to him:

> Mainassara: Alhaji, you see, if you succeed in getting this contract, Alhaji Arzika Rangama, for God's sake, for the Prophet's sake, I'm going to give you a

                           little piece of advice.
Rangama: Fine.
Mainassara: Go to this association they call OPEN. (OPEN/ Office des Petites Entreprises Nigériennes)
Rangama: OPIN, is it?
Mainassara: No, it's not OPIN.
Rangama: OPEL?
Mainassara: OPEN.
Rangama: Oh, OPEN.
Mainassara: This OPEN is the one which looks after the small contractors and the youth who want to get ahead. (Scene 2)(75)

True to his nature, Rangama cannot remember either the name or the useful advice, a joke for the audience but also a foreshadowing of his growing incompetence.

In similar fashion, Rangama bumbles through the scenes at the bank and the office of city planning.(Scenes 4 and 5) At the bank, he again relies on Gimshik'i for help in circumventing the official rules, but he nearly forgets the name of Gimshik'i's accomplice.

Rangama: You'll put me on the right path, won't you?
Gimshik'i: All right.
Rangama: Because you know these clerks, but I don't. The ones that we were used to working with have been sent away....
Gimshik'i: But in spite of that, there's one man here, who they call Hamza.
Rangama: Un hunh, Salisu is it?
Gimshik'i: Oh, you're full of useless talk.
Rangama: Hamza, Hamza, it's Hamza.
Gimshik'i: Look at you, trembling because you didn't get any money, you tremble like that. Wait a bit

	and when you go to his place ask him if he is Hamza.
Rangama:	All right, thanks.
Gimshik'i:	If he says yes, then tell him Alhaji Mahaman Gimshik'i sent you.
Rangama:	Okay.
Gimshik'i:	Then give him these papers.
Rangama:	Okay, fine.
Gimshik'i:	He will fix them for you.
Rangama:	Okay, good, that's good.
Gimshik'i:	But, do you know all this?
Rangama:	If God grants I don't forget, he's Hamisu isn't he?
Gimshik'i:	Ah!
Rangama:	Hamza, Hamza, Hamza.
Gimshik'i:	But you, Alhaji Rangama, what's the matter with you? (Scene 4)(76)

Despite Gimshik'i's simple outline of what he is to do, Rangama cannot master it. He has difficulty negotiating past the secretary to get to Hamza, he naively expresses surprise that Hamza will indeed get the money for him immediately, and he has forgotten his checks--on a Friday afternoon as the bank is about to close.(Scene 4) This is no suave swindle but corruption depicted at its most comic. The Diffa audience laughed at Rangama's stupidity, but the actor retained their sympathy by his ingenuous portrayal. Lobi Aboubacar hesitated and stammered, asking stupid questions with apparent candour--the essence of innocence.(77)

By the time Rangama reaches the office of city planning, he has no time for formalities: he barges past the secretary into the director's office and refuses to wait for the proper clearance for his project from Niamey. Yet when the director telephones the central office in Niamey and reaches the police by mistake, a standard joke about the phones not working, Rangama once again leaps to conclusions, not understanding the French:

Mushe! Mushe! For the
love of God, when I heard you
ask pardon for what you did,
let me ask your pardon, for
God's sake, what is the complaint you're taking to the
police? For God's sake, be
patient, I'll get up and go if
that's how it is. Give me the
papers and I'll go.
(Scene 5)(78)

Despite his fear of being reported to the police, Rangama asks for his papers--a further urging that the director finish their business and let him begin the construction.

Rangama's fawning before those in power contrasts with his stingy hiring practices and his treatment of the laborers at the work-site. He refuses to pay the current wage rates and tries to save money by hiring foreigners and unskilled laborers. Scenes 6 and 7 at the construction site present a variety of problems due to his mismanagement: neither the workers nor the food sellers have been paid, the laborers quarrel among themselves, the Yoruba foreman cannot control the local men, and so on. Both the employees' welfare officer and the director of the office of city planning appear at the site to condemn Rangama and his building. (Scene 7) Here, Rangama's ineptitude reasserts itself; he cannot salvage his failing project in the eyes of these authorities.

By the final scene when a messenger tells Rangama of Bienvenu's flight with his money, the news sends Rangama over the brink of insanity. He begins raving and it requires several men to carry him off in the end.(Scene 8) This powerful final image impresses upon the audience the destiny of the corrupt and incompetent contractor, yet it is nonetheless a comic one. Insanity, like illness and disability, is subject to laughter. But although the audience believes that Rangama has gotten no more than he deserves, that justice and the community's interest have been served, their attention has been sustained throughout the play by the character of Alhaji Rangama--at once corrupt but charming, incompetent but funny. Like the trickster of the stories, he has both cunning and stupid qualities; he attempts to trick the community but finds himself duped instead, both by the authorities and by his own employees.

The Mainé Soroa Troupe's development of ALHAJI SHAGALI focusses even more strongly on the moral character of Shagali than does Maradi's treatment of 'DAN KWANGILA. After the first brief formal scene at the **sous-préfecture**, where Alhaji Shagali is awarded the contract, the troupe presents a scene where other important men in the town gossip about Shagali, who does not appear. These **alhajis** express discontent with the choice of Shagali as contractor:

> Alhaji 2: Well now that they've definitely given him the work and an advance, he's gone out and used the money to buy a car. He's out riding around roaming the streets, and there's the work-site with no supplies. There's no wood, no cement, nothing, the workers are sitting around.
> (Scene 2)(79)

Maître, Shagali's foreman, appears next to confirm the rumors about the construction project; neither he nor the other workers have been paid. He asks Alhaji Ibrahim for a job and arranges with him to report in detail on Shagali's enterprise. (Scene 2)
The third scene confirms this gossip by presenting the work-site itself. The **sous-préfet** and the state's engineer come to inspect the building, informing Shagali that the work has not progressed sufficiently for the seven months he has had it, he has not followed the plans correctly, and the building is inadequate. Moreover, the food seller and the water carriers have not been paid, nor have the workers. Shagali promises to fix everything and to pay everyone after he makes a trip to Maradi.(Scene 3) Instead of a climactic critique, as in Maradi's play, this inspection scene is part of the play's exposition, the given situation in which to observe Shagali's decadence in the scenes to follow.

After these first three short scenes, the play elaborates Shagali's sins in two lengthy, personal scenes: the first at his home and the second at the room of the prostitute, Gimbiya. Scene 4 presents Shagali bargaining with his foreman, arranging with Boka Mai Burgami to rid the project of the zealous engineer, and telling his wives that he will be traveling to Maradi. When his younger wife, Amarya (bride), teases him about where he will sleep on the trip, Shagali slips and addresses his first wife (Hajiya) as Gimbiya.

    Shagali: All right, Gimbiya, er, Hajiya!
    Hajiya: Un huh, un huh, Alhaji, so you do have a Gimbiya, eh, Alhaji?
    Shagali: Oh?
    Hajiya: You have a Gimbiya, don't you, Alhaji?
    Amarya: Well, Hajiya, I told you before, I saw a letter that Gimbiya sent to Alhaji Shagali.
    Shagali: Who said "Gimbiya" just now?
    Hajiya: Well, Alhaji, as for me, I've long since become accustomed to this, that's why I haven't said anything.
    Shagali: No, I said "Hajiya."
    Hajiya: No, Alhaji.
    Amarya: You said "Gimbiya." So who is Gimbiya?
    Shagali: Who said "Gimbiya"?
    Hajiya: So you have another new Gimbiya, Alhaji?
    (Scene 4) (80)

This argument continues with the wives taking all the advantage; Shagali tries to change the subject by offering to buy lace cloth for them, but they are only momentarily dissuaded and Amarya returns to the subject of Gimbiya's letter.

> Shagali: So you said that you saw a letter from Gimbiya on the table, when did you see it?
> Amarya: I saw it but Hajiya said not to show it to you.
> Shagali: Gimbiya can't even write, much less send me a letter.
> Amarya: So you know what I'm talking about!
> Hajiya: Aha! So she really exists, doesn't she, Alhaji? She really exists!
> (Scene 4)(81)

Soundly defeated, Shagali sends them both into the house and hurries to depart on his trip.

With no respect in the community, no command of his construction project, and no control over his own wives, Shagali seeks a bit of pleasure at Gimbiya's place in Scene 5. The audience at Diffa was well prepared for this climactic comic scene by the wives' argument in the previous one; their excited anticipation was rewarded by the most sexually suggestive scene of the entire festival. Although Shagali tells her he is just passing through town, Gimbiya talks him into staying, explaining to him that there is an airplane the next day. He agrees to send his driver on ahead with the truck, and Gimbiya leads him back into her room. The mere sight of her putting her arm around him, walking back into a room with a bed, and her suggesting that he wash up, sent the audience into shrieks of laughter.

Gimbiya asks what he would like to drink, but she pours whiskey into the soft drink he requests while he is in the bathroom.

> Gimbiya: (to herself) There's no Fanta, there's no Coke, why, you always just come, I cook all sorts of things for you, I make everything that you like to eat, you eat

> with pleasure, then
> you get up and leave,
> 1500 francs, 2000
> francs, 500 francs,
> you just say,
> "Gimbiya, I'm going."
> Well, today, your
> steps are finished,
> you'll drink this
> whiskey.
> (Scene 5)(82)

As Shagali becomes progressively more drunk, Gimbiya restrains him from dancing, and asks him about the television set he promised her, the formica bed and the gold that she wants. As he falls asleep, she leads him to the bed and looks into the briefcase he has been so carefully watching. Seeing the money, she takes it and hurries off.(Scene 5)

Like 'Dan Kwangila, Alhaji Shagali is duped in the end. He awakes from his drunken stupor, frantically searching for his briefcase. A friend, Alhaji Lura (attentive/careful), appears, having been told Shagali has gone mad, and asks what has happened. Shagali's repetition of the events with Gimbiya causes a new round of laughter as does his amazement to learn that he was drunk:

> Lura: What's this?
> Shagali: Coca cola.
> Lura: Look and see, Alhaji,
> a man of the world
> like you, don't you
> know coca cola from
> this?
> Shagali: This isn't coke?
> Lura: There is no God but
> Allah and Muhammad is
> his Prophet! This
> thing that she
> brought you, Alhaji,
> a respectable man
> like you.
> Shagali: Gimbiya said it was
> coke.
> Lura: Gimbiya says it's
> coke, Alhaji, if
> you're listening,

Characters in Action 209

> this is whiskey, it's alcohol, Alhaji, this is whiskey.
> Shagali: I just drank alcohol?
> Lura: Really, your briefcase didn't disappear for nothing, Alhaji.
> (Scene 5)(83)

Shagali wants to follow after Gimbiya, but when Lura informs him that she has gone on the plane, Shagali jumps up and down waving his hands at the imaginary airplane overhead. The Diffa audience loudly responded to this ludicrous posture for a well-established man who has been to Mecca, but who has just been outwitted by a very young woman of the world.

Alhaji Zoubeirou Lawal's portrayal of Shagali, like Lobi Aboubacar's 'Dan Kwangila, emphasized his naiveté, his stupidity, his ineptitude. Both actors presented characters of high status as being foolish, laughable and incompetent, in this way demonstrating clearly their faults and wrongdoing while at the same time evoking audience sympathy through laughter. Spectators could feel superior to these characters, who in everyday life would hold tremendous power in the community, and even laugh at their faults. In Beeman's terms, this enables a release of social tension through laughter.(84) As the audience laughs, however, they absorb the troupe's message about corruption in both high and low places.

Mamman Arrivé's major characteristic is arrogance, a belief that his wealth puts him above the rules of the rest of the community. From the outset of the play, Mamman scorns the community's organizations.

> Mamman Arrivé: Well wait, let me ask you something. Don't you, by God and the Prophet, don't you get tired of all that? Always a meeting, another meeting. As for me, I don't see, what do you organize all the time

>   when you go to these
>   meetings?
> Langa Langa: No, they're really very
>   useful. You hear about
>   things you've never
>   heard before. You see
>   things you've never seen
>   before. It's because of
>   that, that I tell you you
>   should attend to joining
>   the community. You
>   see, you're not in the
>   Islamic Association,
>   you're not in the samari-
>   ya, you're not in the
>   Pupils' Parents' Associa-
>   tion. That's why I
>   always say you are ignor-
>   ant. (Scene 1)(85)

Mamman's ignorance is further developed in the same scene: he cannot read his own checks; he argues with Langa Langa not only about his financial affairs and joining the community's organizations, but even over the healthfulness of eating salad. When his son arrives complaining that his teacher hit him, Mamman completely misunderstands the situation, creating the comic climax of the scene.

> Sanussi: Madame hit me over the
>   head because I didn't
>   bring my lesson (leçon).
> Mamman Arrivé: Langa Langa, what's a
>   lesso?
> Langa Langa: Seau like this (pointing
>   to a bucket--le seau).
>   Isn't there a shop where
>   you can go and get one?
>   Here, take this one to
>   her.
> Mamman Arrivé: Stop, just stop, this
>   thing for bringing water?
> Langa Langa: Yes.
> Gimbiya: Now I don't like that....
>   That I don't like. I'm
>   going to have it out
>   between her and me, who
>   will put who in a buc-
>   ket. I will not permit

Characters in Action   211

>   my oldest son to be poked
>   in the eyes. And you,
>   if **you** won't go, **I'll** go
>   and have it out between
>   her and me, who puts who
>   in a bucket.
> Mamman Arrivé: Stop, for God's sake,
>   you've started ruffling
>   your feathers again. I
>   don't see, why can't the
>   government pay a laborer
>   at the school, that they
>   tell the kids they must
>   take buckets and work for
>   nothing? (Scene 1)(86)

The pun on **leçon/le seau** (lesson/bucket) is based on Mamman's ignorance of French, despite the affectation of his name. This misunderstanding stirs the characters' anger and the ongoing action as Gimbiya threatens to confront the teacher and Mamman tells her to stay at home, he will go himself:

>   Me, Mamman Arrivé, I'm not
>   going to sit still when anyone
>   in this town thinks he can
>   crack my son's head and I'll
>   let it go....
>   Me, Mamman Arrivé, there's
>   no one in this town that I'm
>   afraid of, do you hear? You
>   see, no matter how strong he
>   is, there's no one who will
>   beat me! Here. Put this money
>   away for me. Yo! (Scene 1)(87)

Even in his anger, Mamman never forgets his money.

Mamman's confrontation with the teachers in the following scene contrasts with Bartelemi's concern for his son's work at school. Mamman behaves rudely, refuses to listen to anyone's explanations, and betrays how little he knows about his own child when Madame informs him that Sanussi has not been in school for a full week.(Scene 2) After cursing all the teachers, Mamman continues his verbal assault on the authorities assembled at the mayor's office in Scene 4--the school inspector, the mayor, and the police commissioner--as he continually interrupts the meeting even after he has has been ordered not to speak at all. Here, the contrast lies between Mamman and the other parents who have also brought grievances to the school at one time but who now listen to the explanations of the mayor and the other authorities and learn why they were at fault. The repeated opposition between Mamman and the rest of the community intensifies his isolation.

Facing punishment by the police for his behavior at the meeting, Mamman proposes to Langa Langa and his friends that he bribe the commissioner.(Scene 5) They convince him that he cannot do so, that his money will not help him in this case; he must seek pardon at the scene of his crime. They quote a proverb to him, which Yazi Dogo cited as the key point to this scene:

> Icce ta inda aka hau, ta nan ake shi'da.
> (Where you climb in the tree, that is where you must descend from). (Scene 5)(88)

The use of the proverb appears significant because it is a part of traditional wisdom. In this scene, Mamman's belligerence opposes the elders' patience and reasonable requests. The president of the Parents' Association and the head of the **samariya** represent traditional values, particularly respect for the elderly and the powerful. Mamman's recriminations at the mayor's office offend both the government authorities (the mayor, police commissioner, etc.) and those of the local community (the president, Mai Samari, and the other parents). Only in the final scenes of the play, when Mamman asks for mercy and recognizes that he has spoiled his son, does he begin to function as part of the community.(Scenes 7 and 8)

The character Mamman Arrivé delights audiences not with inept charm but with his outrageous lack of decorum. He acts as no proper Hausa person would: he fights with everyone, even powerful authorities; he speaks his mind (ignorant as it might be), tells people off, curses them out. By the later scenes in the play, Mamman Arrivé's mere entrance raised a storm of audience response before he ever spoke a word. In normal social life, audience members could never behave as he does,

Characters in Action

although they might sometimes wish they could. As in Beeman's study of the Iranian clown flaunting characters of authority, Mamman's appeal has a double edge. Hausa audiences admire his audacity at the same time as they laugh at his ignorance; he retains their sympathy even as the prevailing social values condemn his behavior.

Actor Oumarou Nainou's Mamman Arrivé was a masterful portrait of blustery bravado. Oumarou created a character with a quick temper, loud voice and rude assertiveness, both impolite and unpredictable. As with Ibrahim "Gliss" Tando's Boka, the audience never knew what to expect next of Mamman Arrivé. His only prop throughout the performance was a leather purse with a wrist strap, but he used it to great advantage--accentuating his words, waving it about in anger and frustration--so that it soon became a symbol of his wealth, power, and arrogance.(89) By the time the commissioner fined him for his outbursts and Mamman reported to his brother, "They only touched my purse" (Scene 8), the moment echoed all of the earlier scenes in the play.

Talala as a character presents a different face of the trickster, the sly and cunning one. Not a greedy incompetent who is duped, nor a boaster who believes himself better than his neighbors, Talala appears at first as a responsible, trustworthy man, and the community agrees to leave him in charge of his late brother's wealth. (Scene 2) The following scenes, however, reveal his true nature as he arranges to sell his brother's cattle, pays the **malam** to silence the widows, and contracts to build an elegant new house for himself.(Scene 3) At the same time, he refuses to pay his nephew's school fees (Scene 3), denies his niece a loan after she and her husband have been robbed (Scene 5), and makes minimal contributions toward the support of his brother's family.(Scene 6) These actions would define Talala unmistakably as a villain except that he, too, has a comic charm. He cannot control his young wife, Sululu (silently), who leaves for her parents' house in a fit of pique (Scene 3); his former mistress, El Giya (of beer), demands gifts for his neglect of her; and despite his elaborate arrangements with Savon Robb to procure a new young woman for him in his fancy house, she refuses to go

with him into the bedroom and insists that he come
and discuss marriage with her family.(Scene 4)
Talala, reminiscent of Alhaji Shagali, has trouble
with his women. In the end, it is his niece and
his widowed sisters-in-law who bring him to trial
for his failure to provide for them.(Scene 7)

    Central to Talala's comic appeal was Yazi
Dogo's performance.(90) Well known to national
audiences as a master comedian, Yazi arouses
audience interest as soon as he walks on stage, no
matter what role he may be playing. For the
spectators, familiarity with an actor's reputation
and talents functions like their knowledge of the
common character types in the plays: it adds to the
depth of their experience and enjoyment of what is
happening in the play. They know to watch for
Yazi's subtleties, his word play, his understated
remarks, his slight gestures. In TALALA MAI KAMAN
SAKE, Yazi appearing as Talala immediately
signalled that the solemn, pious figure at the
funeral was not all that he seemed.(Scene 2)

    Scenes 3 and 4 develop Talala's deception
first at his home soon after the funeral, where he
begins to sell off his brother's estate and to plan
his own new house and a pilgrimage to Mecca,
and then in his fine house after he has attained
the title of **Alhaji**. The very prospect of this
house brings out Talala's childish delight in what
money can buy:

                Musa
    (the Contractor): What about the paint?
          Talala: Paint?
           Musa: Yes. What kind would
                 you like?
          Talala: Get a paint that's
                 shiny like lightning!
            Musa: Glossy?
          Talala: Yes, a beautiful
                 one.
            Musa: All right....
          Talala: And about the shower.
            Musa: The shower.
          Talala: Don't put in the kind
                 where you stand up
                 and it twists all
                 around you falling so
                 hard.
            Musa: Oh, okay.

> Talala: Put in the kind where you lie down, so that I can lie down and slide in and float like a pigeon. (Scene 3)(91)

This dialogue on house fixtures was animated by Yazi's twinkling eyes, his excited tones and gestures emphasizing the sensuous nature of his dreams for the bathtub. All of these plans foreshadow the next scene where Talala shows his friend the features of the house and they discuss which women they will invite to entertain there (Scene 4).

The subsequent failure of Talala's amorous adventure heightens its comedy. Savon Robb duly delivers Dijé, the very girl Talala and his friend requested, but she arrives veiled in cloth and unwilling to follow Talala into the inner room. Talala sends his friend off to the tailor's and repeats his invitation to Dijé now that they are alone.

> Talala: Just now I know you were ashamed because of him.
> Dijé: No, truly, it's not because of him.
> Talala: Come, I'll rest a little with you. [Standing at the door].
> Dijé: I'm not accustomed to that.
> Talala: What?
> Dijé: Whatever you want to say to me, you can come and tell me, whatever it is you want to say, right here. I'm not accustomed to that, I didn't come for that.
> Talala: What didn't you come for? (Scene 4)(92)

Yazi played this scene with comic credulity, hastily changing tactics as Dijé explained that she had been told he wanted to court her (for marriage). His lascivious looks in the early part of the scene turned to stuttering as he promised to come to her house to discuss marriage, and then to a wistful glance at her backside as she left.(93) Adding to the visual humor of this encounter was the choice of actress for the part of Dijé--a large, well-endowed young woman who overshadowed Yazi Dogo's slight figure, highlighting Talala's lustful ineffectuality.

In the final scene of judgment after all the testimony has been heard against Talala and his sentence announced, the court's officials and the public leave Talala to himself. Typical of Yazi's skill with gesture was his final portrait of Talala silently sinking his head in his lap in defeat, only to have the court clerk yell at him to stand up and go. Yazi's look of startled resignation once again caught the dual essence of his character at the end of the play: morally guilty but comically human.

Although more fully developed than any other characters in the plays, all of these central figures--Talala, 'Dan Kwangila, Mamman Arrivé, and Alhaji Shagali--share a complex role type. They bear the moral message of the plays' themes but they also provide a focus for the humor. Their specific faults differ, but each one is a wealthy and powerful man who threatens the smooth functioning of his society and who is ultimately subdued.

Such characters usually have the title of **Alhaji**, identifying them with a large and powerful class of men in present-day Hausa society, but whose members are not often part of the administrative bureaucracy. The title **Alhaji** suggests an image of wealth even before it connotes piety in Niger due to the expense of the pilgrimage and to the fact that the **hajj** is associated with a great deal of trade. **Alhajis** are often merchants, whether or not they pursue other occupations in the community; long distance commerce has been important to Hausa history for centuries. Satire of this merchant class is comparatively anonymous, far less controversial than critique of high government officials, whose numbers are smaller and whose visibility is greater. Moreover, the **alhaji** character type straddles the traditional and contemporary worlds: merchants and Islamic pilgrims continue to be important members of the community, as they have been in the past.

These **alhaji** characters represent the sort of rich, self-made men often satirized by the traditional Hausa poets (**marok'a**) and comedians (**'yan kama**). Many itinerant minstrels have earned their living by praising important people in each town and village in which they stop. However, if the rewards for praise are not adequate, their song/poems soon become critical, especially toward the wealthy men who have built their own fortunes rather than inheriting noble domains.(94) Thus, when the plays begin to show the negative side of their central characters, the audience feels a strong sense of familiarity and justice in the critique.

Anthony Kirk-Greene explores the Hausa definition of good character in MUTIMIN KIRKII: THE CONCEPT OF THE GOOD MAN IN HAUSA.(95) His list of ten essential qualities of the good man includes:

1. **gaskiya**/truthfulness
2. **bangaskiya**/trustworthiness, reliability
3. **karamci**/generosity
4. **hak'uri**/patience
5. **hankali**/sound judgment, prudence
6. **kunya**/shame, modesty, a sense of the proprieties
7. **ladabi**/good manners, courtesy
8. **mutunci**/human dignity, treating others with due respect (especially those of lower status)
9. **hikima**/wisdom, learning (especially Islamic)
10. **adalci**/scrupulous behavior (in an Islamic sense--godfearing).(96)

These are the very qualities that characters like Talala, Shagali, Rangama, and Mamman Arrivé lack, each with his own emphasis. Talala betrays Muslim morality and the trust of the community when he neglects his wards; Shagali is imprudent and immoral; Rangama has no patience or generosity;

Mamman Arrivé shows no respect toward others or
judgment in his actions. The troupes specifically
intend these moral failings as integral parts of
their themes. As Yazi Dogo stated in a discussion
of BA GA IRINTA BA, one of the troupe's purposes
was to teach ladabi, what Mamman Arrivé defies by
his adventures: "Can Mairie bai yi ladabi ba" (At
the mayor's office, he behaves without courtesy).(97) Even beyond the judgments delivered
against these characters within the plays, the
audience internally feels their violations of Hausa
propriety, the communal code of daily life.

Yet despite the characters' reprehensible
morals and manners, the actors make them likeable.
The humor they inspire transforms villainy into the
ambiguous realm of the trickster. These fictional
characters can break social rules, defy authority,
escape the normal and routine aspect of daily
life--if only temporarily. The actors' skill in
arousing laughter renders these roles much more
interesting and more effective as focal characters
than they would be as single-minded villains. The
moral messages remain important, but as several of
the troupes noted, moral preaching alone can become
boring. The comic skills of experienced actors
sustain audience interest in and add depth to these
central characters who carry the main action and
theme of a play to its conclusion.

Characters in Action 219

ENDNOTES: CHAPTER IV

1. Northrop Frye, "The Mythos of Spring: Comedy," in COMEDY: MEANING AND FORM, ed. Robert W. Corrigan (San Francisco: Chandler Publishing Co., 1965), p. 149.
2. Frye, p. 149.
3. V. Propp, MORPHOLOGY OF THE FOLKTALE, trans. Laurence Scott (Austin: University of Texas Press, 1968), p. 21.
4. Kenneth McKee, Foreword, SCENARIOS OF THE COMMEDIA DELL'ARTE, trans. Henry F. Salerno, (New York: New York University Press, 1967), p. xiii.
5. Giacomo Oreglia, THE COMMEDIA DELL'ARTE (London: Methuen & Co., 1968), p. 12.
6. Pierre Louis Duchartre, THE ITALIAN COMEDY (New York: Dover Publications, 1966), p. 73.
7. McKee, p. xvi, and Duchartre, p. 30.
8. Neil Skinner, trans., ed., HAUSA TALES AND TRADITIONS, Vol. I (London: Frank Cass & Co. Ltd., 1969), p. 290; H.A.S. Johnston, ed., A SELECTION OF HAUSA STORIES (Oxford: Clarendon Press, 1966), p. 184 (footnote).
9. BA GA IRINTA BA, performance by the Troupe Amadou 'Dan Bassa of Zinder for the National Festival in Niamey, Niger, April 1980.
10. Rehearsal notes, Maison des Jeunes (MJC), Zinder, 31 March 1981.
11. This character was called Salamatu in the first performance I saw (28 February 1981), Rabi in the Tanout competitions (9 March 1981), and both Tsaibatu and 'Dayaba (different forms of her own name) at the Diffa Festival performance (8 April 1981). When the troupe re-created the play later that year with a new actress (Elhajiya) in the role, they called her Rabiya (2 September 1981).
12. BA GA IRINTA BA, Scene 8. The transcription of this play is mine with help gratefully acknowledged from Aboubacar Mahamane and Yazi Dogo; the English translation is mine. The original Hausa:

> Yaya: E? Ka duba ka ga lokacin da muke 'yan yara, a gidammu an ta'ba mumu haka?
>
> Mamman: A ina hwa?

>Yaya: Ko zuwa muka yi muka yi hwa'da, aka ba mu kashi muna zo gida da kuka, Baba kashi yake ba mu.
>Mamman: K'warai kuwa.
>Yaya: To, kai wai kai ka samu ku'di ka 'bata yara. Uhm?

13. R.C. Abraham, DICTIONARY OF THE HAUSA LANGUAGE (London: University of London Press, 1962), p. 845.

14. Neil Skinner notes that the titles given to the stories in HAUSA TALES AND TRADITIONS are usually a list of characters, (Personal communication, August 1983).

15. WALWALE, performance by the Troupe from Agadez for the National Festival in Diffa, Niger, 7 April 1981. The transcription of this play is by Aboubacar Mahamane; the English translation is mine. The original Hausa (Scene 8):

>Walwale: Mai Gari, saboda Alla kuma, ka san ni ba sunana ba ne Walwale, sunana Mahammadu hwa Alla....
>Mai Gari: Kai ka yi ma kanka sunan Walwale tunda de duk inda ka ga abun alheri za ka watsar ka ce ina anhwanin shi ka walwale shi, shi ne in de ka bari Walwale daga yau sunanka Mahammadu shi ke nan, kowa ma ya jiya.

16. Personal communication from Connie Stephens, Niamey, Niger.

17. Rehearsal notes, MJC, Zinder, 30 March 1981. The ballet, KIRARIN 'YAN KOKOWA, was performed by the Troupe from Matameye at the National Festival in Diffa, Niger, 11 April 1981.

18. ALHAJI SHAGALI, performance by the Troupe from Mainé Soroa at the National Festival in Diffa, Niger, 12 April 1981.

19. ALHAJI SHAGALI, Scene 1. The transcription of this play is by Aboubacar Mahamane; the English translation is mine. The original Hausa:

Sous-préfet: Shi ya sa na ce to gara in kirai ka gaban Sarki, da Major, da mutumen Société de Développement.
Shagali: Daidai ne.
Sous-préfet: Na 'daya in yi maka godiya bisa ga abin da na gani a tsare cikin takarda.
Shagali: To madalla!
Sous-préfet: Na biyu in jayo hankalinka.

20. A classic pattern of oral narratives sets up, in V. Propp's terms, an **interdiction** which the hero will **violate**, creating the central conflict in the story. See MORPHOLOGY OF THE FOLKTALE, pp. 26-7.
21. ALHAJI SHAGALI, Scene 6.

Sous-préfet: To jama'a 'yan uwa ina so in jawo hankalinku busa abu guda; yau k'asagga tamu in yaro in mace in namiji kowa na in ya tashi wak'a cewa ya kai k'asa ta ci gaba, k'asa ta ci gaba; ni kuma ga yadda na gani yanda Alhaji Shagali ya yi in dai haka za a yi to ha' abada k'asa ba za ta ci gaba ba. Mi ya sa haka? Dan 'daure ma k'arya gindi ake.

Alhaji Shagali duk an sani bai da halin da zai wannan aikin, dan ina bak'o ga wuri ban san komi ba shi kuma dan ya zan ya saba da manyan mutane ya can cuku-cuku yana da dangi masu dogon hannu, ya zo suka taru suka 'daure gindi aka ba shi wannan kwangila. To yau ina anka zo?

> To ina so in jawo hankalinku ku duka, nan dai barikin, matsawan ni an nan gaban wannan bariki to kowa ab ba a sake 'daure ma gindi. Ko an 'daure ma mutun gindi ina walwale shi, in mutun na son aiki ya yi daidai da k'arhinshi.

22. KOWA YA BUGI RUWA IDONAY, (literally, "whoever beats water [will have it in] his eye"), was subtitled in the Troupe's program, "Qui sème du vent récolte la tempête." Performance by the Troupe from Filingué at the National Festival in Diffa, Niger, 13 April 1981.

23. ALHAJI SHAGALI, Scene 1.

   Sous-préfet: Garde!
   Garde: Mon commandant!
   Sous-préfet: Repos. Eh, akwai Sarki nan da Major suna zawwa da wasu mutane ina son ganin su, in sun zo kar ka tsaida su su shigo maza.
   Garde: To.

24. ALHAJI SHAGALI, Scene 6.

   Sous-préfet: ... E, Garde!
   Garde: Mon Commandant.
   Sous-préfet: Ka je ka sa Alhaji ga hannun Commandant dai Brigade, ya adana shi hal in bu'do shi.
   Garde: To.

25. GAADOO K'ARHIN ALLAA (Waasan Kwaykoyoo na Zinder a 1973), transcribed by Abuubakar Mahamman (Niamey: CELHTO, 1977). The recording from which this transcription was taken is no longer available. A later performance of the play was videotaped for television in 1979 by the Troupe Amadou 'Dan Bassa (ORTN Archives, Niamey). I also observed a performance at the **Maison des Jeunes** in Zinder on 13 September 1981.

26. GAADOO K'ARHIN ALLAA, Scene 2, p. 5. The quotations are from the published text; the English translations are mine. The original Hausa (using the UNESCO orthography):

> Waziirii: To! Naa jii da ku kee ceewaa Maynaa Shaahoo, Maynaa Muushee, bak ku luuraa ku ganii yanzu zaamanin baa irin naaku na daa ba nee, koo bu ku sanii ba? Zaamanin daa, da hwaadaawaa da baayin Sarkii su kee gamuwaa su yi sarawtaa; yanzu bu ku san ba duuniyaa taa saakee, baa irin ta daa ba cee: shii Sarkin ma, ay ma'aykacii nee, biyan shi a kee koo bu ku sanii ba? Zaa ku zoo ku cee "Maynaa waane nee! Maynaa Waane nee!" Sarawtaa kuu zaa ku yin ta? Da kuu da liiman kuu zaa ku yin ta? Bu ku san ba sarawta' akway maasu yin ta? ...
> Galaadiima: Waziirii in kaa san haka nee ay bay kamaata ba ku naa tankiyaa, tun 'daazuu ka naa zancen Sous-Préfet ko?

27. GAADOO K'ARHIN ALLAA, pp. 8-9. References to the Party are to the **Parti Progressiste Nigérien**, the ruling political party between 1958 and 1974 when it was dissolved after the military takeover.

28. GAADOO K'ARHIN ALLAA, pp. 34-6.

29. GAADOO K'ARHIN ALLAA, p. 36. See Chapter I for Dan-Inna Chaibou's description of the traditional installation rites. ("La Théâtralité en Pays Hawsa," Memoire de Maîtrise, Université Nationale de Côte d'Ivoire, 1978-79, pp. 20-4).

30. GADO K'ARHIN ALLA, performance by the Troupe Amadou 'Dan Bassa at the MJC, Zinder, Niger, 13 September 1981. For the Député's speech, see GAADOO K'ARHIN ALLAA, pp. 37-40.

31. GAADOO K'ARHIN ALLAA, Scene 7, p. 47.

Sarkii: ... Kuu duka abun da ya saa na kiraawoo ku, kiran na alheeri nee. Kullun i naa gayaa muku i naa ceewaa ku gaanee nii, da aka mini sarawtaa, baa dan in waari da kuu ba. Gidan nan, naamu nee hwa na muu duka: ku san da sanii gidan nan in ya laalaacee muu duka muka laalaacee baa ni ka'day ba da kee busa kujeerag gidan nan.

32. TALALA MAI KAMAN SAKE, performance by the Troupe Amadou 'Dan Bassa of Zinder at the National Festival in Diffa, Niger, 8 April 1981.

33. TALALA MAI KAMAN SAKE, Scene 1. The transcription is mine with help from Yazi Dogo; the English translation is mine. The original Hausa:

Mai Samari: Ba ka sa wannan a kanka? In ya zage ka ai ba kai ba ya zaga. Ai in ka lura, a ka 'dauka daga nan gabas zuwa yamma, k'asar wannan tamu kap! Gaba 'dayanta. Ka ji ko ka shurareni hwa! A nan k'asar nan, Baribari yana wasa da bahulatani. Ka ji ko?
Musa: To.
Mai Samari: In ka yi gaba, za ka tarda Baduwari yana wasa da Bagobiri, ka k'ara yin gaba, ka tarda Bakatsine yana wasa da Bagobiri, ka k'ara yin gaba, ka gan da Ba'are yana wasa da Ba'adare....

Ba ka duba ka ga k'asar tamu duk uwammu 'daya,

Characters in Action 225

> ubammu 'daya, an ka je an ce mutum wane da wane suna wasan nangi.

34. TALALA MAI KAMAN SAKE, performances in Tanout (9 March 1981), Diffa (8 April 1981), and Maradi (1 September 1981).
35. TALALA MAI KAMAN SAKE, Scene 7.

> Alkali: To na rantse da Alla da Annabi, dud mutuman da ya ci dukiyal maraya, daidai da k'ohar allura a k'asata goma ranal tashin kiyama su ne. Cikin wuta yake wannan.

36. Interview with Yazi Dogo, Zinder, Niger, 14 August 1981.
37. 'DAN KWANGILA, performance by the Troupe from Maradi at the National Festival in Diffa, Niger, 9 April 1981.
38. 'DAN KWANGILA, Scene 3. This transcription is by Aboubacar Mahamane; the English translation is mine. The original Hausa:

> President: Messieurs les membres de la commission, l'ordre du jour de la présente réunion comporte un seul point. Il s'agit comme vous le savez de l'examen des dossiers concernant l'avis d'appel d'offre numéro 007 du 3 mars 1981 rélatif à la construction d'un dispensaire à Maigémé village situé dans l'arrondissement de Dakoro.
> Je voudrais avant d'entrer dans le vif du sujet attirer votre attention sur certains points: le choix du dossier qui doit s'opérer dans la plus grande objectivité et si l'Etat

consent l'accroissement
du FNI, il est de notre
devoir en tant que
techniciens de retenir un
entrepreneur sérieux et
de veiller surtout a
l'exécution des travaux.
Sur ce, chers Messieurs,
sans plus tarder, nous
allons passer au dé-
pouillement. Monsieur
Ruwa, présentez-nous les
dossiers.

39. 'DAN KWANGILA, Scene 4.

Directeur: Ça c'est grave ça,
comment Hamza demande
'din fonctionnaires za
ka tsaya sai ka yi une
semaine gare ta, c'est
normal qu'ils te fassent
du bruit, ce sont les
premiers venus tu les as
negligés. Décidément
c'est ton habitude,
kala ina ji har ga shi na
gani kullum ana gaya min
haka nan. Bai kyautu ba
mutane su baro aikinsu ka
zo ka wulakantasu,
alhali mu ko clients muke
nema. Tsakanin clients
que ça soit fonctionnaire
ou commerçant ba ta
kamata ba ka yi banbanci
ba duka 'daya ne wurinka.

40. 'DAN KWANGILAA, mimeographed text by the Troupe from Maradi, Scene 3, pp. 12-13.
41. 'DAN KWANGILA, Scene 7 (transcription from the Diffa performance).

Chef Urbanisme
(Hamidu): A'a ba shi yiwuwa, kuma
ni ab ba za ni zawwa da
sunan gwamnati in 'dauki

Characters in Action 227

> wanga gida in ba
> gwamnati a sa 'yan malati
> ciki ba ya yiwuwa.

42. William O. Beeman, "Why do They Laugh? An Interactional Approach to Humor in Traditional Iranian Improvisatory Theater," JOURNAL OF AMERICAN FOLKLORE, no. 374 (1981), pp. 506-26.
43. Beeman, pp. 513-15.
44. Beeman, pp. 523-5.
45. TALALA MAI KAMAN SAKE, Scene 4.

> Talala: To ita muke son ku huddo muna.
> Abokin: I.
> Agogo: Kaiii, wannan ta hi k'arhina ni.
> Talala: Haba!
> Abokin: Ashe!
> Agogo: Alla. I ta hi ...
> Abokin: Haba, Agogo, ka yi tsatsa dan Alla dan Annabi.
> Agogo: Wannan sai su Savon Robb.
> Abokin: Wa?
> Talala: Savon Robb?
> Agogo: E. Ma su yanzu-yanzu.

46. Personal communication from Mamman Lawal, Zinder, Niger, April 1981.
47. GADO K'ARHIN ALLA, performance in Zinder, 13 September 1981.
48. GAADOO K'ARHIN ALLAA, Scene 4, p. 22.

> Shaho: Yanzu ko. Laa'buu'buu! Kay Laa'buu'buu!
> Laa'buu'buu: Ee, biyaa maraadi.
> Shaho: Kay in an kiraayee ka bak ka zawwaa! Ba ka san ba goobe sarawtaa? Bi maalan ku tahi.

(The published text spells this character's name La'buu'buu; the troupe called him La'baa'baa in the performances I observed).
49. GAADOO K'ARHIN ALLAA, Scene 4, p. 23.
50. Interview with Abdou Louché and Yazi Dogo, Zinder, Niger, 22 April 1981. See discussion in Chapter II.

51. ALHAJI SHAGALI, Scene 4.

    Shagali: Wallahi tallahi ka gani in da malummai in ka sa su suna yi yau bai ya kwana a garin nan.
    Maître: Malummai bas sa yi ai.
    Shagali: Yanzu in ka gaya musu sai k'ungiya addinin islam ya hana, wannan Alla bai ya so, mi ne ne haka za su ce.

52. ALHAJI SHAGALI, Scene 4.

    Shagali: Ka san inda za ka yi da shi.
    Mai Burgami: To Alhaji.
    Shagali: E.
    Mai Burgami: Mu wannan wurin mu ba ta da wuya.
    Shagali: E.
    Mai Burgami: Don in mun yi niyya abunda muka gani yi muke aikinmu, yanzu za mu soma bakin aikin za mu kama.

(The use of mu/"we" is common in Hausa; Mai Burgami is referring to himself.)
53. 80,000 francs (cfa) at the time of the play was worth about $320, a small fortune compared to the workers' 3,000 ($12) and 5,000 ($20) in wages.
54. Ibrahim "Gliss" Tando performed this role both for the 1979 videotape and for the performance I witnessed in Zinder in September 1981. At one scheduled rehearsal, members of the troupe spent an entire evening trying to find him, while the rest waited at the **Maison des Jeunes**. They cancelled the planned performance of GADO K'ARHIN ALLA when they learned that he was out of town. (Rehearsal notes, MJC, Zinder, 25 August 1981).
55. Abraham, DICTIONARY, p. 220.
56. Abraham, DICTIONARY, p. 868; and personal communication from Neil Skinner.
57. James T. Brink, "Organizing Satirical Comedy in **Kote-tlon:** Drama as a Communication

Strategy Among the Bamana of Mali," Diss. Indiana University 1980, pp. 124-5.
 58. KOWA YA BUGI RUWA IDONAY, performance in Diffa, 13 April 1981.
 59. Instrumental Ensemble entry of the Département of Niamey at the National Festival in Diffa, Niger, 7 April 1981.
 60. Brink, p. 26.
 61. Skinner, pp. 176-211.
 62. M.G. Smith in Skinner, p. xviii.
 63. TALALA MAI KAMAN SAKE, performance at the Diffa Festival, 8 April 1981.
 64. Neil Skinner suggests that **dofiya** may be the English "don't fear" (Hausa: **babu shakka**). (Personal communication, August 1983).
 65. 'DAN KWANGILA, Scene 8.

> Rangama: Wanga anne, wanga anne ya cuce ni, wanga anne ya cuce ni....
> Sai da Inspecteur ya ce mini in yi aiki da 'yan k'asa, inda 'yan k'asa ne na 'doka ka ji ko da ku'din nan na tare su.

 66. BA GA IRINTA BA, Scene 2.

> Bartelemi: Ah! Nous, éducation pour nous c'est pas ça. L'enfant venu l'école, il dit, heh! Poser, garder cahier pour toi ... Mais pas éducation pour nous, pour vous, papa ba luwani, maman ba luwani ... Yaro ta ka zo lakwal, eh, ka doki lance pierre margouillat hwuh! monter bourico hwuh! hwuh! hwuh! ... Mais nous, jamais.

 67. GAADOO K'ARHIN ALLAA, p. 26.
 68. The troupe saves these costumes; while many of the expensive robes and other costumes have "disappeared" over the years, the Boka's attire has not found its way into anyone's personal wardrobe.

69. GAADOO K'ARHIN ALLAA, Scene 4, p. 27.
70. GAADOO K'ARHIN ALLAA, Scene 4, pp. 27-30.
71. GADO K'ARHIN ALLA, performances for ORTN (videotape) and in Zinder, 13 September 1981.
72. Propp, pp. 39-50.
73. 'DAN KWANGILA, Scene 1.
Rangama: To ni ina tsammanin shiga za ni yi in jarraba in gani.
Issa: Ab.
Sale: Ab Alhaji Rangama da wace kama za ka shiga?
Rangama: Ab.
Sale: To mi ke gare ka?
Rangama: To kai mai arziki sai na shiga duk abunda take zama ta zama....
Sa'idu: To Alhaji Arzika, wannan dai za ka hwara rangamat taka. Wannan haraka ce wadda ta shahi 'yan kongila.
Taro: Un hun, gaskiya ne.
Sa'idu: Shi kau hwa gini ba saida 'bosho ne ba.

74. The name **Arzika** (wealth) **Rangama** (barter) refers to a rich petty trader, but it connotes a person who jumps from one thing to another. (Personal communication from Aboubacar Mahamane, CELHTO, Niamey, October 1981).
75. 'DAN KWANGILA, Scene 2.

Mainassara: Alhaji ka ga in ka dace da wannan kasuwa, Alhaji Arzika Rangama, dan Alla dan Annabi zan ba ka wani 'dan galga'di.
Rangama: Yauwa.
Mainassara: Ka biya wata k'ungiya wadda ake ce mata OPEN.
Rangama: A OPIN ko?
Mainassara: A'a ba OPIN ba.
Rangama: OPEL.
Mainassara: OPEN.
Rangama: A OPEN.

Mainassara: OPEN kin nan ko ita ce ta ke kulawa da 'yan kwangila k'ank'ana da manya matasa wanda suke so su ci gaba.

(OPEN/Office des Petites Entreprises Nigériennes).
76. 'DAN KWANGILA, Scene 4.

Rangama: Ka sa ni ga hanya, ka ji ko?
Gimshik'i: E.
Rangama: Dan saboda ka san wa'anga kwamumuwan ba san su ba, wanda muka saba aiki da su an tada su....
Gimshik'i: To amman duk da haka nan, akwai mutume na ya na nan guda yana nan ana ce mishi Hamza.
Rangama: E anhan, Salisu ko?
Gimshik'i: Ab kai hwa kwaramniya gare ka.
Rangama: Hamza Hamza haba Hamza
Gimshik'i: Diba kai karkarwa tun ba ka kama ku'di ba kana karkarwa haka, ka dakanta in ka je wurin shi ka tambaya in shi ne Hamza.
Rangama: E, to madalla.
Gimshik'i: In ya ce e to sai ka ce mishi Alhaji Mahamman Gimshik'i ya aiko ka.
Rangama: To madalla.
Gimshik'i: Sai ka ba shi wa'annan takardun.
Rangama: To madalla.
Gimshik'i: Zai ya gyara maka su.
Rangama: To madalla, madalla.
Gimshik'i: E, amma hwa, ka sani ko?
Rangama: In Alla ya yarda ban mancewa, ba Hamisu ba yake ko?
Gimshik'i: Ab.
Rangama: Hamza, Hamza, Hamza.
Gimshik'i: Amma kai, wai kai Alhaji Rangama mi ya same ka?

77. 'DAN KWANGILA, performance at Diffa, 9 April 1981.

78. 'DAN KWANGILA, Scene 5.

Rangama: Mushe! Mushe! Ka wa Alla ka ga sai da na, na ji kuna tambayag gahwara wanga abun da ka yi, sai da na tambaye ka gahwara da Alla mi ne ne abun kai k'ara ta komsariya, da Alla ka yi hak'uri, in ma tashi zan yi in tahiyata in ma abun haka yake. Ba ni takardun in tahiyata.

79. ALHAJI SHAGALI, Scene 2.

Alhaji 2: To yanzu aikin da an ba shi labudda an ba shi aiki kuma an ba shi **avance**, da aka ba shi **avance** sai ya je ya sayi mota da ku'din. Yana nan yana yawo yana bin titi-titi, ga kuma **chantier** ba kaya na kirki. Ba katako, ba **ciment**, ba komi, leburori ga su can zamne.

80. ALHAJI SHAGALI, Scene 4.

Shagali: To Gimbiya, e Hajiya!
Hajiya: Anha anha Alhaji ashe da man kana da wata Gimbiya ko Alhaji?
Shagali: E?
Hajiya: Kana da wata Gimbiya ko Alhaji?
Amarya: Ai da man Hajiya na ce miki na ga lettre kin da Gimbiya ta ma Alhaji Shagali.
Shagali: Yanzu wa ya ce Gimbiya?

Characters in Action

>
> Hajiya: To Alhaji ni na riga na saba ne saboda shi ne ban miki magana ba.
> Shagali: A'a ni na ce Hajiya.
> Hajiya: A'a Alhaji.
> Amarya: Gimbiya ka ce, to wace ce Gimbiya?
> Shagali: Wa ya ce Gimbiya?
> Hajiya: Had da wata Gimbiya gare ka daban Alhaji?

81. ALHAJI SHAGALI, Scene 4.

> Shagali: To ke kin ce wai kin gani wasik'an Gimbiya a busa **table** ne, yaushe kin gani?
> Amarya: Na gani dan Hajiya ce ta ce kar in gwada ma.
> Shagali: Gimbiya ba ta iya ko rubutu ba balle ta yi mini **lettre**.
> Amarya: Ai ka san da zancen.
> Hajiya: Anha ashe akwai ta ko Alhaji? Ashe akwai ta ko?

82. ALHAJI SHAGALI, Scene 5.

> Gimbiya: Ba **fanta** ba, ba **coca** ba, wai kullun kana zuwa kawai ina maka dahe dahe ina maka komi abunda kake so ka ci, ka ci da'di kawai ka tashi ka tahiyakka daga dari ukku, jikka biyu, dala dari ka ce mini Gimbiya na tahi. Yau taka ta k'are, ka sha **whiskey** kin ma.

(In Hausa, ci/"to eat" is also one of the verbs used for sexual intercourse; this speech carries greater innuendo than the literal translation would imply in English).

83. ALHAJI SHAGALI, Scene 5.

Alhaji Lura: Mi ne ne?
Shagali: **Coca**.
Lura: Diba ka gani Alhaji, yanzu kai 'dan duniya kamak ka ba ka san **coca** ba sai wannan.
Shagali: Ba **coca** ba ne wannan?
Lura: La'ilahwa illallahu mahamada rasulalla, kuma ga wanga abun ta kai ka Alhaji mutun da daraja kamak ka.
Shagali: Gimbiya dai ta ce **coca** ne.
Lura: Gimbiya za ta ce ma **coca**, Alhaji in ka ji ana **whiskey**, giya wannan **whiskey**, Alhaji wannan ita ce.
Shagali: Yanzu na sha giya?
Lura: Ashe ba banza ba sakosh kin ka ta 'bace Alhaji.

84. Beeman, p. 525.
85. BA GA IRINTA BA, Scene 1.

Mamman Arrivé: Wai ni, tsaya in tambaye ka. Wai ku, saboda Alla da Annabi ba ku gajiya da wannan. Kullum ranyo, ranyo. Wai, ni, wai ni mi ku ke k'uk'k'ullawa a can wurin in kun je ranyo? (ranyo= French **réunion**)
Langa Langa: A'a ya na da amhwani mana. Ka ji abin da ba ka ta'ba ji ba. Ka ga abin da ba ka ta'ba gani ba. Dan wannan ni ke ce maka ka rik'a shiga cikin jama'a. Ka gani, k'ungiya' addinin musulunci bak ka shiga ciki. Ranyo na samariya bak ka shiga ciki. K'ungiya ta asosiyasiyon ta paran na elev ba ka shiga ciki. Don wannan ni ke ce ma hak kullum jahili ne.

(asosiyasiyon ta paran na elev = French **Association des Parents d'Eleves**)

Characters in Action 235

86. BA GA IRINTA BA, Scene 1.

Sanussi: Wai madan ta hwasa min baki dan ba 'doki ba leso.
Mamman Arrivé: Langa Langa, mi ne ne leso?
Langa Langa: Seau, seau irin wannan. Ba akwai kanti ba ba ka zuwa ka 'dauka? To ga shi ka 'dauka ka kai mata mana.
Mamman Arrivé: A'a tsaya, tsaya, wannan na 'dauka ruwa?
Langa Langa: E.
Gimbiya: Ni yanzu ba wannan ni ke so ba.... Zuwa nike tsakanin ni da ita. Wani ya sa wani a cikin butili. Ba na yarda ba 'da na 'daya a hudda mishi ido. An kai ba ka je ba ni in tahi in je in tarda ta tsakanin ni da ita wani ya sa wani cikin butali.
Mamman Arrivé: Tsaya dan Alla kin hwara halin naki. Wai kai ni, lebaran da gwamnati ke biya a can lakwal 'din kuma sai an ce su 'dauki wani leso su yi badala?

87. BA GA IRINTA BA, Scene 1.

Mamman Arrivé: Yo ni Mamman Arrivé a garin nan a zo a ma 'dana rotse tsammmani ka ke kwanci za ni yi in bari ... Ni yanzu Mamman Arrivé da kike ji a garin nan ba wani ba ni ke tsoro. Kin ga da k'arhi ma mutun ba kashi ba za ya ba ni. Ungo. Adana mini wannan ku'din. Yo!

88. Yazi Dogo, 14 August 1981. The proverb is used in the play by the town gossip K'arawrawa (the Bell), (Scene 5).
89. BA GA IRINTA BA, performance at the Niamey Festival, April 1980
90. TALALA MAI KAMAN SAKE, performances in Zinder (28 February 1981), Tanout (9 and 11 March 1981), Diffa (8 April 1981), and Zinder (1 September 1981).

91. TALALA MAI KAMAN SAKE, Scene 3.

    Musa: Wannan **peinture**.
    Talala: **Peinture**?
    Musa: E. Kamar wacce iri ce kake so?
    Talala: **Peinture** a samu mai walk'iya.
    Musa: Mai walk'iya?
    Talala: I, mai kyau.
    Musa: To....
    Talala: To zancen wannan **doucheur**.
    Musa: **Doucheur**.
    Talala: Kada ka sa min ta tsaye wanda aka mir'dawa tana shar.
    Musa: U hun.
    Talala: Sa mini ta kwance in na kwanta in lutse ina muymuya kin kamar tantabara.

92. TALALA MAI KAMAN SAKE, Scene 4.

    Talala: Da ma na san shi kike kunya.
    Dijé: A wallahi ba don shi ba.
    Talala: Zo in dan ta'bawa da ke.
    Dijé: Ban saba ba ne.
    Talala: E?
    Dijé: Abin da za ka gaya mana, ka zo nan ka gaya min abin da za ka gaya ma ka gaya ma nan gurin. Ban saba ba ne, ban zo ba don wannan.
    Talala: Ba ki zo ba dom mi?

93. TALALA MAI KAMAN SAKE, performance at the Diffa Festival, 8 April 1981. This performance did not include Talala's crotch gesture, although other rehearsals and performances did (See discussion in Chapter II).

94. See M.G. Smith, "The Social Functions and Meaning of Hausa Praise Singing," IBADAN, 21 (October 1965), pp. 81-92; C.G.B. Gidley, "'Yankamanci--The Craft of the Hausa Comedians," AFRICAN LANGUAGE STUDIES, 8 (1967), pp. 52-81; C.G.B. Gidley, "Rok'o: A Hausa Praise Crier's Account of His Craft," AFRICAN LANGUAGE STUDIES, 16 (1975), pp. 93-115.
95. Anthony H. Kirk-Greene, MUTUMIN KIRKII: THE CONCEPT OF THE GOOD MAN IN HAUSA (Bloomington: African Studies Program, Indiana University, 1974).
96. Kirk-Greene, pp. 4-12.
97. Yazi Dogo, 14 August 1981.

CHAPTER V
PERFORMANCE: THE TROUPES AND THEIR AUDIENCES

> Drama is an expression of community, feeling the pulse of an age or of a moment in time like no other art. A play is a social event or it is nothing.
> J.L. Styan (1)

In developing their plays, the Hausa troupes remain acutely aware of their audience, either their own community or the wider, national audiences for festival or television performances. During rehearsal, some troupes invite community members to observe and participate in the discussions as they create their scenic scores. Yet even when no one from outside the troupe comes to offer early responses and comments, the members of the troupe serve as spectators if they are not themselves acting. The troupes incorporate as much community feedback as possible into their developing score, but they also allow for spontaneous interaction with future audiences in the open spaces left for improvisation.

Bernard Beckerman analyzes the interaction between performers and audiences in what he terms selection and feedback.(2) Theatre artists select the activities of their plays to produce a certain effect, intuitively judging the appropriateness of each choice within the prevailing theatrical conventions. Audiences, in turn, test the activities they experience in performance against their artistic and personal experiences and signal their acceptance back to the actors. This process continually modifies the range of materials a performer draws upon in the complex balance between established conventions and a desire for variety.(3) Because the present Hausa theatre is such a recent development in Niger, its actors are quite conscious of their selective process and audience reactions. They are working to establish dramatic conventions and to involve audiences in their emerging art form.

Beckerman further divides audiences into random and communal types. A communal audience consists of people whose social experiences are similar to those of the performers; a random group is never totally random, but performers seldom know what kind or degree of similarity (economic, intellectual, etc.) has brought a particular audience to the theatre. Random audiences have dominated the western theatre for a long time, according to Beckerman.(4)

Nigerien audiences, however, would largely fall into his communal category. Social divisions between traditional lifestyles and more western, urbanized patterns are rapidly developing in Niger, but most members of the educated elite still have strong ties to families in rural areas. In a poor country with a comparatively small population, no one lives very far from the farms and herds. Indeed, the theatre takes as its subject matter many of the problems of the nation's development efforts, portraying the strains on cultures undergoing change. Both the troupes and their audiences include people involved in the process of change at many different levels, whether voluntarily or involuntarily. Moreover, one of the purposes of the government in fostering the annual cultural festivals is to develop a sense of national community among the diverse population groups in the country. With this in mind, the theatre troupes develop themes from current community problems and concerns; they work to forge a deeper sense of nationalism through audiences' participation in their performances.

Significant differences appear in the work of the troupes when they move from a known, local audience to the national audiences of the festival and television plays. The language used often changes; costumes, scenery and properties may become more elaborate; the emphases on theme, improvisational style, and type of humor may all be altered to suit the expected audience. Changing from their own community to national exposure not

only means performing before strangers, but also
the addition to the audience of women, members of
other ethnic groups, and powerful national leaders. In between these extremes are the audiences
of live productions on tour--although usually
strangers to the performers, they are often much
like their home audience in background.
   For local play productions, audiences consist
primarily of young men with a scattering of children and middle-aged men. Respectable married
women rarely attend public performances, and many
families also forbid their young daughters to
attend evening plays. Even the wives of actors do
not come to see their performances. At one performance I attended in Zinder, the only other women in
the audience were actresses from the Troupe Amadou
'Dan Bassa coming to observe the Radio Club Troupe
perform; at another performance, an American friend
and I were the only women present.(5) These
audiences of young people, mostly men, mirror the
composition of the troupes themselves, which
include relatively few women and older people. The
plays compete with films in towns large enough to
have a cinema, attracting very similar audiences--
young men going out to be entertained.
   With the competitive cycle for the festival
plays, the audiences begin to alter in
composition. A greater number of prominent citizens appear; a few, though by no means all, bring
their wives and children. The first two or three
rows of chairs are normally reserved for the
judges and other guests; the theatre then becomes a
social occasion for the **fonctionnaire** elite. Plays
performed in honor of visiting officials attract a
similar audience even when they are not part of the
festival series. Sometimes the price of admission
is raised for these events, or they are limited to
those with invitations in order to exclude the
poorer young people wandering in off the streets.
But the crowd of young men usually comes in any
case, merely sitting and standing behind the
important people in the reserved rows.(6)
   At the National Festival, the status level of
the audience shifts upward to the highest officials
in the country. President Kountché himself did not
appear at the Diffa Festival but several ministers,
préfets, sous-préfets, and invited guests, including the Governor of Borno State in Nigeria, did
attend the performances as well as members of the

foreign diplomatic corps, the press, and officials from all ranks of the Nigerien civil service.

Since 1979, television coverage of the festivals has extended to virtually all regions of the country. Even the smallest villages lacking electricity now often have televisions powered by car batteries or solar energy. Thus, festival performances reach new multi-ethnic audiences of all income and status levels, in addition to the women and older people who do not normally come to live performances. Although still a communal audience, the community takes on a national character, a broader scope, with corresponding changes in the performances.

One of these major changes between local performances and the national arena is the language used in a play. Troupes perform in the predominant local language in their regions but switch to Hausa when the audience diversifies. The Mainé Soroa Troupe performs in Kanuri within the Diffa **Département** but in Hausa for the festivals. Their director explained this change as a direct result of early festival experiences: when the troupe performed in Kanuri at the Zinder Festival (1976), they were given a low ranking in the competition; when they performed in Hausa the following year, they were awarded first prize. Since then there has been no question of which language to use outside their Kanuri-speaking département.(7)

In some regions of the country, several languages are spoken interchangeably and the plays reflect these linguistic and ethnic mixtures. The students' play I attended in Tchin Tabaraden, an isolated northern community, was performed in a combination of Hausa, French and Tamashek. Between each scene, the action was summarized by the head of the **samariya** in Tamashek, and then by a teacher from the CEG in Hausa. French appeared in the office scenes of the play and several jokes centered on characters not understanding one another's languages.(8)

Similar mixtures of language appear in the festival performances as well, particularly the use of French interspersed in the scenes with **fonctionnaire** characters in government offices. Or in the dance performances, Hausa may be used for the dialogue to clarify what is happening, with the songs kept in their original languages, as in the

Agadez **Ballet** in 1981 with its songs in Tamashek, and the Gaya **Ballet** with its songs in Zarma.(9)

Some of the troupes can perform in French, but many do not have enough French-speaking actors to create an entire play in French. To attract the widest possible audience the troupes find that Hausa is necessary. The majority of Nigeriens speak little or no French, and very few people outside of distinct regions speak Zarma, Kanuri, Tamashek or Fulfulde. As a teacher in Tchin Tabaraden described the situation, their school (CEG) troupe could perform in French, but the play is not meant for the actors alone; they want to bring a message to the community, so they must use Hausa because everyone understands it. However, he added, people understand a lot from the action in a play even if they do not know the language, so it is possible in any play to incorporate a little of the performers' other languages.(10)

Hausa remains the most widely used **lingua franca** within Niger and across the southern border with Nigeria. Nonetheless, the dialects of Hausa vary considerably and the troupes must also take dialect differences into account in performance. Yazi Dogo noted that his troupe often changes their Hausa to make it familiar to their audience. When in Dogondoutchi, for example, they reduce their eastern dialect expressions; when in Niamey, they increase their use of French.(11) Here again, the troupes' facility in different languages reflects the composition of its members: formally educated actors speak French, while actors from different regions bring their linguistic skills with them and can advise the troupe on adjusting the dialogue of a play to be readily understood by a given audience.

For local productions, which are often quickly produced with little funding, costumes generally come from the actors' personal wardrobes. Since the actors portray contemporary people living in communities like their own, they select clothing appropriate to the character's age, sex, and social status. **Alhajis** wear robes and embroidered caps; servants wear used clothing from the markets, often torn t-shirts and blue jeans; young men and **fonctionnaires** wear western clothing or the damask suits that are currently popular (a modified form of traditional clothing without the extra yards of loose robe--**babban riga**--over them). Wealthy women characters wear expensive wax cloth or lace outfits with gold jewelry, while their poorer companions wear worn and unmatched cloth. Colors, styles, and combinations of clothing reflect current Nigerien fashion for most roles.

The exceptions to these ordinary sorts of clothing draw attention to the characters they adorn. As suggested in Chapter IV, short pants immediately identify foreigners and men of low status. The **bokas**, as comic figures and outsiders with magical associations, often wear strikingly odd clothing. For instance, in GADO K'ARHIN ALLA the **boka**, wearing black shorts, bells, cowry shell decorations, charms and an unusual hat, dominated the stage as soon as he appeared.(12)

Another extreme in clothing was used by the Radio Club Troupe to emphasize the decadence of the young people's party in DARAJAR K'ASA AL'ADARTA: Taxi and another girl wore pants. This drew a general wave of laughter, and loud, rather rude, comments from men sitting in the audience.(13) Respectable Muslim women do not wear trousers in Nigerien society; in this, the smaller towns remain considerably more conservative than the city. In Zinder, the troupe made their point instantly--Taxi has transgressed the bounds of all propriety--at the same time as she stimulated audience interest in the scene. However, the shock value of this choice of costume would diminish significantly if the play were performed in Niamey, or if the idea were used repeatedly in different plays.

Within the festival cycle, production budgets increase with each level of competition from the local **samariyas** to the departmental eliminations, culminating in the festival performances themselves. With increased funding, artistic choices of costume become more apparent as troupe members direct tailors to make clothing for their roles in specific styles, fabrics and colors. For the songs and **ballets** the performers usually dress in identical costumes. Many groups select locally printed cloth with appropriate motifs--the Development Society emblem or the commemorative print for the year's national wrestling competition. Identical costumes emphasize the unity of the group of singers, dancers or musicians. Similarly, in the Diffa performance of ALHAJI SHAGALI, his two wives were dressed alike in the fourth scene, underscoring their unity in opposing his prospective visit to Gimbiya.(14)

The plays' costumes for the festival productions appear no different in kind from those in the local productions; both aim at verisimilitude. Festival costumes become more theatrical, however, in that they are designed. In BA GA IRINTA BA, Mamman Arrivé's suit was made from mint green damask in the typical style of wealthy merchants. The bright green is an available choice for anyone to buy in the market, but not a common one; most Hausa men prefer the traditional white or conservative blues. The green costume thus drew visual attention to Mamman on stage among the plainer colors of the other men's robes, while it also suggested something of his character: brash, vivid, and unconventional.(15) Similarly, Savon Robb in TALALA MAI KAMAN SAKE appeared in the Diffa Festival performance (for the first time) in a bright purple, embroidered suit. The costume joined his effeminate walk in signalling his role as pimp.(16)

Conversely, between the preliminary Tanout performance and the Diffa Festival performance of TALALA, the young wife's costume was changed to a plainer, more conservative style. In Tanout, the actress wore one of her own dresses of a flowing, sheer scarf material made into the year's latest fashion with no seams under the sleeves; both the filmy cloth and the open sides of the blouse were meant to be revealing. In contrast, the costume sewn for her for the Diffa performance was of flowered cotton cloth in a demure style with the extra cloth wrapper over the blouse worn by married women. The new dress clearly labelled her as a properly modest wife.(17)

As in western theatre, costumes serve to visually identify the occupations and status of characters. Consequently, Nigerien troupes pay considerable attention to accurately costuming police officers, guards, doctors, and other roles which require uniforms in real life, as well as the range of clothing signifying wealth and aristocracy. If possible, these costumes are borrowed rather than reproduced. One instance indicating the importance attached to appropriate costumes occurred when the Troupe Amadou 'Dan Bassa performed GADO K'ARHIN ALLA in Zinder, an event organized on a day's notice in September 1981. Despite the fact that they had not performed the play for two years and were scheduled for that evening, members of the troupe put rehearsal aside in order to search for the robes and turbans needed for the play's traditional characters--the **sarki**, the courtiers, the princes, and others.(18) This placing of priority on costumes over rehearsals is also true for Zinder's WASAN KARA, where all the actors must look as much as possible like their real counterparts; what they say and do in character seems less significant than the visual effect of audience recognition.(19)

Like the costumes, the scenery and properties for the plays provide a sense of familiarity, drawing audiences into the world of the play. Usually, everyday objects are utilized as they would be in any Nigerien community. In the rehearsals I observed, the troupes employed no special sets; often they did not even act on the stage but in a smaller room or with a cluster of chairs outdoors. Rudimentary props might be brought into rehearsal--a mat, a bowl, a piece of cloth--but the actors often went through their scenes without any objects at all, or they took whatever was at hand to represent what they should be holding.

Local performances rarely include a painted or constructed set; instead, the troupes suggest the surroundings with appropriate props. Mats create traditional environments such as a man's **zaure** (where he receives visitors) or the women's rooms in a compound. Often the actors, as part of the scene, will bring out a mat to unroll for a guest to sit on or instruct a servant to bring chairs. Plastic string chairs, readily available and not very expensive, denote a more "modern" household, while stuffed furniture signals wealth. Metal tables and chairs correspondingly suggest a government office. In TALALA MAI KAMAN SAKE, the funeral scene took place on mats, Talala's first house had string chairs, his new house sported stuffed armchairs, while a metal table and benches served the judges and witnesses in the final scene.(20) The conventions of these settings are simple, but they nonetheless convey a sense of real Nigerien milieux.

Within these settings, the actors make use of objects appropriate to their characters' activities in the scene. Government workers use telephones for conversations with distant officials; wives bring their husbands dishes of food; vendors carry trays of items to sell. As noted earlier, radios have become a common means of relaying messages and announcements. In 'DAN KWANGILA, Alhaji Rangama brings a pile of presents as bribes for Mainassara, including a large box containing a color television set. However, he himself does not carry these things, as a man of his status would not lift heavy objects, so the servant Dodo is sent to haul them in after he leaves.(Scene 2)(21)

As is true for the costumes, suitable props are sought carefully. Yazi Dogo teased me repeatedly about giving him my knapsack. Only later did I learn that he played an American tourist in one of his troupe's past productions, RIGA BA WUYA, a play they might someday want to perform again.

In moving upward in the festival competition, the troupes often elaborate their basic scenery and props as well as creating new costumes. Several of the preliminary performances at Tanout included painted cloths as backdrops, usually of village scenes. By the time they performed at the Diffa Festival, most of the troupes used such hanging cloths as scenery. In the month between being chosen to represent the Zinder **Département** in the Tanout competition and performing in Diffa, the Zinder Troupe had three scenic pieces made for TALALA MAI KAMAN SAKE. The first, a painted cloth, depicted the outer walls of typical village houses; it was unrolled during the scene for the funeral ceremonies.(Scene 2) The second set combined a painted cloth representing the inside of Talala's modern house (a wall with light fixtures) and a functioning door in a wooden frame. The structure greatly excited the troupe's members when they saw it for the first time the day before they left to travel to Diffa.(22) Although used in only one scene, this set focussed audience attention on Talala's unsuccessful seduction; this was the door to the bedroom that Dijé would not enter.(Scene 4) The third set construction was a curved stand for the final scene at court. With nearly the entire troupe present on stage as spectators and witnesses to Talala's trial, the wooden stand served to focus on the central dialogue--the testimony--at any particular moment. (Scene 7)(23)

In a similar manner, the painted wooden airplane in KUSKURE KARATU NE that carried the successful pilgrims off to Mecca, the piped water flowing from the school pump in WALWALE, and the brick wall that crumbled under the foot of the building inspector in 'DAN KWANGILA, all served to heighten interest in the scenes in which they were used and to spotlight the central actions in the plays.(24) These stage effects are not always possible in performances in the smaller towns or on tour, and the plays can be performed effectively without them. However, with increased financial support for festival entries and the prospect of television recording, the troupes take delight in strengthening and embellishing their creative work with scenery, properties and costumes.

Along with the material aspects of performance, the themes and range of improvisation also change with the shift in audience. As discussed in earlier chapters, the themes chosen for local performances are often different, even at the outset, from those developed with a view toward the festival competition. Local plays stress local problems, but they also lean more heavily toward entertainment than instruction. These productions must attract their audiences, luring people away from the cinema or from their homes. While issues of morality frequently figure among the themes, such themes also open up the possibilities for bawdy comedy. For example, as an institutionalized moral force, the police arrest Taxi and her wild young friends in DARAJAR K'ASA AL'ADARTA, but not before one young woman asks an officer to zip up her dress for her.(Scene 3) And while the drunken son in GIRMAN KAI RAWANIN TSIYA ultimately loses his inheritance, the play centers in the humorous scenes of debauchery at the bar.(25)

Home audiences know the performers well. This familiarity creates an intense climate of interaction for both humor and critique. Local performances can be quickly organized, allowing great latitude for improvisation because the actors know who will be in the audience and how to communicate easily with them. Thus, Zinder's traditional WASAN KARA needs little rehearsal; parts are assigned and arrangements made for costumes, vehicles, microphones, etc., with minimal time to rehearse the activities that will occur during the day of the celebration. The townspeople become actors for the day as they portray important people; their actions are improvised from a schedule of typically real events that would take place should the President of Nigeria (or Benin or Cameroon or any other country) visit Zinder. The audience responds to seeing their neighbors in those roles and to the actors' quite varied ability in imitating their real counterparts--the way they walk, stand, speak, dress, and so on.(26)

This knowledge of the performers as individuals--neighbors, friends, relatives--pervades the locally staged plays as well as community events like the WASAN KARA. Part of the success of a totally improvised play like GIRMAN KAI RAWANIN TSIYA lies in the audience's personal acquaintance with the actors. Yazi Dogo as the prodigal son, wearing a young man's loud plaid suit, reeling around the stage, would be comic in any context. But for those who know him as a devout Muslim who does not drink, and whose wife was a pilgrim in Mecca at the time of the troupe's performance in Zinder, his antics on stage were even funnier.(27) With their home audience, the Zinder troupe, like any other, works from an established rapport. They know they will be warmly received and can therefore take greater risks with new material and spontaneous decisions on stage.

Satire may be more stringent in a local setting as well. Hausa culture has strong traditions of satirical poetry and conversational innuendo (**habaici**); people quickly take note of and discuss the faults and foibles of others. The plays create an ideal environment not only for witty verbal commentary on fellow townspeople, but for physical mimicry of them as well. Unfortunately, this is one of the aspects of the plays that I had least access to as a foreigner. As Neil Skinner notes, the point of **habaici** is its obscurity to an outsider.(28) During one performance, I asked the man sitting next to me why everyone laughed at the entrance of one character before he did anything at all; he told me that the actor had walked in like the mayor. Such a level of common referents--for humor or subtle critique--is only possible between performers and a limited, intimately familiar, audience.

Alhaji Abdousalam Adam, Director of the Radio Club Troupe of Zinder, discussed the importance of this special ability of the plays to criticize faults within the community. He divided the audiences of live productions into two groups: those who come just for amusement and those who come to see the critiques (gugar zana). According to Alhaji Abdousalam, a lot of people come to see the troupes' criticism of local officials, including the officials themselves, who want to see the faults others in the community may perceive in their actions. If they find themselves or others in similar positions portrayed critically, they take note and sometimes make changes. "Su 'dauki abun da suka 'dauka" (They will take out of it what they take).(29) As an actor, Alhaji Abdousalam said that the plays enable him and other members of the troupes to show situations they cannot criticize as individuals in real life. The plays offer an opportunity to express points of view more powerfully and less personally than a direct statement to someone in the community.(30)

Local plays thus present a public forum at one remove from personal confrontation but within a community that recognizes their referents as easily as the individuals for whom the criticism is intended. The plays can bring public attention to controversial issues and focus pressure or embarrassment on those who must initiate changes and solutions to the problems. In Alhaji Abdousalam's words:

> Our experience has been that when we do a lot of plays, you'll see something get fixed. Some things will be improved.(31)

In this regard, the plays seem to function more actively than the traditional poets' praise-songs and critiques of wealthy men, which prompted donations to the clever poet rather than reform within the community.

In taking their plays to a national audience, the troupes lose some of this specificity of reference. For example, in the gossip scene in BA GA IRINTA BA, the men discuss Alhaji Jimmy's missing truck before Mamman Arrivé appears among them. The brief conversation sets the tone of the scene, with the name Jimmy adding an ironic note with its American flavor linked to a Hausa trans-

port merchant (Jimmy Carter was President of
the United States at the time of the play). The
local Zinder audience, however, could catch more of
the joke--Jimmy is the nickname of Adamou Hassane,
one of the youngest actors in the troupe, who rides
a dilapidated **mobylette;** the grandeur of a president's name, ownership of a truck, and the title
Alhaji associated with this Jimmy created a comic
oxymoron. While the troupe could play this joke to
comic effect at home, their festival performance
moved quickly on to the major subject of the scene,
Mamman Arrivé's delinquency.(32)

   Ethnic jokes and references may also change in
view of national audiences which are more ethnical-
ly diverse. At the 1981 Tanout competitions for
the Zinder **Département,** two of the plays portrayed
the conflict between Hausa farmers and Fulani
herdsmen. Since they were produced by troupes from
predominantly Hausa communities, both plays used
traditional "bush" Fulani characters in broad comic
caricature: exaggerated nasal voices, clumsy
movements, ignorant remarks.(33) Although an
important issue in certain communities, this
ethnic conflict is not a theme authorities would
wish to stress in a festival celebrating national
unity. These plays were passed over in the departmental competition in favor of TALALA MAI KAMAN
SAKE, which still included a comic Fulani character
but in a minor role. Indeed, far from being the
cause of the conflict, 'Dan Hulani is one of the
characters who testifies against Talala in the
final trial scene of the play.(34)

   In the national festival atmosphere, development themes have begun to dominate the plays, and
their instructive emphasis often overshadows the
spontaneous comedy. Competition remains a central
factor in the festival performances: the judges sit
in the front row, and all audience members evaluate
and compare the week's series of performances to
each other and with past plays. Although aesthetic
judgments are part of the official final ranking,
the political content is a more readily apparent
factor to troupe and audience members alike.
National recognition, prestige, and support from
the government, as well as invitations to perform
before the president and in other towns, reinforce
the choice of popular national themes for these
plays.(35)

The judges at the Zinder departmental competitions before the Diffa Festival gave points to each play in four categories: choice of theme, interpretation, production (**mise en scène**), and settings and costumes.(36)   I believe this scoring is standardized for all of the regional competitions and for the final festival performances. As noted in Chapter I, most of the organizational structure for the festivals dates back to the French colonial arts competitions.

Seasoned actors and spectators make their own judgments of the plays, taking the official categories into account. When asked to describe the qualities of theatrical excellence, Yazi Dogo listed three. First, the theme chosen should reflect recent news, the events that concern people (**abin da ya dami mutane**). Second, the actors should know their roles thoroughly and perform with care (**hankali**). Finally, everything in the play should be integrated appropriately (**daidai**) into the main theme.(37)

Troupes guard their current themes jealously. None of the troupe members I interviewed before the 1981 Festival would discuss their current work, and even after the Diffa Festival, the Mainé Soroa actors would not name the ideas for themes they had eliminated that year in case they might want to work them into future plays.(38) According to Alhaji Zoubeirou Lawal, actors from different troupes do not discuss their work when they are all gathered together at the festivals because of the competition between them; they are afraid other actors might steal their ideas. No one knew why both Mainé Soroa and Maradi used the theme of a corrupt entrepreneur, he said, but each felt the other had copied it.(39) However, once the plays have been performed publicly, the troupes may take good themes and produce them in their own towns. This was done more frequently before the arrival of television; now the original festival plays are available for everyone in the country to see, both during the festival and throughout the year on re-broadcasts.(40)

Before the current regime took power, the government prescribed the themes for the plays to be performed for the **Semaine de la Jeunesse** (Youth Week) each December. With the change in government, the troupes have been permitted to choose their own themes for the plays of the **Festival**

National de la Jeunesse each April.(41) In a critique of the 1980 Festival performances, Kélitigui A. Mariko quotes the government's instructions on themes as follows:

> Themes can be chosen freely but should be inspired by Nigerien realities and aspirations. They are left to the judgment of their creators but should be inspired by Niger's cultural inheritance. The compositions should take into account the cultural, economic, and social concerns of the nation.(42)

This sense of nationalism pervades not only the plays' themes, but the entire festival. In an address to the nation during the Seventh Annual Festival of 1982, President Kountché cited the objectives of the Supreme Military Council and the government when they instituted the festivals in 1976:

> The first goal has been to make our young people aware of the exciting realities of our new Niger. Our ideals of unity and brotherhood, of patriotism, the value of work; vigilance in the preservation of our security, and the resounding affirmation of our identity--in short, all of our mottoes and leitmotifs have been magnified and our national consciousness has been exalted....
> The second goal stems from the need to provide our **départements** with a better infrastructure for the social, cultural, and sports events necessary for body and spirit to blossom....
> The third goal, and without doubt the principal one, has been the rehabilitation of our cultural inheritance, which has been demoralized by foreign beliefs

> and the bad habits of a consumer society attempting to overshadow it and break it up. Here also, the festival has served as a springboard for a remarkable and irreversible renaissance of our philosophy.(43)

Publicity for the festivals echoes this presidential mandate for nationalism. In Niger's official newspaper, LE SAHEL, Babacar L. Mariko described the festival as an opportunity for collective reflection.

> It serves as a positive celebration of all youth--urban and rural, male and female, literate and illiterate. All are homogenized, made equal by the shared conditions of existence, by the shared means of expression, and by the common ideal of elevating the uniqueness of being Nigerien.(44)

The ideal that Mariko expresses recalls Beckerman's communal audience--artist/performers and audience members sharing common social experiences, values and aspirations--here set in nationalistic terms.

Given the tremendous significance awarded to national performances, the troupes mold their festival plays with great care. As suggested above, the right theme becomes all important; each troupe seeks a theme that will illuminate a national concern, but also one that they can instill with their own insight. The plays that 'Dan-Inna Chaibou summarized in his thesis on Hausa theatre, which were produced prior to 1978, emphasized the newly established military regime, the changes in its policies, and the aftermath of the drought.(45) By 1981, the new program of the Development Society began to dominate the plays, along with continuing exposés of selfish, non-cooperative citizens desiring to make a profit from cheating others or the government. The themes are similar to those Chaibou outlines, but each play reflects its specific time in its emphasis.

The construction of these festival plays as well as the choice of theme demonstrate the troupes' over-riding concern for the messages they want to project. As discussed in Chapter II, the scores of the festival plays are rehearsed more thoroughly than those for local productions; much less of the action is left open to improvisation and comedy. The ninety-minute time limit for the competition entries also encourages a set score with comparatively little room for change in the final performance. The troupes minutely detail the key didactic points of the plays, the ones the actors must not forget under any circumstances, since these points carry the thematic thrust of the work.(46) And it is with an awareness of the important government officials in the festival auditorium and the potentially vast television audience, that the troupes bring in local officials to critique their rehearsals and early versions of the play in order to forestall negative reactions.(47) Everyone--performers, spectators, and government officials--places great importance on the festival performances. This widespread belief in their utility reinforces their effectiveness as agents of change in the society.

From an official standpoint, Babacar L. Mariko's article in LE SAHEL eloquently expresses this confidence in the educational power of the theatre:

> ... The theatre is also (and I believe especially) an art of socio-political criticism and thus a medium of popular education. It has the capacity to transform a scene into a mirror mimicking customs, social flaws, or malfunctions--whether normal or provoked--of certain social structures, beliefs and behavior. Or, in contrast, it can praise positive, humane values. The theatre should be for us a proud, communal force for social transformation.(48)

Among theatre participants throughout Niger, I found recurring statements about social consciousness as the purpose of theatre, supporting Mariko's view. Nawaki Abdou, the **animateur** at the **Maison des Jeunes** in Matameye, quoted the proverb, "Zuwa da kai ya hi sak'o" (Coming yourself beats a message). Seeing a play, he felt, was far better than hearing what it had to say:

> Because of the theatre, yes, the times are changing now. Years ago, people preferred to laugh at plays. But now they want to be shown the problems of the people of this country.(49)

As quoted in Chapter II, Mahamadou Lido of Mainé Soroa also emphasized the instructive purpose of the plays. When asked what benefits actors receive from their work in the theatre, he responded:

> What do we get from it? First of all, we know that we are doing the work of our country. That is, if a person comes ... and puts his best efforts toward the nation's struggle, that is useful.(50)

A primary school inspector in Maradi, Kaka Doka, had this to say about the purpose of the theatre:

> There are bad things in this world that are done and perhaps if they do a play with a good idea, because of that play, a person will see that he must stop what he is doing, that people don't condone that action. So it happens that he will leave that road and return to a good road because of the play. Also we laugh, but laughter alone isn't enough. It is not for us alone, no, we do it to put a person back on the right road.(51)

Alhassane Yacouba, a member of the **samariya** in Dogondoutchi, which does not produce plays, described his reactions as a spectator in similar terms.

> For myself, well, in the actions of a play, I understand the comic things. In the plays, if you watch them, even if you don't do them, if you watch them you will see there is progress in them. What progress? It's.... You see things you've never seen before, and you hear things you've never heard before. In my opinion, the theatre is a very interesting thing with progress incorporated into it.(52)

That governmental officials and villagers, actors and spectators share this faith in the theatre as a force for change reflects the range of this dramatic art form. Although a comparatively new introduction to Niger, theatre in national languages has demonstrated a unique ability to bring diverse social groups into contact with one another--men and women, members of different age and ethnic groups, people with western education and those who have never been to school--to work on current issues. The plays they produce fuse serious themes and humor within a broad continuum from local communities' comedies to the nationalistic festival pieces. The troupes adjust their work to their audience, spicing it with more comic improvisation when entertainment is primary, or intensifying the key moments of instruction when that purpose becomes paramount.

Audiences flock to the **Maisons des Jeunes**, listen to the radio serials week after week, and crowd around television sets to watch plays. The plays involve spectators in their messages through familiar language, settings, costumes, characters and incidents. Comic actions sustain audience attention while serious themes and satiric references engage their thought. Nigeriens appreciate the artistic abilities of actors in improvising new versions of well known stories and character types. They enjoy the performances of friends and neighbors in community productions as well as the skills and talents of famous actors from other towns. Within only a few years, the troupes have earned both this immense popularity and their praise.

ENDNOTES: CHAPTER V

1. J.L. Styan, DRAMA, STAGE AND AUDIENCE (London: Cambridge University Press, 1975), p. 11.
2. Bernard Beckerman, DYNAMICS OF DRAMA: THEORY AND METHOD OF ANALYSIS (New York: Alfred A. Knopf, 1970), pp. 22-27.
3. Beckerman, p. 24.
4. Beckerman, p. 135.
5. Performance notes, Zinder, Niger, 21 June 1981 and 31 July 1981.
6. The price of admission to local plays was usually 100 or 200 francs (CFA) in 1980-81, equivalent to that of most films. Tickets for the Diffa Festival were 3,000 francs ($12) for the seven evening performances, or 500 francs for a single evening. I was always admitted to performances as a guest without charge and usually shown to the reserved seats.
7. Interview with Alhaji Zoubeirou Lawal, Mainé Soroa, Niger, 18 April 1981.
8. MADAME SIDIKOU, performance by the CEG Troupe, Tchin Tabaraden, Niger, 17 December 1980.
9. **Ballet** Entry of the **Département** of Agadez for the National Festival in Diffa, Niger, 10 April 1981; **Ballet** Entry of the **Département** of Dosso for the Diffa Festival, 9 April 1981.
10. Interview with the director, several teachers and members of the students' troupe of the CEG, Tchin Tabaraden, Niger, conducted by Aboubacar Mahamane, 18 December 1981.
11. Interview with Yazi Dogo, Zinder, Niger, 14 August 1981.
12. GADO K'ARHIN ALLA, performance by the Troupe Amadou 'Dan Bassa at the **Maison des Jeunes** (MJC), Zinder, Niger, 13 September 1981.
13. DARAJAR K'ASA AL'ADARTA, performance by the Radio Club Troupe at the MJC, Zinder, Niger, 21 June 1981.
14. ALHAJI SHAGALI, performance by the Troupe from Mainé Soroa at the National Festival in Diffa, Niger, 12 April 1981.
15. BA GA IRINTA BA, performance by the Troupe Amadou 'Dan Bassa at the National Festival in Niamey, Niger, April 1980.
16. TALALA MAI KAMAN SAKE, performance by the Troupe Amadou 'Dan Bassa at the National Festival in Diffa, Niger, 8 April 1981.

17. Performance notes, TALALA MAI KAMAN SAKE, in Tanout, Niger (9 March 1981), and in Diffa (8 April 1981).
18. Performance notes, MJC, Zinder, 13 September 1981.
19. Performance notes, Zinder, 21 June 1981. See also the discussion in Chapter II, pp. 76-8.
20. TALALA MAI KAMAN SAKE, performances in Tanout (9 March 1981), Diffa (8 April 1981), and Maradi (1 September 1981).
21. 'DAN KWANGILA, performance by the Troupe from Maradi at the National Festival in Diffa, Niger, 9 April 1981.
22. Rehearsal notes, MJC, Zinder, 2 April 1981.
23. Performance notes, TALALA MAI KAMAN SAKE, in Diffa, 8 April 1981.
24. Performance notes, KUSKURE KARATU NE (10 April 1981), WALWALE (7 April 1981), and 'DAN KWANGILA (9 April 1981), at the National Festival in Diffa, Niger.
25. GIRMAN KAI RAWANIN TSIYA, performance by the Troupe Amadou 'Dan Bassa at the MJC, Zinder, Niger, 12 September 1981.
26. Interview with Alhaji Abdousalam Adam, President of the 1981 WASAN KARA, Zinder, Niger, 30 June 1981.
27. Performance notes, MJC, Zinder, 12 September 1981.
28. Personal communication, November 1983.
29. Interview with Alhaji Abdousalam Adam, conducted by Aboubacar Mahamane, Zinder, Niger, 13 January 1981.
30. Alhaji Abdousalam Adam, 13 January 1981.
31. Alhaji Abdousalam Adam, 13 January 1981.
32. BA GA IRINTA BA, performance in Niamey, April 1980 (Scene 5).
33. COHABITATION ENTRE ELEVEURS ET CULTIVATEURS, performance by the Troupe from Matameye in Tanout, Niger, 7 March 1981; COHABITATION ENTRE ELEVEURS ET CULTIVATEURS, performance by the Troupe from Magaria in Tanout, 10 March 1981. The plays were remarkably similar in more than their titles; much off-stage discussion went on as to which troupe stole the theme from the other.
34. TALALA MAI KAMAN SAKE, performance in Tanout, 9 March 1981 (Scenes 3 and 7).

35. At the conclusion of the Diffa Festival, President Kountché invited the winning troupes to Niamey to perform for him along with an audience of invited guests, including the Diplomatic Corps, the faculty of the University of Niamey, and the higher levels of government officials, many of whom had not made the difficult journey to Diffa.

36. The **Inspecteur de la Jeunesse** for the Zinder **Département** gave me blank copies of the judges' score sheets and their final determinations of rank for the plays, **ballets**, instrumental ensembles and songs for the **Eliminatoires** held in Tanout in March 1981. The government has published a guide for the festival, but I was unable to obtain a copy.

37. Yazi Dogo, 14 August 1981.

38. Interview with members of the Troupe Théâtrale de Mainé Soroa, 17 April 1981.

39. Alhaji Zoubeirou Lawal, 17 April 1981.

40. Alhaji Zoubeirou Lawal, 17 April 1981.

41. Interview with Yazi Dogo and Abdou Louché, conducted by David Hofstad for the Voice of America, Niamey, Niger, 30 October 1981.

42. Kégitigui A. Mariko, "Le Cinquième Festival National de la Jeunesse--1980--Essai d'examen critique des prestations des Troupes engagées--Observations et suggestions pour l'avenir," Unpublished paper (Niamey, 1980), p. 2. The original French:

> Les thèmes sont libres mais doivent s'inspirer des réalités ou aspirations nigériennes. Les thèmes sont laissés à l'appréciation des créateurs, mais doivent s'inspirer du patrimoine culturel nigérien. Les compositions tiendront compte des préoccupations culturelles, économiques et sociales du pays.

43. "Message adressé à la Nation par S.E. le Colonel Seyni Kountché, Président du Conseil Militaire Suprême, Chef de l'Etat, à l'occasion du huitième anniversaire de la prise de pouvoir par les Forces Armées Nationales," SAHEL HEBDO, 15 avril 1982, p. 15. The original French:

> Le premier fut tout d'abord celui de sensibiliser nos jeunes aux palpitantes réalités de notre Niger nouveau. Nos idéaux d'unité et de fraternité, l'amour de la Patrie, la mystique du travail, la vigilance dans la préservation de notre sécurité et l'affirmation éclatante de notre identité bref, tous nos mots d'ordre comme nos leitmotiv se sont trouvés magnifiés et la conscience nationale largement exaltée....
> Le deuxième objectif procède en l'occurrence, de la nécessité de doter chacun de nos départements, d'infrastructures sociales, culturelles et sportives, indispensables à l'épanouissement du corps et de l'esprit....
> Le troisième objectif, sans doute le principal, est celui de la réhabilitation de notre patrimoine culturel, que l'action dissolvante de certaines moeurs lointaines et les errements d'une certaine société de consommation ont tenté d'occulter et de désagréger. Là aussi, le festival a servi de tremplin à une irréversible et remarquable renaissance de notre philosophie.

44. Babacar L. Mariko, "La fête de toute la jeunesse," LE SAHEL, 14-15 février 1981, p. 8. The original French:

> Il présente la particularité positive d'être la fête de la jeunesse tout entière (urbaine et rurale, filles et garçons, lettrés ou analphabètes), homogénéisée et égalitarisée par l'identite de leurs conditions d'existence, de leurs moyens d'expression et par l'idéal commun de porter le plus haut

possible l'originalité de sa nigérienneté.

45. Dan-Inna Chaibou, "La Théâtralité en Pays Hawsa," Memoire de Maîtrise, Université Nationale de Côte d'Ivoire, 1978-79. See discussion of Chaibou's work and his synopses of several plays in Chapter I, pp. 40-45.
46. Interview with Yazi Dogo and Abdou Louché, Zinder, Niger, 22 April 1981.
47. Interview with members of the Troupe Théâtrale de Mainé Soroa, conducted by Aboubacar Mahamane, 18 April 1981.
48. Babacar L. Mariko, p. 8.

> ... le théâtre est aussi (et surtout je crois) un art de la critique socio-politique et c'est en cela qu'il est un médium d'éducation populaire. Pour sa capacité à transformer une scène en un mirroir mettant en jeu les moeurs, les tares sociales, les disfonctionnements normaux ou provoqués de certaines structures de la société, certaines croyances et des comportements négatifs, ou au contraire en exaltant d'autres valeurs parce que humainement positives. Le théâtre devrait être chez nous une force de transformation sociale collective et profonde.

49. Interview with Nawaki Abdou and members of the Troupe Théâtrale de Matameye, conducted by Aboubacar Mahamane, 17 January 1981. His original statement in Hausa:

> Saboda shi teyatur, e, yanzu zamani ya sauya. Teyatur 'din da, wato an hi son na dariya. Na yanzu ko, an hi son wanda za a gwada laihin kaman mutanen k'asa.

50. Mahamadou Lido, Mainé Soroa, 18 April 1981. His original statement in Hausa:

>Amfanin da munkai? Na 'daya mun san aikin k'asa nan munkai. Ke nan mutum in ya zo ... ya kawo nashi k'ok'ari cikin aikin k'asa, to ya yi amfani.

51. Interview with members of the Troupe Théâtrale de Maradi, conducted by Aboubacar Mahamane, 8 January 1981. Kaka Doka's original statement in Hausa:

>Akwai su haraka da duniya da ake yi to, kila, in an yi théâtre wato dubara masu kyau ba don an yi théâtre wanda ya ga kamar haraka nan da shike yi yana hita, mutane wato ba su yarda da irin wannan haraka ba, shi ne samu shi ke nan shi hito wancan hanyarshi shi koma hanya mai kyau saboda shi ne théâtre nan. Kuma ana dariya, to dariyarmu kuma 'dai bai isa ba. Ba mu 'dai wato an yi shi na a maida mutum na hanya daidai.

52. Interview with members of the Samariya of Dogondoutchi, conducted by Aboubacar Mahamane, 14 December 1980. Alhassane Yacouba's original statement in Hausa:

>To ni, lalle, cikin haraka teyatur, na gane abu na mai ban dariya. Cikin shi teyatur, in kana kallon shi, ko ba ka yin shi, in kana kallon shi za a k'aruwa a ciki. Me ya k'aruwa? Saboda ... ka ga abin da ba ka ta'ba gani ba, kuma ka ji abin da ba ka ta'ba ji ba. Cikin zancenai teyatur dai abu ne mai ban sha'awa da k'aruwa ciki.

CONCLUSION
GADO K'ARHIN ALLA
(Inheritance, Strength from God)

Hausa theatre in Niger is creating a new form of oral art, making use of both traditional and inherited western forms and adapting them to the social changes and needs of a developing nation-state. The oral nature and the communal development of the plays provide the flexibility that is the basis for their popularity among diverse audiences throughout the country. This theatre is an eclectic art, drawing from traditional ceremonies, current community problems, history, politics, satiric poetry, radio commentaries, oral narratives, **bori** spirit possession, French comedy, observations of people in daily life. Anything which troupe members know, experience or can research may be incorporated into their work. The test of the effectiveness of any new idea will be the troupe's reactions and modifications, and later, the audience's responses. The plays change continuously through this interaction, revealing fresh insights and humor to audiences in every new performance. Yet once developed, a play retains its own identity: a theme, a series of characters and incidents crafted into a unique pattern. A play may rest for months or years without performance, but it remains within the troupe's repertoire to create again whenever they wish.

One of the most successful of the Hausa plays, GADO K'ARHIN ALLA, epitomizes this tradition. First produced in the early 1970's by the Troupe Amadou 'Dan Bassa of Zinder, the play was chosen to represent Niger at FESTAC in Lagos in 1977, and it was among the first of the plays to be videotaped when television was introduced in 1979. The troupe still performs it on occasion in Zinder; I was privileged to observe one such unrehearsed performance in September 1981.(1) Locally, nationally, and internationally, GADO K'ARHIN ALLA has demonstrated a universal appeal in its union of traditional and topical elements, its merging of ritual, comedy, and political instruction.

The troupe has taken a traditional process, the election of a **sarki** (chief), and created a fictional drama from it divided into scenes like those of conventional western plays. This use of traditional custom as the basis of plays and of **ballets** dates back to the early Ponty School's dramatic productions and the French encouragement of indigenous themes for them.

In the first scene of GADO K'ARHIN ALLA, the old **sarki** dies after calling on his courtiers to see that his favorite son, Baydu, succeeds him. The courtiers convene in the second scene to discuss the other eligible princes, and the **sous-préfet** for the district comes to establish the official list of candidates. Scenes 3 and 4 follow the comic attempts of two of the princes to guarantee their own election: Mushe (Monsieur) uses his **fonctionnaire** position to bribe his influential friends with grain from the government, and Shaho (hawk) seeks a series of magical aids to insure his success. In Scene 5, the **préfet** announces the government's choice of Salihi (honesty) as **sarki**, and he is installed formally by the ritual official who dresses him in the **sarki's** robes and turban. The other princes meet later to protest his election, but they are interrupted by Salihi's messenger commanding them to come to the court. (Scene 6) In Scene 7, Salihi awards each of the princes a new title and asks that they all work in harmony together. Scene 8 presents a mimed portrayal of the **hawan daba** (durbar), with the princes mounted on horseback saluting the new **sarki**.

This play incorporates far more ritual material than any of the other plays I saw in 1980 and 1981. The use of music, mime, and the representations of the durbar and the installation ceremony greatly enrich the production and connect it to events which are still important parts of Hausa culture. As Dan-Inna Chaibou describes the installation ceremony, it is itself a drama with the **sarki** and the **doka** playing formal, ritual roles.(2) The troupe places these symbolic actions within a scene that also includes the secular formalities of governmental speeches to the assembled villagers.

Conclusion

In addition to the ritual forming the basis of Scenes 5 and 8, the troupe includes authentic details which recall real customs, such as the **jekahwadiya's** shrill wailing announcing the **sarki's** death in Scene 1. Shaho prays at the beginning of Scene 4, an action which establishes a familiar Muslim context, in contrast to the charlatans he sends for later in the scene. The **boka's** wild incantations on Shaho's behalf take the comedy beyond specific traditional practices; Ibrahim "Gliss" Tando's uninhibited **boka** parodies false **malams**, magicians, "pagans" and foreigners of all types.(3) Yet Boka's antics indirectly parody **bori** spirit possession as well, a practice still very much a part of Hausa communities although it is accepted with varying degrees of belief and respect. Thus, within the same play, the troupe represents seriously certain aspects of traditional Hausa culture lending verisimilitude to the **sarki's** death and the election procedure, while the actors choose other customs to satirize in comic portrayal. A complex balance results which both respects the audience's sense of propriety and indulges their sense of humor.

The troupe further fuses their theme of the traditional process of election with topical political concerns. As the courtiers argue with one another over the eligibility of the princes in Scene 2, the **waziri** reminds them that the court no longer has control of the election, that the national officials will make the final choice.(4) In the scenes that follow, the play demonstrates the wisdom of the government's choice and the ideal harmony between traditional rulers and the modern state. This message appears structurally in the corrupt actions of Mushe (Scene 3) and the folly of Shaho (Scene 4), which are immediately juxtaposed with the **sous-préfet's** speech admonishing against corruption and the **préfet's** speech warning against hasty actions and announcing Salihi as **sarki**. Salihi's pronouncements in this investiture scene (Scene 5), and later as he awards his brothers titles to forestall their enmity (Scene 7), also contrast with the other princes' actions--their comic attempts to sway the election and their conspiracy afterwards to try to oust him from power.(Scene 6) The troupe unequivocally aligns the government's power of selection with the superior moral qualities of Salihi, the administration's choice.

Within this overall theme of authoritative harmony, the troupe incorporates discussion of current problems, primarily the Sahelian drought of the 1970's. Mushe's offical duty is to distribute grain provided by the government and the international relief agencies to the people who are suffering as a result of the drought. However, he ignores the group of poor and crippled people who come to beg for food, while he arranges to transfer a truckload of grain to his rich friend to sell and gives several sacks to his well-dressed mistress, Alhajiya.(Scene 3) This is a highly comic scene but it nonetheless indicts Mushe's corruption. Other topical references appear in the serious speeches by the government officials in Scene 5, including appeals for national unity and cooperation with Nigeria and warnings against treachery and selfishness during the difficult times brought by the drought.

As with all of this troupe's plays, the instructive messages are masterfully blended with comedy throughout GADO K'ARHIN ALLA. Mushe's and Shaho's scenes center in comic activity, but even the more serious scenes include humorous elements. The **liman** in Scenes 1 and 2 is played by Ibrahimm "Gliss" Tando as a slightly foolish old man, not quite understanding what is going on around him.(5) In Scene 5, as the announcement of the new **sarki** is about to be made, all the candidates leap up and run to the microphone with silly smiles of anticipation, except Salihi who sits waiting with appropriate modesty. Among the princes in Scenes 2, 5, 6 and 7, appears Juju (fetich), a prince by birth but a fool. He wears tattered robes, stumbles through the formal meetings, eats meat while lying on his back in the middle of serious discussions, and yet constantly demands his rights as a prince. Salihi wisely confers upon him the title of **Sarkin Kassuwa**, chief of the market, allowing him to eat whatever and wherever he likes at will.(Scene 7) Through a few brief but well-placed appearances, Juju provides comic relief to the serious political process of the election.(6)

The play's structural framework follows the normal social process of a Hausa election. In Victor Turner's terms for social drama, the breach in the ordinary functioning of the society occurs with the death of the reigning **sarki**.(Scene 1)

Conclusion

The crisis emerges in the competition among the princes (Scenes 2, 3 and 4); the redressive action appears in the **préfet's** choice of the new **sarki** and the ritual installation.(Scene 5) This play emphasizes the reconciliation phase by re-introducing the crisis--the princes' continuing dissatisfaction with the choice of Salihi.(Scene 6) It then provides a transformation of their discontent into reconciliation through Salihi's diplomacy in granting his brothers the titles to high offices in his court.(Scene 7) The final scene further strengthens this reintegration through the durbar's symbolic salute of allegiance.(Scene 8)(7)

Within this process and its parallel to actual events in a Hausa community, the troupe uses conventional scenes and devices from the developing theatrical tradition. The **sarki's** court where pronouncements are made (Scenes 2, 5 and 7), the gossip scene among the princes (Scene 7), and the domestic scenes with their series of visitors (Scenes 3 and 4) are all stock units which the troupe adapts to its particular purposes in this play. Here, the court scenes introduce and then resolve the conflict of the election; the domestic scenes, including the gossip session, further that conflict. The ritual elements--music, rich costumes, and formal actions--emphasize the dual resolution, first in the election results (Scene 5), and then in the personal reconciliation of the contending princes.(Scenes 7 and 8)

Repetition, a technique important both to drama and to the oral narrative tradition, also forms a crucial part of the play's structure. As noted in Chapter III, Shaho's adventures involve a series of encounters with magicians who he believes can guarantee his election. The repetitions of his attempts, physically portrayed one after another and then verbally related to his friend, add to the comedy of his folly.(Scene 4) On the serious side, the speeches during the installation ceremony by the **sous-préfet, préfet, sarki,** and **député** repeat and reinforce one another's messages and the solemnity of the event.(Scene 5) The troupe has developed the score of the play with these types of repetition as central elements--stressing both the message and the comedy. Even to Hausa audiences who may be unfamiliar with western staged drama, the troupe's use of repetition as a basic structuring device recalls the oral tradition that audience members know well, allowing them to anticipate the play's actions and experience its deeper themes.

Animating this framework of scenes are the roles created by the troupe's talented actors. GADO K'ARHIN ALLA presents a classic set of characters, both serious and comic. The serious types include the traditional authorities (the **sarki** and his courtiers) and the governmental officials (the **préfet, sous-préfet,** and **député**). Salihi joins them as the ideal choice for **sarki**--honest and wise, reconciling all conflict from the start of his rule. Balancing these serious roles are the comic types: the handicapped beggars; Juju, the crazy prince; La'ba'ba, the bumbling servant; Malam Gobe da Nisa, the false **malam**; Boka, the foreign charlatan; Mushe, the corrupt **fonctionnaire**; Shaho, the superstitious dupe. These character types derive from Hausa stereotypes of people in everyday life: the city man--here, Mushe--as a swindler; servants as stupid; insane people as comic. The types also resemble characters common in the narrative tradition: the wise prince, the stupid trickster who is duped, the clever **malam**, and so on. These types have all entered the dramatic tradition, sometimes directly in their customary form (Salihi), and at other times in contemporary guise (Mushe).

Yet, unlike most of the later plays I observed, this one has no central character. The princes competing for power share the stage and each dominates a different scene. Mushe and Shaho satirize the newly educated, westernized elite and the traditional elite respectively, while Salihi portrays the ideal qualities of a **sarki** without comic flaws. In this respect, the play presents the troupe's communal talent perhaps most clearly of all their productions. The men at the head of the troupe--Yazi Dogo, Abdou Louché, Oumarou Nainou, Kailou Bako, Ibrahim "Gliss" Tando--have developed a variety of roles matched to their individual abilities, rather than creating a star vehicle for just one of them (as BA GA IRINTA BA is for Oumarou Nainou as Mamman Arrivé, or TALALA MAI KAMAN SAKE is for Yazi Dogo as Talala). The scenic structure of GADO K'ARHIN ALLA and its balance among the princes allows each of these skilled actors to improvise within the limits of one or two scenes. Yazi Dogo plays both Prince Mushe, speaking in a comic mixture of French and Hausa and strutting about in his western business suit, and later the **boka's** interpreter. Abdou Louché lends his deep voice and most serious demeanor to the absurd orders of Malam Gobe da Nisa. Oumarou Nainou provides a foil to Shaho as his friend, as well as playing the exemplary Salihi. Kailou Bako as Shaho and Ibrahim "Gliss" Tando as Boka rival each other in outrageous nonsense.(8)

In 1981, for their home audience who knew the play very well, these actors performed with far greater abandon than for the television videotape in 1979. The live audience's anticipation electrified their performance, making it difficult to judge who was enjoying it most. The emphasis was very much on the comic performances, the audience watching well-known actors in roles they had played many times before, since the story and political message of the play were quite familiar.(9)

The television performance was more stately and more lavishly produced than the local one. Filming allowed changes of location for the different scenes; the **sarki's** room was decorated authentically with rugs and tapestries on the wall, and Mushe's visitors met him on the porch of a modern house. The staged performance in Zinder suggested these locations with less detail--a rug for the **sarki** to lie on (Scene 1), and the conventional string chairs for Mushe's house.(Scene 3) After experiencing the **boka** and Shaho hopping all over the stage and leaping toward the audience, yelling "Yubana!"--I found the taped version of the scene cramped. It was done in a small room, giving less latitude to Gliss's wild gestures (Scene 4), besides being removed from the spectator because of the medium itself. The costumes for the videotaped production were more elegant in sumptuous fabrics; they were the quality of robes that the troupe had aspired to obtain the day they searched Zinder for appropriate apparel.(10)

The elaboration of the production for national television reinforced the ritual aspects of the play, the message linking symbolic Hausa customs to the contemporary political hierarchy. This message has universal connotations in the union of the past with the modern nation-state. The mimed salute on wooden horses, the court musicians playing instruments associated exclusively with royalty, the magnificent costumes of the princes, and the

robes and turban tied in the unique fashion of a
sarki--all contribute to the play's invocation of
tradition, whether for a Hausa audience which knows
the symbolic associations, or for people outside
that particular culture who still sense the solemn
significance. Woven around this central theme is
the comedy ranging from the slapstick, physical
humor of Juju, or La'ba'ba or Boka, to the linguistic chicanery of the **boka's** interpreter. The
Troupe Amadou 'Dan Bassa has created an intricate
pattern indeed of comedy and political message in
GADO K'ARHIN ALLA.

The Hausa theatrical tradition continues to
evolve. Even within the few short years between
the creation of GADO K'ARHIN ALLA, the plays
Chaibou discusses, and those that I saw, changes
have taken place. GADO K'ARHIN ALLA has only two
minor women's roles, and one of these--Mushe's
mistress--does not appear in the 1973 transcription, implying a later addition. By 1981, the same
troupe had eight actresses, several of whom had
significant roles in TALALA MAI KAMAN SAKE. From
GADO K'ARHIN ALLA'S focus on the drought and relief
efforts, and Chaibou's accounts of plays praising
the downfall of the corrupt civilian regime, the
plays have moved on to portray optimistic development plans. Active construction efforts appear in
'DAN KWANGILA, ALHAJI SHAGALI, and WALWALE; the
extension of the health care system provides a
backround to KOWA YA BUGI RUWA IDONAY; the efforts
of an entire community to improve their local
schools propels the action of BA GA IRINTA BA.
These plays continue to focus on the problems
within development efforts, but they also try to
suggest changes and innovative ways of solving
those problems. New themes continually join the
repertoire of this theatre along with corresponding
modifications of its characters, scenes, and
conventions.

As a popular art form, the Hausa theatre in
Niger has an enormous potential for future development. The troupes' open membership and their basis
in the **samariyas** give individual communities a
strong voice in their work. Government support has
encouraged the growth of new troupes and promoted
their patriotic themes. Yet once nurtured, such a
theatre takes on a life of its own. It may forge a
national consensus on certain issues, but it also

Conclusion

creates a potential forum for criticism, one that would be difficult to control. The Hausa troupes have successfully joined humor with vital social commentary, traditional theatrical forms with western drama. They have captivated diverse audiences and earned national respect. With so rich a heritage behind them and such strong support at present, the Hausa theatre will play a key role in Niger's future.

Conclusion

ENDNOTES: CONCLUSION

1. GADO K'ARHIN ALLA, performance by the Troupe Amadou 'Dan Bassa at the MJC, Zinder, Niger, 13 September 1981. The videotape of the 1979 performance is in the ORTN Archives, Niamey. Aboubacar Mahamane's transcription of a 1973 performance has been published by CELHTO, GAADOO K'ARHIN ALLAA (Niamey, 1977)--the only Nigerien play in Hausa published to date.
2. See Chapter I, pp. 13-16; Dan-Inna Chaibou, "La Théâtralité en Pays Hawsa," Memoire de Maitrise, Université Nationale de Côte d'Ivoire (1978-79), pp. 20-2.
3. See Chapter IV, pp. 198-200.
4. See Chapter IV, p. 176-7, for this speech.
5. See Chapter IV, pp. 191; 197-200 for discussion of Ibrahim "Gliss" Tando as a comedian.
6. GADO K'ARHIN ALLA, performance in Zinder, 13 September 1981, and the ORTN videotape, 1979. The role of Juju was played by Mamane Lawal who specializes in crazy characters (see Chapter IV, p. 186).
7. See discussion of Turner's terms and social drama models in Chapter III, pp. 151-4.
8. See Chapter IV, pp. 176-8; 188; 190-1; 198-200.
9. GADO K'ARHIN ALLA, performance 13 September 1981. Abdou Louché was not in town the evening of this performance, and members of the troupe felt Scene 3 was not at all the same without him in the role of Malam Gobe da Nisa.
10. See discussion in Chapter V, pp. 244-6, and in Chapter II, pp. 104-5.

BIBLIOGRAPHY

Abraham, R.C. DICTIONARY OF THE HAUSA LANGUAGE. London: University of London Press, 1962.
Acquaye, Saka. "The Language Problem of the Developing African Theater." AFRICAN ARTS, II, no. 1 (Autumn 1968), 58-9.
Adedeji, J.A. "Oral Tradition and the Contemporary Theater in Nigeria." RESEARCH IN AFRICAN LITERATURES, 2, no. 2 (Fall 1971), 134-49.
AFRICAN LITERATURE TODAY: DRAMA IN AFRICA, no. 8 (1976).
Ahmed, Umaru, and Bello Daura. AN INTRODUCTION TO CLASSICAL HAUSA AND THE MAJOR DIALECTS. Zaria, Nigeria: Northern Nigerian Publishing Company, 1970.
Ahmed, Umaru Balarabe. BORA DA MOWA. Zaria, Nigeria: Northern Nigerian Publishing Company, 1972.
Akyea, E.O. "The Atwia-Ekumfi Kodzidan: An Experimental African Theatre." OKYEAME, IV, no. 1 (December 1968), 82-84.
Amadou, Diado. MAIMOU OU LE DRAME DE L'AMOUR. Niamey, Niger: Imprimerie Générale du Niger, 1972.
Amon d'Aby, F.-J., Bernard Dadié and G. Coffi Gadeau. LE THEATRE POPULAIRE EN REPUBLIQUE DE COTE-D'IVOIRE. Abidjan, Ivory Coast: Centre Culturel et Folklorique de Côte d'Ivoire, 1966.
Aristotle. POETICS. Trans. Gerald F. Else. Ann Arbor: University of Michigan Press, 1977.
'Balewa, (Alhaji Sir) Abubakar Tafawa, Umaru Ladan and Dexter Lyndersay. SHAIHU UMAR. Zaria, Nigeria: Northern Nigerian Publishing Company, 1974.
Bame, K.N. "Drama and Theatre in Traditional African Societies." THE CONCH, VI, no. 1-2 (1974), 80-98.
Banham, Martin and Clive Wake. AFRICAN THEATRE TODAY. London: Pitman Publishing Ltd., 1976.
Barry, Jackson G. DRAMATIC STRUCTURE: THE SHAPING OF EXPERIENCE. Berkeley: University of California Press, 1970.
Beckerman, Bernard. DYNAMICS OF DRAMA: THEORY AND METHOD OF ANALYSIS. New York: Alfred A. Knopf, 1970.

Beeman, William O. "Why Do They Laugh? An Interactional Approach to Humor in Traditional Iranian Improvisatory Theater." JOURNAL OF AMERICAN FOLKLORE, 94, no. 374 (1981), 506-26.

Bentley, Eric. "The Psychology of Farce." Introduction to LET'S GET A DIVORCE! AND OTHER PLAYS. New York: Hill and Wang, 1958, pp. vii-xx.

Besmer, Fremont E. "Boɗrii: structure and process in performance." FOLIA ORIENTALIA, Tome XVI (1975), 101-30.

Bovin, Mette. "Ethnic Performances in Rural Niger: An Aspect of Ethnic Boundary Maintenance." FOLK (Denmark), Vol. 16-17 (1974-75), 459-74.

Brink, James Thomas. "Organizing Satirical Comedy in Kote-tlon: Drama as a Communication Strategy Among the Bamana of Mali." Diss. Indiana University 1980.

Brook, Peter. THE EMPTY SPACE. New York: Atheneum, 1969.

Centre d'Etudes Linguistique et Historique par Tradition Orale. "Final Report: Meeting of Experts on the Harmonization of the Orthography of the Hausa Language." Niamey, Niger: Organization of African Unity, January 1980.

Chaibou, Dan-Inna. "La Théâtralite en Pays Hawsa." Memoire de Maîtrise, Université Nationale de Côte d'Ivoire 1978-79.

Clark, J.P. "Aspects of Nigerian Drama." In AFRICAN WRITERS ON AFRICAN WRITING. Ed. G.O. Killam. Evanston: Northwestern University Press, 1966, pp. 19-32.

Collins, E.J. "Comic Opera in Ghana." AFRICAN ARTS, IX, no. 2 (January 1976), 50-7.

Cornevin, R. LE THEATRE EN AFRIQUE NOIRE ET A MADAGASCAR. Paris: le livre africain, 1970.

Corrigan, Robert W., ed. COMEDY: MEANING AND FORM. San Francisco: Chandler Publishing Co., 1965.

Crow, Brian, and Michael Etherton. "Wasan manoma: Community Theatre in the Soba District, Kaduna State." SAVANNA, 8, no. 1 (June 1979), 5-12.

Dandobi, Mahamane. "L'Aventure d'une chèvre: pièce satirique en quatre tableaux." TRAITS D'UNION (Dakar), no. 9 (1955), 76-83.

Bibliography

Decalo, Samuel. HISTORICAL DICTIONARY OF NIGER. Metuchen, New Jersey: The Scarecrow Press, 1979.

'Dan Goggo, (Malam) Adamu, and (Malam) Dauda Kano. TABARMAR KUNYA: A HAUSA COMEDY. Zaria, Nigeria: Northern Nigerian Publishing Company, 1975.

Distler, Paul Antonie. "The Rise and Fall of the Racial Comics in American Vaudeville." Diss. Tulane University 1963.

Duchartre, Pierre Louis. THE ITALIAN COMEDY. 1929; rpt. New York: Dover Publications, 1966.

Edebiri, Unionmwan. "French Contributions to African Drama." RESEARCH IN AFRICAN LITERATURES, 6, no. 1 (Spring 1975), 40-3.

Esslin, Martin. AN ANATOMY OF DRAMA. New York: Hill and Wang, 1976.

Frye, Northrop. "The Mythos of Spring." ANATOMY OF CRITICISM: FOUR ESSAYS. Princeton: Princeton University Press, 1957.

GAADOO K'ARHIN ALLAA (Wasan Kwaykoyoo na Zinder a 1973). Transcription by Abuubakar Mahamman. Niamey, Niger: Centre d'Etudes Linguistique et Historique par Tradition Orale, 1977.

Gidley, C.G.B. "**Rok'o**: A Hausa Praise Crier's Account of His Craft." AFRICAN LANGUAGE STUDIES, 16 (1975), 93-115.

"'**Yankamanci**--The Craft of the Hausa Comedians." AFRICAN LANGUAGE STUDIES, 8 (1967), 52-81.

Goffman, Erving. FRAME ANALYSIS: AN ESSAY ON THE ORGANIZATION OF EXPERIENCE. New York: Harper & Row, 1974.

Graham-White, Anthony. "The Characteristics of Traditional Drama." YALE/THEATRE, 8, no. 1 (Fall 1976), 11-24.

THE DRAMA OF BLACK AFRICA. New York: Samuel French, Inc., 1974.

"Ritual and Drama in Africa." EDUCATIONAL THEATRE JOURNAL, XXII, no. 4 (December 1970), 339-49.

"West African Drama: Folk, Popular, and Literary." Diss. Stanford 1969.

Hill, Errol. THE TRINIDAD CARNIVAL: MANDATE FOR A NATIONAL THEATRE. Austin: University of Texas Press, 1972.

Hopkins, Nicholas S. "The Modern Theater in
    Mali." PRESENCE AFRICAINE, no. 53 (1965),
    English Edition Vol. 25, 159-93.
  "Persuasion and Satire in the Malian Theatre."
    AFRICA, XLII, no. iii (1972), 217-28.
Iyi-Eweka, Ademola. "The Development of Dramatic
    Troupes in Benin." Diss. University of Wisconsin--Madison 1979.
Johnston, H.A.S., trans., ed. A SELECTION OF
    HAUSA STORIES. Oxford: Clarendon Press, 1966.
Jones-Quartey, K.H.B. "Tragedy and the African
    Audience." OKYEAME, 3, no. 1 (1966), 50-6.
Keita, Joseph. CORRUPTION: PIECE INEDITE EN
    CINQ TABLEAUX. Niamey, Niger: Imprimerie
    Nationale du Niger, n.d.
Kennedy, Scott. IN SEARCH OF AFRICAN THEATRE.
    New York: Charles Scribner's Sons, 1973.
Kidd, Ross. "From Outside In to Inside Out:
    The Benue Workshop on Theatre for Development." THEATERWORK, 2, no. 4 (1982), 44-54.
  "Liberation or domestication: Popular theatre
    and non-formal education in Africa." EDUCATIONAL BROADCASTING INTERNATIONAL, 12, no. 1
    (March 1979), 3-9.
  "People's theatre, conscientisation, and struggle." MEDIA DEVELOPMENT, 27, no. 3 (1980),
    10-14.
King, A.V. "A Bòorìi Liturgy from Katsina."
    AFRICAN LANGUAGE STUDIES, 7 (1967), 105-25.
Kirby, E.T. "Indigenous African Theatre." THE
    DRAMA REVIEW, 18, no. 4 (December 1974),
    22-35.
Kirk-Greene, A.H.M. HAUSA BA DABO BA NE: A COLLECTION OF 500 PROVERBS. Ibadan, Nigeria: Oxford
    University Press, 1966.
  MUTUMIN KIRKII: THE CONCEPT OF THE GOOD MAN IN
    HAUSA. Bloomington, Indiana: Indiana University, African Studies Program, 1974.
Kountché, Seyni (Président). "Message adressé
    à la Nation par S.E. le Colonel Seyni Kountché, Président du Conseil Militaire Suprême,
    Chef de l'Etat, à l'occasion du huitième
    anniversaire de la prise de pouvoir par les
    Forces Armées Nationales," SAHEL HEBDO,
    (Niamey) 15 avril 1982, pp. 10-15.
Labouret, Henri and Moussa Travélé. "Le théâtre
    mandinque (Soudan français)." AFRICA, I, no.
    1 (January 1928), 73-97.

Bibliography

Ladipo, Duro. THREE YORUBA PLAYS: OBA KOSO, OBA MORO, OBA WAJA. English Adaptations by Ulli Beier. Ibadan, Nigeria: Mbari Publications, 1964.
Lea, K.M. ITALIAN POPULAR COMEDY; A STUDY IN THE COMMEDIA DELL'ARTE, 1560-1620 WITH SPECIAL REFERENCE TO THE ENGLISH STAGE. 1934; rpt. New York: Russell and Russell, 1962.
"Les Misères du théâtre au Maroc." JEUNE AFRIQUE. (Tunis) no. 162 (décembre 1963), 28-9.
Leshoai, Bob. "The African Theatre and African Actor: Political Dimension." UMMA. (Nairobi) 5, no. 2 (1975), 107-116.
Mahood, M.M. "Drama in New-Born States." PRESENCE AFRICAINE, English Edition, Vol. 32 (1966), 23-39.
Mariko, Babacar L. "La Fête de toute la jeunesse." LE SAHEL, (Niamey), 14-15 février 1981, pp. 3; 8.
Mariko, Kélitigui A. "Le Cinquième Festival National de la Jeunesse--1980--Essai d'examen critique des prestations des Troupes engagées-observations et suggestions pour l'avenir." (Unpublished paper, Niamey, Niger, 9 mai 1980).
Mark'arfi, (Malam) Shu'aibu. JATAU NA KYALLU. Zaria, Nigeria: Northern Nigerian Publishing Company, 1970.
Mayo, (Alhaji) Muhammadu and Mary Pollock. LADI'S HUSBAND: A PLAY IN TWO ACTS. London: Hodder and Stoughton, 1978.
Meillassoux, Claude. "The 'Koteba' of Bamako." PRESENCE AFRICAINE, English Edition, no. 24 (1964), 38-53.
Monfouga-Nicolas, Jacqueline. AMBIVALENCE ET CULTE DE POSSESSION: CONTRIBUTION A L'ETUDE DU BORI HAUSA. Paris: Editions Anthropos, 1972.
Muhammad, Bello. MALAM MAHAMMAN. Zaria, Nigeria: Northern Nigerian Publishing Company, 1974.
Newman, Paul, et al. SABON K'AMUS NA HAUSA ZUWA TURANCI. Ibadan, Nigeria: Oxford University Press, 1974.
Nicolas, Jacqueline. "LES JUMENTS DES DIEUX": RITES DE POSSESSION ET CONDITION FEMININE EN PAYS HAUSA. Niamey, Niger: Etudes Nigeriennes No. 21, n.d.
Ogunba, Oyin, and Abiola Irele, eds. THEATRE IN AFRICA. Ibadan, Nigeria: Ibadan University Press, 1978.

Oreglia, Giacomo. THE COMMEDIA DELL'ARTE. London: Methuen & Co., 1968.
Pageard, Robert. "Théâtre Africain à Ouagadougou." PRESENCE AFRICAINE, No. 39 (1961), 250-3.
Peacock, James. RITES OF MODERNIZATION: SYMBOLIC AND SOCIAL ASPECTS OF INDONESIAN PROLETARIAN DRAMA. Chicago: University of Chicago Press, 1968.
———. "Society as Narrative." FORMS OF SYMBOLIC ACTION. Ed. Robert F. Spencer. Seattle: University of Washington Press, 1969.
Propp, V. MORPHOLOGY OF THE FOLKTALE. Trans. Laurence Scott. Austin: University of Texas Press, 1968.
Ricard, Alain. "The Concert Party as a Genre: The Happy Stars of Lome." RESEARCH IN AFRICAN LITERATURES, 5, No. 2 (Fall 1974), 165-79.
———. "The ORTF and African Literature." RESEARCH IN AFRICAN LITERATURES, 4, No. 2 (Fall 1973), 189-91.
Ringel, Pierre. MOLIERE EN AFRIQUE NOIRE, OU LE JOURNAL DE QUATRE COMEDIENS. Paris: Presse du livre français, 1951.
Rotimi, Ola. "Traditional Nigerian Drama." In INTRODUCTION TO NIGERIAN LITERATURE. Ed. Bruce King. New York: Africana Publishing Co., 1972.
Roukbah, Bashari Farouk. MATAR MUTUM KABARINSA. Zaria, Nigeria: Northern Nigerian Publishing Company, 1974.
Rowe, Sylvester Ekundayo. "Sierra Leone's Newly--Born Theatre." AFRICAN ARTS, IX, no. 1 (1975), 56-9.
Sada, (Alhaji) Mohammed. UWAR GULMA: A HAUSA PLAY FOR SCHOOLS AND COLLEGES. Zaria, Nigeria: Northern Nigerian Publishing Co., n.d.
Saivre, Denyse de. "Le Théâtre au Niger." RECHERCHE, PEDAGOGIE ET CULTURE, 20 (1975), 42-3.
Salerno, Henry F., trans. SCENARIOS OF THE COMMEDIA DELL'ARTE: FLAMINIO SCALA'S IL TEATRO DELLE FAVOLE RAPPRESENTATIVE. Foreword by Kenneth McKee. New York: New York University Press, 1967.
Salifou, André. TANIMOUNE: DRAME HISTORIQUE EN SEPT ACTES. Paris: Presence Africaine, 1973.

Schechner, Richard. ESSAYS ON PERFORMANCE THEORY, 1970-1976. New York: Drama Book Specialists, 1977.
"Performers and Spectators Transported and Transformed." KENYON REVIEW, 3, no. 4 (1981), 83-113.
Schechner, Richard, and Mady Schuman, eds. RITUAL, PLAY, AND PERFORMANCE: READINGS IN THE SOCIAL SCIENCES/ THEATRE. New York: Seabury Press, 1976.
Scherer, Jacques. "Le théâtre en Afrique noire francophone." In LE THEATRE MODERNE DEPUIS LA DEUXIEME GUERRE MONDIALE. Ed. Jean Jacquot. Paris: Editions du Centre National de la Recherche Scientifique, 1967.
Scheub, Harold. "Body and Image in Oral Narrative Performance." NEW LITERARY HISTORY, VIII (1977), 345-67.
"Oral Narrative Process and the Use of Models." NEW LITERARY HISTORY, VI (1975), 353-77.
"Parallel Image-Sets in African Oral Narrative-Performances." REVIEW OF NATIONAL LITERATURES, 2 (1971), 206-23.
"Performance of Oral Narrative." In FRONTIERS OF FOLKLORE. Ed. William R. Bascom. Boulder, Colorado: Westview Press, 1977.
"The Technique of the Expansible Image in Xhosa **Ntsomi** Performances." RESEARCH IN AFRICAN LITERATURES, I, No. 2 (1970), 119-46.
Serumaga, Robert, and Janet Johnson. "Uganda's Experimental Theater." AFRICAN ARTS, III, No. 3 (Spring 1970), 52-5.
Sigel, John. WASAN BAHAUSHE GASKIYARSA (WHAT THE HAUSA SAYS IN PLAY, HE REALLY MEANS). Madison: University of Wisconsin, African Studies Program Occasional Paper No. 10, 1982.
Skinner, Neil. AN ANTHOLOGY OF HAUSA LITERATURE IN TRANSLATION. Madison: University of Wisconsin, African Studies Program Occasional Paper No. 7, 1977.
trans., ed. HAUSA TALES AND TRADITIONS: AN ENGLISH TRANSLATION OF **TATSUNIYOYI NA HAUSA**, ORIGINALLY COMPLIED BY FRANK EDGAR. Vol. I. London: Frank Cass & Co., 1969. Vols. II and III. Madison: University of Wisconsin Press, 1977.

K'AMUS NA TURANCI DA HAUSA (English-Hausa Dictionary). Zaria, Nigeria: Northern Nigerian Publishing Company, 1970.

"Realism and Fantasy in Hausa Literature." REVIEW OF NATIONAL LITERATURES, II, No. 2 (1971), 167-87.

Smith, M.G. "The Social Functions and Meaning of Hausa Praise Singing." IBADAN, 21 (October 1965), 81-92.

Soyinka, Wole. DEATH AND THE KING'S HORSEMAN. London: Eyre Methuen, 1975.

THE LION AND THE JEWEL. London: Oxford University Press, 1963.

MYTH, LITERATURE AND THE AFRICAN WORLD. London: Cambridge University Press, 1976.

THREE SHORT PLAYS. London: Oxford University Press, 1969.

Stephens, Connie L. "The Relationship of Social Symbols and Narrative Metaphor: A Study of Fantasy and Disguise in the Hausa Tatsuniya of Niger." Diss. University of Wisconsin--Madison 1981.

Styan, J.L. DRAMA, STAGE AND AUDIENCE. London: Cambridge University Press, 1975.

THE ELEMENTS OF DRAMA. London: Cambridge University Press, 1967.

Sypher, Wylie, ed. COMEDY. Garden City, New York: Doubleday & Company, 1956.

THE DRAMA REVIEW: AFRICAN PERFORMANCE ISSUE. (T92), 25, No. 4 (Winter 1981).

THE DRAMA REVIEW: INTERCULTURAL PERFORMANCE ISSUE. (T94), 26, No. 2 (Summer 1982).

Traoré, Bakary. THE BLACK AFRICAN THEATRE AND ITS SOCIAL FUNCTIONS. Trans. Dapo Adelugba. Ibadan, Nigeria: Ibadan University Press, 1972.

Tremearne, A.J.N. THE BAN OF THE BORI: DEMONS AND DEMON-DANCING IN WEST AND NORTH AFRICA. London: Heath, Cranston & Ouseley, 1914.

HAUSA SUPERSTITIONS AND CUSTOMS: AN INTRODUCTION TO THE FOLK-LORE AND THE FOLK. 1913; rpt. London: Frank Cass & Co., 1970.

Turner, Victor, ed. CELEBRATION: STUDIES IN FESTIVITY AND RITUAL. Washington, D.C.: Smithsonian Institution Press, 1982.

Turner, Victor. DRAMAS, FIELDS, AND METAPHORS: SYMBOLIC ACTION IN HUMAN SOCIETY. Ithaca, New York: Cornell University Press, 1974.
Introduction. FORMS OF SYMBOLIC ACTION. Ed. Robert F. Spencer. Seattle: University of Washington Press, 1969.
FROM RITUAL TO THEATRE: THE HUMAN SERIOUSNESS OF PLAY. New York: Performing Arts Journal Publications, 1982.
Waters, Harold A. BLACK AFRICAN THEATER IN FRENCH: A GUIDE. Sherbrooke, Québec: Editions Naaman, 1978.
Yahaya, Ibrahim Yaro. "Nazari Kan Yanayin Wasan Kwaikwayon Hausa." Unpublished Paper from the Conference on Hausa Language and Literature, Center for the Study of Nigerian Languages, Bayero University College, Kano, Nigeria, July 1978.
Yoka, Lye Mu-daba. "Le Griot dans le théâtre africain." AFRIQUE LITTERAIRE ET ARTISTIQUE, No. 40 (1976), 61-9.
Zarrilli, Phillip. THE KATHAKALI COMPLEX: ACTOR, PERFORMANCE, STRUCTURE. New Delhi: Abhinav, 1983.

RECORDED INTERVIEWS

Abdoullahi Bagoudou, Theatre Director. Gaya, Niger. 10 December 1980.
Abdousalam Adam (Alhaji), Director of the Radio Club Troupe. Zinder, Niger. 13 January 1981.
Abdousalam Adam (Alhaji), President of the WASAN KARA. Zinder, Niger. 30 June 1981.
Boubé, Director, Maison des Jeunes. Dogondoutchi, Niger. 12 December 1980.
CEG Student Theatre Troupe. Dogondoutchi, Niger. 12 December 1980.
CEG I Student Theatre Troupe. Tahoua, Niger. 15 December 1980.
CEG Student Theatre Troupe, with their director and several teachers. Tchin Tabaraden, Niger. 18 December 1980.
Chaibou Begu with the director and members of the Troupe Théâtrale, Maison des Jeunes. Maradi, Niger. 27 April 1981.
Director (MJC), the theatre director, and members of the Troupe Théâtrale, Maison des Jeunes. Tahoua, Niger. 15 December 1980.
Director and members of the Troupe Théâtrale, Maison des Jeunes. Madaoua, Niger. 7 January 1981.
Inspecteur de la Jeunesse (Maradi) and two members of the Troupe Théâtrale, Maison des Jeunes. Maradi, Niger. 8 January 1981.
Mahamadou Lido, (Alhaji) Zoubeirou Lawal, and members of the Troupe Théâtrale, Maison des Jeunes. Mainé Soroa, Niger. 18 April 1981.
Nawaki Abdou, Director, and members of the Troupe Théâtrale, Maison des Jeunes. Matameye, Niger. 17 January 1981.
Souley Kanoua (Alhaji), Theatre Director, Maison des Jeunes. Magaria, Niger. 16 January 1981.
Yazi Dogo, Director of the Troupe Amadou 'Dan Bassa, Maison des Jeunes. Zinder, Niger. 14 August 1981.
Yazi Dogo and Abdou Louché of the Troupe Amadou 'Dan Bassa, Maison des Jeunes. Zinder, Niger. 22 April 1981.
Yazi Dogo and Abdou Louché of the Troupe Amadou 'Dan Bassa, interviewed by David Hofstad for the Voice of America. Niamey, Niger. 30 October 1981.

Zakari (Alhaji), Theatre Director, Maison des
    Jeunes. Birni N'Konni, Niger. 22 December
    1980.
Zoubeirou Lawal (Alhaji), Director, and members of
    the Troupe Théâtrale, Maison des Jeunes.
    Mainé Soroa, Niger. 17 April 1981.

     Copies of all of these interviews are
on deposit at IRSH (Institut de Recherches en
Sciences Humaines, Université de Niamey) and
CELHTO in Niamey, as well as in my personal
collection.

RECORDED PLAYS

A KULA DA YARA MAYAN GOBE. Performance by the Troupe Théâtrale de Mirriah. MJC, Tanout, Niger. 5 March 1981. (CELHTO)
ALHAJI SHAGALI. Performance by the Troupe Théâtrale de Mainé Soroa. MJC, Diffa, Niger. 12 April 1981. (CELHTO, ORTN)
BA GA IRINTA BA. Performance by the Troupe Amadou 'Dan Bassa of Zinder. MJC, Niamey, Niger. April 1980. (CELHTO, ORTN)
BABBAN RUMBU MATARSHI TUKUNYA. Five episodes for national radio by the Troupe Théâtrale ORTN. Zinder, Niger. August and September 1981.
CHAME ABOKIN BADDA KIBIYA. Performance by the Troupe Théâtrale de Tanout. MJC, Tanout, Niger. 6 March 1981. (CELHTO)
COHABITATION ENTRE ELEVEURS ET CULTIVATEURS. Performance by the Troupe Théâtrale de Magaria. MJC, Tanout, Niger. 10 March 1981. (CELHTO)
COHABITATION ENTRE ELEVEURS ET CULTIVATEURS. Performance by the Troupe Théâtrale de Matameye. MJC, Tanout, Niger. 7 March 1981. (CELHTO)
LA CONFIANCE MET LE DINER DES MALHONNETES. Performance by the Troupe Théâtrale de Gouré. MJC, Tanout, Niger. 8 March 1981. (CELHTO)
'DAN KWANGILA. Performance by the Troupe Théâtrale de Maradi. MJC, Diffa, Niger. 9 April 1981. (CELHTO, ORTN)
DARAJAR K'ASA AL'ADARTA. A final rehearsal by the Radio Club Troupe, Zinder, Niger. 19 June 1981.
GADO K'ARHIN ALLA. Performance by the Troupe Amadou 'Dan Bassa. MJC, Zinder, Niger. 13 September 1981.
GADO K'ARHIN ALLA. Videotaped performance by the Troupe Amadou 'Dan Bassa. Niamey, Niger. 1979. (CELHTO, ORTN)
GIRMAN KAI RAWANIN TSIYA. Performance by the Troupe Amadou 'Dan Bassa. MJC, Zinder, Niger. 12 September 1981.
KOWA YA BUGI RUWA IDONAY. Performance by the Troupe Théâtrale de Filingué. MJC, Diffa, Niger. 13 April 1981. (CELHTO, ORTN)

KUSKURE KARATU NE. Performance by the Troupe
  Théâtrale de Tahoua. MJC, Diffa, Niger. 10
  April 1981. (CELHTO, ORTN)
SOJAN DA. Videotaped performance by the Troupe
  Amadou 'Dan Bassa. Produced by Mamane Bakabé.
  Niamey, 1979(?). (ORTN)
TALALA MAI KAMAN SAKE. Performance by the Troupe
  Amadou 'Dan Bassa of Zinder. MJC, Tanout,
  Niger. 9 March 1981. (CELHTO)
TALALA MAI KAMAN SAKE. Performance by the Troupe
  Amadou 'Dan Bassa of Zinder. MJC, Diffa,
  Niger. 8 April 1981. (CELHTO, ORTN)
WALWALE. Performance by the Troupe Théâtrale
  d'Agadez. MJC, Diffa, Niger. 7 April 1981.
  (CELHTO, ORTN)

   My recordings of these plays are audio tapes, as are those in the CELHTO collection (as noted above). The ORTN Archives include videotapes of the festival plays (those marked ORTN).

APPENDIX

Synopses of Scenes
and
Character Lists

ALHAJI SHAGALI
BA GA IRINTA BA
'DAN KWANGILA
DARAJAR K'ASA AL'ADARTA
GADO K'ARHIN ALLA
KOWA YA BUGI RUWA IDONAY
KUSKURE KARATU NE
TALALA MAI KAMAN SAKE
WALWALE

(I have included Cast Lists with the individual performers where possible.)

ALHAJI SHAGALI
(Alhaji Pleasure-seeking)

Performed by the Troupe Théâtrale de Mainé Soroa for the National Festival in Diffa, Niger, 12 April 1981.

Scene 1. At the **Sous-préfet's** office.

The **sous-préfet** holds a meeting with the **sarki** and other community leaders to announce the award of the clinic contract to Alhaji Shagali. The **sous-préfet** thanks Shagali for his low bid and reminds him of the importance of the project to the **département** and to the national development efforts; he arranges for Shagali to be shown the site and to receive an advance payment for the work.

Scene 2. At the home of Alhaji Ibrahim.

Alhaji Ibrahim and a neighbor discuss the misguided choice of Shagali as contractor and his neglect of the project in favor of driving around in a new car. Shagali's foreman, Maître, arrives to confirm their assessment: he has not been paid for three months and is looking for a new job. Alhaji Ibrahim asks him to bring further information about Shagali's affairs and says that he will help him.

Scene 3. At the work site.

Alhaji Shagali arrives with the **sous-préfet** and the state's engineer to inspect the construction. The officials are appalled at the state of the work after seven months and the mistakes made in the design. The **sous-préfet** warns Shagali that he promised to complete the project in ten months-- he has three months left to finish it properly. After they leave, a food seller presents her complaint that the (unpaid) workers owe her a lot of money; Shagali pays her. The workers and water carriers also demand their wages. Shagali promises to pay them after his trip to Maradi.

Scene 4. At the home of Alhaji Shagali.

Maître visits Shagali at home to report on the

Appendix 293

project's debts. They curse the meddlesome engineer, who won't take bribes, and Maître suggests that Boka Mai Burgami could help get rid of him. Shagali calls his chauffeur and tells him to prepare for their trip, but first to bring Mai Burgami.

Mai Burgami comes and discusses the problem of the engineer with Shagali and assures him that he will take care of him. After he leaves, Shagali calls his first wife, Hajiya, to tell her about his prospective trip. She calls Amarya, the second wife, who needles him about where he will sleep on the trip. Flustered, Shagali calls Hajiya "Gimbiya" and the wives tease him mercilessly about his girlfriend Gimbiya.

Scene 5. Gimbiya's room.

Shagali knocks at Gimbiya's door as she listens to her radio. He says he has only come to greet her but she tells him there is a plane the next day and convinces him to stay; he sends his chauffeur ahead with the car. While he is washing up, Gimbiya pours whiskey into his soft drink. As he becomes progressively more drunk, Gimbiya reminds him of gifts he has promised--a television set, a formica bed, gold jewelry. He falls asleep and she puts him to bed and then examines the briefcase he has guarded so carefully. Finding it full of money, she hurries off with it.

He wakes up frantically searching for her and his briefcase. Alhaji Lura a friend passing by, hears the commotion and stops by to inform him that Gimbiya has gone off on the plane. Lura and Shagali decide to tell the **sous-préfet** that he lost the money in a car accident on his trip.

Scene 6. At the **sous-préfet's** office.

The **sous-préfet** gathers the town elders to discuss Shagali's incomplete construction and sends his guard to bring Shagali. Shagali limps in telling his story of the accident, claiming that they announced it on the radio at 3:00 a.m. (before radio programming begins for the day). The **sous-préfet** orders the guard to take Shagali to jail and asks the others what they should do about the construction. They suggest that Alhaji Cuncun be put in charge. The **sous-préfet** warns them against the sort of collusion that led to the choice of Shagali; it will not be tolerated in the future.

Alhaji Shagali
by Members of the Troupe Théâtrale de Mainé Soroa

Sous-Préfet..........................Mahamadou Lido
Garde (guard)............................Ba Adame
The Town Elders:
    Major..........................Amadou Yacouba
    Sarki (chief)....................Boulama Issa
    Alhaji Ibrahim, an entrepreneur ....Makurta
    Alhaji Cuncun, an entrepreneur..........Hassan
Alhaji Shagali.............. Alhaji Zoubeirou Lawal
(pleasure seeking)
Maître, Shagali's foreman....................Ba Kaw
Boka Mai Burgami.....................Hassan Souley
(wizard with a goatskin bag)
Ingenieur (engineer)..................Guéro Namata
The Construction Crew:
    Maître Maçon (head mason)..............Ba Gana
    Vendeuse (a food vendor)..................Zara
    Menusier (carpenter)................Souleymane
    Manoeuvre 1 (laborer)...................Adamou
    Manoeuvre 2...........................Mamadou
    Manoeuvre 3.................Mamadou Mounkaila
    Manoeuvre 4...........................Zanzama
    Manoeuvre 5..........................Aminansi
Hajiya, Shagali's first wife................Gamandi
Amarya (bride), Shagali's second wife.......Hadjara
Gimbiya..................................Ladi Garba
(short, squat woman, or a princess)
Chaffeur, Shagali's driver.................Mamadou
Alhaji Lura.........................Gumarou Moussa
(to look after), Shagali's friend

BA GA IRINTA BA
(There's nothing like it!)

Performance by the Troupe Amadou 'Dan Bassa of Zinder for the National Festival in Niamey, Niger, April 1980.

Scene 1. At the home of Mamman Arrivé.

This scene introduces the central character, Mamman Arrivé, at home arranging business with his friend and lackey, Langa Langa. Mamman's son Sanussi returns home crying because his teacher hit him. Mamman and his wife react angrily, each ready to upbraid the teacher.

Scene 2. At the Primary School.

The teachers gather for a meeting to grade a set of examinations and to discuss school affairs. Bartelemi (a Yoruba man) comes to inform his son's teacher that the boy missed class because of illness and to ask how he is progressing in his studies. After he leaves, Mamman Arrivé appears, and without so much as greeting anyone, demands to see Madame, Sanussi's teacher, and curses the other teachers and the director as they try to calm him down.

Scene 3. At the school inspector's office.

The teachers cannot solve the problem at their level and so the director goes to consult the primary school inspector, who sees that some of the teachers as well as the parents are at fault in the series of complaints. Because the issue has wider implications, the inspector refers it on to the mayor by telephone. The mayor then calls for a town meeting to discuss the problems at school.

Scene 4. At the mayor's office.

The mayor convenes the town meeting--the director, the inspector, the police commissioner, representatives from the Parents' Association and other community groups, along with Mamman Arrivé and three other parents who have caused confrontations at the schools. The authorities listen to their complaints--teachers who drink or who do not come to class, misunderstandings about the school's programs (why the young girls wear short pants for sports, etc.)--and they work to resolve their questions. Mamman Arrivé, however, continually disrupts the meeting showing no respect for anyone, and he is told to report to the commissioner of police the next morning.

Scene 5. At Langa Langa's house.

While Mamman is at the meeting, other men in town gather to gossip about him. Mamman appears in the midst of their discussion, gives his version of the story, and receives the advice of his neighbors. They feel he is in the wrong and that the only way to repair the damage is to go back to the school where it all started. They agree that he should ask the president of the Parents' Association and Mai Samari to accompany him to add their plea for leniency in his punishment.

Scene 6. At the primary school.

Mamman and the elders return to the school to ask for pardon. Sanussi's teacher withdraws her complaint, but only because of the elders' intercession.

Scene 7. At the police station.

The commissioner refuses to pardon Mamman, even though Madame has withdrawn her complaint, and he gives Mamman a stiff fine and a severe warning.

Scene 8. At Mamman Arrivé's house.

Mamman returns to face his family, including his older brother, and shows that he has learned his lesson when Sanussi comes in crying with a new story about being beaten. Mamman decides to investigate the matter and not act rashly.

Appendix

BA GA IRINTA BA
by Members of the Troupe Amadou 'Dan Bassa of Zinder

Mamman Arrivé........................Oumarou Nainou
(Mamman who has "made it")
Langa Langa (a long, slender person).....Ali Kasoum
   (Langa Langa is also the nickname of a famous wrestler in Zinder--the irony is that both the actor and the wrestler are large, heavy-set men)
Gimbiya.........................Hajiya Hadiza Musa
(a princess, or a short, squat woman)
Sanussi, Mamman's son.................Na Maikwashi
The School Staff:
   Directeur (of the Primary School)....Yazi Dogo
   Monsieur 1, a teacher............Abdou Louché
   Monsieur 2.....................Mamman Abarchi
   Monsieur 3.........................Sinni Sanda
   Monsieur 4........................Rabilou Sabo
   Monsieur 5....................Souleymane Keita
   Monsieur 6........................Lawan Sabo
   (Skant), a drunken teacher
   Madame, Sanussi's teacher........Amina N'Dette
Bartelemi, a Yoruba man.......Ibrahim "Gliss" Tando
Inspecteur....................Abdouramane N'Diaye
Directeur de Brousse...............Adamou Hassane
(Director of "the bush")
Maire (mayor).........................Lawali Dango
Commissaire....................Dodo Abdou Nagondja
(police commissioner)
Président..........................Amadou Ciroma
(of the Parents' Association)
Mai Samari (head of the **samariya**)..............Illo
The Townspeople:
   Malam Na Kullu, a parent........Amadou NaKullu
   Sakan Dami, a parent...............Illo Grand
   Musa Mai Kaji......................Musa Akusa
   (Musa the chicken farmer)
   Délégué................................Harouna
   Aboki 1 (Friend).................Lawali Abass
   Aboki 2........................Mamman Abarchi
   Aboki 3..........................Lawan Harou
   Aboki 4.........................Rabilou Sabo
   K'arawrawa (the bell).........Ibrahim Issoufou
Policier (policeman)..................Rabilou Sabo
Jatu........................Jatikuru Malam Garba
Yaya, Mamman's older brother...........Abdou Agali

'DAN KWANGILA
(The Contractor)

Peformance by the Troupe Théâtrale de Maradi for the National Festival in Diffa, Niger, 9 April 1981.

Scene 1. At the home of Alhaji Gimshik'i, a conversational meeting place (Maradi).

    A group of townsmen hears news over the radio of the government's intention to build clinics in the Maradi **Département**; bids will be taken for the construction projects. The men discuss the importance of people working together for national development. Alhaji Rangama wants to bid for the contract, but the others warn him against it because he knows nothing about construction.

Scene 2. At the home of Mainassara, a member of the commission to choose the contractor (Niamey).

    The prospective contractor, Alhaji Rangama, travels to Niamey to visit Mainassara, a personal friend of Alhaji Gimshik'i. Rangama brings a pile of presents (including a color television set) to this man's house, and discusses his desire to get the contract.

Scene 3. The meeting of the Commission (Niamey).

    The commission members discuss the dossiers submitted for the construction project. Mainassara weighs the discussion in favor of Rangama.

Scene 4. At the bank (Maradi).

    Rangama meets Gimshik'i at the bank and receives advice about which clerk to see to obtain his loan. While Rangama gets his money quickly (even arranging payment after hours because he has forgotten his checkbook), two government **fonctionnaires**, who have waited for days, receive no attention. They raise a complaint and the bank's director, coming out to quiet the fight, begins an investigation of the corrupt clerk.

Appendix 299

Scene 5. At the office of city planning (Maradi).

Rangama interrupts a meeting between the director and another government official to demand that they show him the site for his project. His official clearance papers have not yet arrived from Niamey, but he is too impatient to wait for them.

Scene 6. At the construction site (Village of Maigêmê, outside of Maradi).

The workers complain about not having been paid and the foreman complains that there are not enough workers and they have no skills. Rangama will not pay the official wages and hires foreign laborers at lower rates. One of the dissatisfied workers leaves to take a complaint to the inspector.

Scene 7. At the construction site (Maigêmê).

The workers fight with the foreman until the inspector of employee welfare comes to review the situation. He informs Rangama that he is at fault for failing to hire Nigerien workers and for not paying them adequate wages for their over-time work. Rangama must pay all of the back wages, so he sends his accountant to the bank. After the inspector leaves, the director of city planning arrives to inspect the foundation of the clinic building. He discovers that the bricks shatter easily because Rangama has increased the regulated ratio of sand to cement. He declares the building to be sub-standard and orders Rangama to destroy it.

Scene 8. At Rangama's home.

Rangama, at home with his wife, receives the news that his building has been torn down and his accountant has left the country with the workers' wages. He loses his senses and has to be carried off by his brother-in-law and Alhaji Gimshik'i.

'DAN KWANGILA
by Members of the Troupe Théâtrale de Maradi

(This cast list is taken from the Troupe's mimeographed version of the play; it reflects their own Hausa orthography. Additions in parentheses are mine.)

Elhaji Bakway (seven)................Mahamane Meydo
   (later this character was named Alhaji
   Gimshik'i, "supporting pillar")
Maalan Iisaa...........................Buuzu Dayma
Elhaji Saale.......................Saabi'u Ashuuraa
Sa'iidu...........................Baawa Ubandawaaki
'Dan Kwangilaa (the contractor)....Loobi Abuuubacar
Maynasaraa............................Sheerif Iisaa
Maatar Maynasaraa (Maynasaraa's wife).......Hadiiza
Doodo................................Haamisu Laadan
(a spirit, ogre; Maynasaraa's servant)
Four Members of the Commission (along with
   Maynasara):
   Burayma, Directeur..............Lawwalii Askaa
   Ruwa (water)......................Abdu Shaaway
   Agaali........................Lawwalii Gwandaa
   Kacella............................Isuhu Marii
   (a traditional slave title)
Kadi (secretary at the bank)............Raabi Hasan
Hamza (clerk at the bank)..............Tankari Banaw
Bukari (a teacher)....................Siidi Haruuna
Likita (doctor)............................Hak'iilu
Directeur de Banque....................Isaaka Iisaa
Haashimu (clerk at the bank)............Isuhu Marii
Hajo.......................................Raabi Ali
(secretary at the city planning office)
Chef Service Topo.....................Haruuna Salaw
(head of the topography office)
Hamidu, Chef d'Urbanisme.............Sha'aybu Beegu
(head of city planning)
Planton (orderly)..........................Hak'iilu
The Construction Crew:
   Joseph (the Yoruba foreman).....Lawwalii Askaa
   Bienvenu........................Haruuna Salaw
   (welcome; Rangama's Yoruba accountant)
   Ma'aazu, Maître Maçon..............Saani Hasan
   (chief mason)
   Naayu (the worker who complains).....'Dandulla
   Sadda (to bend down)...............'Dan Dawraa
   Gwaggobilii...................Abuu 'Dan Adama
   (Bagobiri, a man from Gobir)

Appendix

```
     Loggon Banja...................Siraaji Aadamu
     ("worthless worker")
     May Gaadii (guard).....................Bonhoo
     'Dan Caawaa-raggoo (grass seller)...Hasan Kane
     Landoo  (a food seller)............Raabi Hasan
     Haadii................................Hak'iilu
     Kacella...............................May Musa
Inspecteur de travail...........Usman 'Dan Twasshii
(of employee welfare)
Balki (Rangama's wife)...................Raabi Aali
Gambo (Rangama's brother-in-law)...Lawwalii Gwandaa
```

DARAJAR K'ASA AL'ADARTA

(The Value of a Country is in its Customs)
Performed by the Radio Club Troupe as part of the **Wasan Kara**, Zinder, Niger, 21 June 1981.

Scene 1. At the home of Alhaji Na Alla.

Alhaji Na Alla calls his two wives and forbids them to allow their daughters out of the house while he is gone. The girls are too old now to go wandering the streets without trouble; he hopes to find husbands for them this year. He tells his wives to call the girls, Taxi and Cha-cha-cha, and he repeats his instructions to them.
Gagarau and Mai Hangin Nesa, friends of Na Alla, come to visit him and the men discuss the growing problems with controlling their children. After the men leave, the women come out again to discuss the situation; Hajiya Pantaika, the older wife, disagrees with Na Alla, but Hajiya K'arama says they must do as he wishes. Monsieur Mazari arrives to invite the girls to a party at his house that evening. He leaves and Pantaika asks who he is; learning that he works at the bank and has a lot of money, she tells her daughter Taxi to go to the party. K'arama objects and refuses to allow Cha-cha-cha to go.

Scene 2. At the home of Gagarau.

Gagarau's wife sends their daughter, Rariya, on an errand and receives a rebuke from her husband when he returns home; he says that whenever Rariya leaves the house, she returns with a pack of men following her like dogs. A young man comes calling for Rariya and Gagarau chases him off in anger. Then Taxi arrives to take Rariya to the party; her mother forbids her to go. Rariya defies her mother and leaves with Taxi.

Scene 3. The party at the home of Monsieur Mazari.

The young people arrive one by one, greet each other, dance, drink beer, and go in and out of the back room in couples. The police arrive to investigate the loud noise and arrest everyone present.

Appendix 303

Scene 4. At the home of Alhaji Na Alla.

Na Alla's friends come at his invitation to discuss the arrangements for husbands for his daughters, according to custom. They invite Taxi's prospective father-in-law, a pious scholar, to tell him of their decision to give Taxi to his son without asking for bridewealth. A policeman appears informing Na Alla that his daughter is being held at the station. Na Alla refuses to believe him until he calls his wives and daughters, and Pantaika admits that she lied. Taxi is not ill in her room; she has not returned home.

Scene 5. At the Police Station.

Na Alla and the other fathers come to the police station to bail out their children. They are shocked to find their daughters wearing trousers and their sons in long-haired wigs. The Commissioner informs Na Alla that someone hit Taxi at the party, so they took her to the doctor; the doctor has notified them that she is three months pregnant. Na Alla collapses in shock. The police release the girls to their fathers with a warning, but they continue to hold the young men in jail, particularly Mazari, an employee of the state.

Scene 6. At the home of Alhaji Na Alla.

Na Alla calls Pantaika and Taxi and repudiates both of them; he refuses to recognize Taxi as his daughter because of her pregnancy, and he sends Pantaika back to her family, holding her responsible for Taxi's behavior. He then announces the divorce to K'arama and tells her to prepare Cha-cha-cha for her wedding. Gagarau and his friends arrive to arrange a new marriage for Na Alla, and to confirm Cha-cha-cha's marriage settlement with Alhaji Manaja.

Scene 7. At the home of Alhaji Na Alla.

Na Alla's wedding is celebrated with music, joyful shouts, and general celebration.

Scene 8. At the compound of Malam Zargewa.

Pantaika and Taxi come to Malam Zargewa's to tell him of their situation--that Na Alla has cast them out and Taxi is pregnant. Pantaika wants him to prepare an amulet that will cause her pregnancy to miscarry. Zargewa pretends to arrange it for her by sending his pupil Saluhu off to bring Malam Almajiri. Almajiri, a police officer, handcuffs Pantaika and takes the two women off to jail.

A stranger arrives who introduces himself as Malam JaGaba and explains that he has just returned from the distant north. There he studied under a great prophet who has founded a new religion with a new book, which he gives to Zargewa along with a large sum of money. He would like Zargewa to help him reach the other **malams** in the town, promising him a car and more money for his efforts. Zargewa sends for Saluhu to bring Malam Almajiri and other **malams** to hear the stranger's message; Almajiri comes and arrests JaGaba.

DARAJAR K'ASA AL'ADARTA
by Members of the Radio Club Troupe of Zinder

Alhaji Na Alla (Alhaji of God)...Habubakar Sha'aibu
Hajiya Pantaika............................Maryama
(Hajiya fried cakes), his first wife
Hajiya K'arama..............................Salmai
(little Hajiya), his second wife
Taxi, his daughter............................Zara
Cha-cha-cha, his daughter..................Hawwa'u
Gagarau (warrior), his friend.................Adam
Mai Hangin Nesa (far-seeing), his friend.....Camago
Makwabciya, a neighbor......................Hadiza
Monsieur Mazari................Alhaji Yahaya Isa
(a greedy man), a bank employee
Matar Gagarau, Gagarau's wife...............Hadiza
Rariya (tramp), Gagarau's daughter.........Maryama
Samari (young man), Rariya's boyfriend....Muhammadu
Sanussi, a neighbor..................Adamu Abubakar
Afolo, a young man at the party..............Amadu
Rastaman, a young woman at the party..........Gado
Mushe (**monsieur**), a guest at the party..Maman Manzo
Policiers.........................Lawwali and Ali
Abokin Alhaji 1 (Na Alla's friend).....Alhaji Manzo
Abokin Alhaji 2..............................Siraji
Abokin Alhaji 3..............................Saluhu

Appendix

```
Abokin Alhaji 4..............................Idi
Chef de Poste, a district officer.........Muhammadu
Bak'auye (a villager)...............Habubakar Hamza
Gardo Uban Garson............................Adam
(Gardo, the father of Garson)
Commissaire (police commissioner).......Maman Manzo
Garson (garçon/boy)..........................Abdu
Malam Zargewa (arresting)..........Alhaji Abdusalam
Tawada (ink), Zargewa's wife.................Jaru
Saluhu, Zargewa's pupil.............Habubakar Hamza
Malam Almajiri (pupil), a police office.....Lawwali
Malam JaGaba (guide), a stranger.......Maman Manzo
```

GADO K'ARHIN ALLA
(Inheritance, Strength from God)

Performed by the Troupe Amadou 'Dan Bassa of Zinder in 1973.

Scene summary from the published Hausa text, GAADOO KARHIN ALLAA (WAASAN KWAYKOYOO NA ZINDER A 1973), transcribed by Abuubakar Mahamman (Niamey: CELHTO, 1977).

Scene 1. In the **sarki's** room.

The **sarki**, on his deathbed, calls for his courtiers to bring his son Baydu, whom he names as his successor just before he dies.

Scene 2. At the **sarki's** court.

The courtiers discuss the selection of a new chief from among the eligible princes. The **waziri** reminds them that the **sarki** now also works for the national government and that the courtiers no longer have the final choice. The **sous-préfet** comes to pay his respects to the family of the deceased and to establish the official list of candidates: Baydu, Shaho, Mushe, and Salihi. He tells them that the **préfet** will announce the person who is best suited for the job of **sarki**, someone who has worked well with the Party and the government, and then they will hold the investiture.

Scene 3. At the home of Mushe.

An **alhaji** visits Mushe to discuss the grain shipment and to buy grain for himself; Mushe agrees to supply him with grain in return for a Land-Rover. A friend then visits Mushe and they discuss the distribution of grain and milk he is supposed to give to the poor on behalf of the government. Mushe complains about all the people begging for food from him because of his position. A group of beggars comes to ask for food; Mushe refuses and rudely sends them off. But he arranges to give several sacks to his friend.

Scene 4. At the home of Shaho.

Shaho's friend reports on purchases of food he

Appendix

has bought for him and tells him that he overheard men at the market saying the the investiture ceremony will take place the next morning. Shaho sends for Malam Gobe da Nisa, who prays with Shaho and then listens to his request for help in becoming **sarki**. Malam leaves with Shaho's servant and reappears with a large clay water pot. Malam explains that the name of everyone in the region is written in the pot, and that Shaho is to drink the entire contents before morning, but on the condition that he does not urinate during the night. Shaho sends Malam home and calls La'ba'ba to fetch Boka.

Boka and his interpreter then appear and Boka sends for the great spirit Yubana. The interpreter translates back and forth, informing Shaho what the great spirit is conveying to Boka: that he sees Shaho receiving the **sarki's** turban, but that he must put on a black turban, mount a black donkey, and ride through the crowd calling, "Yubana! Yubana!" After the two leave, Shaho reports it all to his friend and tells him they must now go off to see the blind **malam**.

Scene 5. At the door to the **sarki's** palace (with drumming and trumpeting).

As the crowd gathers for the investiture ceremony, the series of speeches begins. The **sous-préfet** warns against those who cheat the government; the **préfet** expresses his regret for the death of the **sarki** and announces the new **sarki**, Salihi. The new ruler is dressed in his robes and turban and then he addresses his people, praying for God's blessings on everyone. Finally, the region's **députe** speaks at length about national unity and the work of the government and the Party to relieve the drought.

Scene 6. At the home of Shaho.

Shaho sends for Baydu and Mushe to discuss their common discontent with the choice of Salihi. A messenger comes from the new **sarki** to ask them to see him at court.

Scene 7. At the **sarki's** court.

Shaho, Baydu and Mushe arrive and **Sarki**

Salihi announces that the inheritance belongs to all of them, not just to him. Before the durbar salute, he wants to give Shaho the title of Yakudima, Baydu the title of Yarima, and Mushe the title of Magaji. He also warns the courtiers that he will hear no slander against his brothers.

Scene 8. The Durbar Salute (in mime).

The princes mounted on horseback ride to salute the **sarki** under his umbrella, surrounded by his courtiers. Each raises his sword to the new **sarki** who acknowledges their allegiance.

GADO K'ARHIN ALLA
by Members of the Troupe Amadou 'Dan Bassa of Zinder

Character List

Sarki
Members of the Court:
    Liman (imam)
    Waziri, a titleholder
    Wakilan Waziri (representative of the Waziri)
    Galadima, a titleholder
    Ciroma, a titleholder
    Sarkin Dogaray (head of the **sarki's** guards)
    Jajako, a messenger

The princes (**mayna**/son of a chief)
    Mayna Baydu
    Mayna Juju (fetich, spirit), a crazy man
    Mayna Shaho (hawk)
    Mayna Mushe (**monsieur**)
    Mayna Salihi (honesty)

Alhaji, a friend of Mushe
Shaho's Friend
Ma'aykin Ciroma, messenger of the Ciroma
Manemin Dawa (seekers of corn)
La'ba'ba (newborn), Shaho's servant
Malam Gobe da Nisa (tomorrow is far)
Boka (wizard)
Interpreter
Secrétaire-Général
Sous-Préfet
Préfet
Député

Appendix

KOWA YA BUGI RUWA IDONAY
(Whoever beats water [will get it in] his eye)

Performance by the Troupe Théâtrale de Filingué for the National Festival in Diffa, Niger, 13 April 1981.

Scene 1. At Mai Gari's compound.

The men of the village gather at Mai Gari's courtyard for the arrival of the first doctor for the new clinic. An herbal peddler, Boka, passes by selling his remedies; Mai Gari informs him that they will have no more need for him, the town is to have a modern doctor as part of the development of the region. A government official brings the doctor, Saluhu, and introduces him formally to the group. Saluhu announces that anyone who feels ill, at any time, is to come to see him; the government's health care is for everyone and he is at their service.

Scene 2. At the clinic.

Mai Gari comes to greet Saluhu on his first working day at the clinic and to arrange for a worker to assist him. Saluhu explains his duties to Gimshik'i, who does not want to touch the sick people or to clean the latrine, and who chases the patients away. Saluhu tells Gimshik'i to call them one by one, and he treats each in turn: a man with a rash, a young woman with a headache, a young man with venereal disease, an old man who has been sick for years but refuses to go to the hospital in the larger town, and a Fulani man who wants medicine for his sick donkey and fights with Gimshik'i. After the patients have gone, Mai Gari returns to suggest that he and the doctor sell the government's medicines; Saluhu readily agrees, telling Mai Gari of the wealth he received by doing so at his last post.

Scene 3. At Mai Gari's compound.

Mai Gari receives a series of visitors at his compound. Bahillace, the Fulani, brings his complaint about the doctor's refusal to treat his donkey. Sata, the veteran's wife, says that the clinic has no more medicine; Mai Gari sends her back with his instructions to buy some of the medicine Saluhu has set aside. Doctor Saluhu himself appears to tell Mai Gari how much money they are making by the arrangement and hurries back to work.

Mai Samari comes to discuss the government's plans to help the destitute and handicapped people in their district. He and Mai Gari overhear Boka hawking medicines again; they call him in to stop him. He replies that people have asked him to return because the new doctor is too expensive. The veteran arrives to complain about his wife's instructions to buy medicine, saying that he will carry his complaint to the higher authorities. Three other elders also bring grievances against the new doctor and his illegal sales. Despite Mai Gari's attempts to quiet the complaints, Mai Samari insists on investigating the matter.

Scene 4. At the **Sous-préfecture**.

The region's **sarki** meets with the **sous-préfet** over two problems--a divorce between a deaf man and his young wife, and the village doctor selling medicine. The **sous-préfet** telephones the chief medical officer of the district for a report on the doctor and his supplies, and then he calls the **gendarmes** to inform them of the situation.

Scene 5. A village meeting.

The **sous-préfet** and the **sarki** arrive in the village to meet with the assembled elders. The **sous-préfet** denounces the corruption of the doctor and Mai Gari, who have been arrested, and promises to send a new doctor. They also install Karo as the new headman; he makes a speech accepting his responsibilities.

Appendix

KOWA YA BUGI RUWA IDONAY
by Members of the Troupe Théâtrale de Filingué

Character List

Elders of the Village:
    Kotso (a type of drum)
    Mai K'wali (one who beats with a stick)
    Sangam (huge)
    Karo
    Shartar
    Gojirgo
    Katam'bari (a type of tree)

Mai Samari (head of the **samariya**)
Mai Gari (headman)
Boka (herbalist)
Bak'o (stranger), a government bureaucrat
Saluhu, the new doctor
Tsohon Soji (old soldier), a veteran
Zamnau, a boy
Gimshik'i (supporting pillar), Saluhu's assistant

Patients at the clinic:
    Mai Goge (fiddler)
    Banzugu (handsome), a young woman
    Katam'bari
    Tsoho (old man)
    'Dan Tsoho, the old man's son
    Bahillace (a Fulani man)
    Sata, Matar Tsohon Soji (the wife of the veteran)

Garde (guard)
Sous-préfet
Sarki
Kurma (deaf man)
Matar Kurma, his wife

KUSKURE KARATU NE
(A Mistake is a Lesson)

Performed by the Troupe Théâtrale de Tahoua for the National Festival in Diffa, Niger, 10 April 1981.

Scene 1. At Arzika's home.

Arzika tells his wife of the good harvest in cotton and his plans to go to Mecca on the pilgrimage. Madugu comes to visit and announces his own plans for the pilgrimage, but unlike Arzika, he does not want to join the Nigerien group arrangements. A friend, Udu, then stops by on his way to help with a **samariya** building project, a communal activity Madugu will not participate in.

Scene 2. At the Travel Agency in Illela.

Malam Musa, Secretary for the local Islamic Association, brings the group of prospective pilgrims to pay for their tickets, to have their identity cards checked, and to receive instructions about the necessary innoculations for the trip. Arzika is among this group, as are Hajiya Rahamu (an experienced pilgrim), a Fulani man and his wife, and an infirm old man and a pregnant woman who are not permitted to go.

Scene 3. Somewhere abroad.

Madugu takes his friends, Udu, Mahamman and Assibit, across the border to arrange their journey to Mecca with 'Dan Kamasho. Madugu hands over their money without asking for a receipt, relying on the promises of 'Dan Kamasho that he will do everything for them. Udu questions the difference in cost from what the group paid in Niger, but they laugh at him. Mahamman questions their lack of receipts and asks about innoculations; dissatisfied, he demands his money back and curses 'Dan Kamasho. After the group leaves, 'Dan Kamasho and his accomplice discuss the car and the trip to Cairo they will buy with Madugu's money.

Scene 4. At Madugu's home.

Madugu asks his wife and son if they have prepared his things for the journey. His daughter

Appendix

and her husband and two friends arrive to bring gifts and to say goodbye to Madugu, requesting that he buy things for them in Mecca. Madugu entrusts the care of his family to 'Dan Baki while he is gone and bids farewell to everyone as he leaves to join Udu and Assibit on the road.

Scene 5. At the Tahoua Airport.

The Nigerien airline officials call the list of passengers for the departure to Mecca: Arzika, Hajiya Rahamu, the Fulani man (who is told he must leave his hat and stick behind), and a doctor and nurse who will accompany the group for their well-being. The scene ends with the sound of the plane taking off.

Scene 6. At the foreign airport.

The last plane to Mecca is about to depart; the officials call the final names, but none of Madugu's group is among them. The officials ask for their receipts, which they do not have, and listen to their story. The police go to find 'Dan Kamasho, but they return with only his accomplice who tells them 'Dan Kamasho left for Cairo with Madugu's money. The airport officials apologize to Madugu and his friends but tell them they must return home and wait until 'Dan Kamasho can be arrested. Udu leaves Madugu, accusing him of breaking his trust and declaring that he will not return with him.

Scene 7. At the customs post at the border.

The customs officers greet Mai Samari, who warns them of a young man who looks and acts funny coming through with two old people. When Madugu, Assibit and the young man appear, the officials uncover the youth's smuggled drugs. Madugu knows nothing about the drugs although he took some for a headache while they were traveling together. They send Madugu off as they telephone the **gendarmes** to come and arrest the young man.

Scene 8. At Madugu's home.

'Dan Baki visits Madugu's wife to tell her that the group did not leave for Mecca after all; Maryama refuses to believe his story. When Madugu himself returns, she begins to wail. Their daughter and son-in-law and Mai Riyoji come to visit; Madugu must repeat his sad story and face the full shame of his mistake.

Scene 9. Under the tree of conversation.

Mai Riyoji tells the gathering that Madugu was left behind at the airport, and they lay the blame on Madugu's lack of cooperation and his refusal to listen to anyone else. Madugu arrives in time to hear them discuss Alhaji Arzika's return from Mecca. He then leaves and the men note that he seems ill.

Scene 10. At Arzika's home.

The men come to greet Alhaji Arzika, including Madugu. 'Dan Baki tells Arzika about Madugu's story. Arzika tells them all of the pilgrimage and distributes gifts, while Madugu repents.

KUSKURE KARATU NE
by Members of the Troupe Théâtrale de Tahoua

Character List

Arzika (wealth)
Zalewa, Arzika's wife
Tinni, Arzika's daughter
Madugu (caravan leader)
Udu (miser)

Staff at the Nigerien Travel Agency:
    Planton
    Secrétaire
    Agent

Malam Musa, Secretary of the Islamic Association
Prospective pilgrims:
    Zambado Barto, a Fulani
    Makki, his wife
    Tsoho (old man)
    Macce mai ciki (a pregnant woman)
    Basaru Sani

Appendix

'Dan Kamasho (son of commission)
Yaro (boy), 'Dan Kamasho's accomplice
Prospective pilgrims with Madugu:
- Mahamman
- Assibit, an old woman
- Maryama, Madugu's wife
- Abuzaidi, Madugu's son
- Amina, Madugu's daughter
- Alkatum, Amina's husband
- Mai Riyoji (owner of wells), Madugu's friend
- 'Dan Baki, Madugu's friend
- Airline officials in Tahoua
- Likita (doctor)

Pilgrims at the foreign airport:
- Maigizo Naino
- Iyo Dogari
- Assuman Mai Karhi

Foreign airline officials and airport police
Customs officials:
- Basaru
- Sarmangadi
- Chef de douanes

Travelers at the customs post:
- Tsohuwa (old woman)
- Mai Samari (head of the **samariya**)
- Yarinya (young girl)
- Yaro (boy), a smuggler of drugs

Madugu's and Arzika's neighbors:
- Kanta
- Akadama
- Alkasum
- Jatau
- Alhaji Turke (tether), Arzika's companion on the pilgrimage

TALALA MAI KAMAN SAKE
(A Long Tethering Rope Is Like Freedom)

Performed by the Troupe Amadou 'Dan Bassa of Zinder for the National Festival in Diffa, Niger, 8 April 1981.

Scene 1. Outside the home of Mai Samari.

Mai Samari receives a visit from Dodo who brings Zangina and Musa, members of the **samariya** who are in conflict; Mai Samari solves their dispute after listening to their cases and reminding them of the mutual relationships among all of the peoples of Niger. Major then appears with three visitors from abroad who inquire about the function of Niger's **samariyas**, which Mai Samari outlines for them. Major asks to listen to the radio news and the group is shocked to hear the obituary for one of their **samariya** members. Major and Mai Samari prepare to go to the funeral in another town.

Scene 2. At the funeral.

A large group of men, religious leaders, friends, and neighbors of the deceased have gathered to pray and to distribute the funeral offerings. Then they call the widows to settle the estate in the presence of the **liman** and the elders. Talala is entrusted with his late brother's money and property and agrees to take care of his family, rather than dividing the estate among them.

Scene 3. At Talala's home.

Talala's younger wife (Sululu) leaves to visit her family before he returns home, angering Talala when he does arrive. He gives his first wife explicit instructions about grilling a leg of lamb he has bought and mentions that he plans to go to Mecca on the pilgrimage.

After his wife leaves for the kitchen, Talala's nephew Sule visits to request money for the family since they are nearly out of food. Talala tells him that he has no money and no time for their constant requests. The contractor Musa then pays a visit to discuss the final fixtures for Talala's new house--paint, lights, the bathtub, etc.--and the payments in millions of francs; Talala pays him a large sum of money as he leaves. Malam appears next to tell Talala what he has seen in the oracles for his future; Talala arranges with him to silence his brother's widows and children and gives him money as he leaves.

Next appears 'Dan Hulani, who looks after the estate's cattle; Talala tells him to sell nearly all of his late brother's herds. Finally, Sululu reappears and accuses Talala of neglect; they argue heatedly but he cannot stop her from packing her things and leaving to go to her parents' house (the first step toward divorce).

Scene 4. At Talala's new house.

After his return from Mecca, Alhaji Talala shows a friend his elaborate new house. The friend suggests that instead of moving into the house right away with his wives and children, Talala should use it as a retreat, a place to entertain friends and young women. They discuss an attractive girl Talala would like to meet and they call Agogo, Talala's servant, to bring her to the house. Agogo says that he cannot arrange such a rendez-vous, but that Savon Robb can; he brings Savon Robb, a pimp, who agrees to bring the girl immediately for a price.

Once brought, Dijé refuses to accompany Talala into the bedroom, even after he sends his friend off an an impromtu errand. She tells him he must come to court her properly (for marriage), at her father's house. Agogo reappears to announce that Talala's niece is waiting at his old house to see him.

Scene 5. At Talala's home.

The niece, Tsaibatu, and her husband have come to ask for a loan from Talala because their house has been robbed along with a neighborhood collection they had been holding. Talala refuses to give her her share of the inheritance, saying that it was not meant as a neighborhood fund. His wife argues against his injustice, pointing out his trip to Mecca and his new house. Talala leaves to warn the widows against Tsaibatu's "slander."

Scene 6. At the widows' home.

The widows, with no money and no food, plan to sell some of their dowry goods to Hajiya as a last resort. Major, who has not made a trip from his town for the three years since the funeral, arrives with sacks of grain and gifts of cloth and money. Talala then appears, greets Major, and tells them all not to listen to Tsaibatu's lies; he gives the women some money and leaves. The widows then inform Major of the real situation, that Talala has never given them enough money for food.
Tsaibatu returns and tells them all of her recent visit to Talala. She wants the estate apportioned out properly and Major agrees that they should take their case to court.

Scene 7. The court.

The judge hears Tsaibatu's complaint against Talala, his side of the case, an account of the estate's money and how he has provided for the family, and the widows' testimony. The Islamic judges pronounces the Qur'an's condemnation of those who steal from orphans, and the government's judge pronounes Talala's earthly sentence: he must repay everything he has spent from the estate or go to prison.

TALALA MAI KAMAN SAKE
by Members of the Troupe Amadou 'Dan Bassa of Zinder

Mai Samari (head of the **samariya**).......Kailou Bako
Dodo...........................Dodo Abdou Nagondja
Zangina.....................................Zanguina
Musa.....................................Musa Akusa
Major..............................Oumarou Nainou

Three visitors from abroad:
    Dauda Mai Burodi...................Ali Kasoum
    (Dauda/David the breadmaker)
    Sanussi Kominaka...................Lawan Sabo
    (Sanussi, everything is yours)
    Malam Muhamadu.................Amadou Nakullu
Talala (a tethering rope)................Yazi Dogo
Abokin Talala (Talala's friend)........Abdou Louché

Appendix

Mai Unguwa..........................Ciroma Amadou
(the headman of the district)
Liman (imam, Muslim prayer leader)......Sinni Sanda
Ladan (Muslim muezzin)...................Illo Grand
Na'ibi (deputy imam).......................Suleman
Malam 1............................Adamou Hassane
Malamin Tudu (Malam of the hill)...........Galadima
Munde, the first widow..................Hadiza Musa
Mata 2.......................................Jatikuru
(the second wife), the second widow
Sule, Talala's nephew..............Souleymane Keita
Tsaibatu, Talala's niece....................'Dayaba
Zainabu, Talala's first wife................Dumbule
Sululu (silently), Talala's second wife.......Amina
Malam Musa, a contractor.................Musa Akusa
Malam....................................Sinni Sanda
'Dan Hulani, a Fulani man..........Délégué Harouna
Agogo (a watch), Talala's servant .....Mamman Lawal
Savon Robb (a beauty cream).....Dodo Abdou Nagondja
El Giya.......................................Murza
(of liquor), one of Talala's girlfriend
Dijé, a young woman......................Ladi Saley
Soja (soldier), Tsaibatu's husband.....Lawali Abass
Hajiya, a rich woman......................Elhajiya
Planton, the court clerk.............Adamou Hassane
Juge (judge).........................Lawali Dango
Premier Plaignant (first defendant)......Illo Grand
Alkali (Muslim judge)..............Ibrahim Issoufou
Malam 2....................................Suleman
Secrétaire (Court secretary)............Sinni Sanda

WALWALE
(Unravelled)

Performance by the Troupe Théâtrale d'Agadez for the National Festival in Diffa, Niger, 7 April 1981.

Scene 1. A meeting of the Parents' Association of the village of Muntaru (we have gathered).

The leaders of the Parents' Association meet with the primary school director to discuss the problems at the school. Chief among these are the lack of water, the children's lack of cleanliness, and the chores that they must do at home, tiring them out too much for their studies. Various solutions are proposed to bring water to the school; the group decides to ask Mai Gari to call a town meeting in order to collect money to connect a pipeline to the village water tower.

Scene 2. In front of Mai Gari's compound.

The town crier announces the community meeting at Mai Gari's compound. When everyone assembles, Mai Gari and President Tumka of the Parents' Association address the crowd, informing them of the school's problems and the plan of the Association. Walwale is the lone voice of dissent, arguing that the children would not be overworked or thirsty if the teachers did not tire them out in the middle of the day.
   He refuses to participate in the fundraising, claiming that the government workers always keep the money to themselves and never complete their projects. After arguing with Mai Gari and insulting Sassak'e, he leaves in disgust, as the others contribute their money for the school's pump.

Scene 3. At the home of Walwale.

Walwale argues with his wife about the meeting; even she agrees that the community has a good project. Alhaji, Sinadiri and several other leaders pay Walwale a visit and he explains to them that they will never see their money again or the pump, because Mai Gari and President Tumka will pocket the money. They argue heatedly and leave in a huff.

Scene 4. At Mai Gari's compound.

   Sinadiri visits Mai Gari to tell him about Walwale's statements about them embezzling the money. President Tumka then appears to inform Mai Gari that he has talked to the plumber Issa about the project. They agree that Walwale's appropriate punishment, shame, will fall on him when the pump is completed.

Scene 5. At the office of the **sous-préfet**.

   Mai Gari and President Tumka bring the collected money and explain their plans for the pump to the **sous-préfet**. He adds a contribution and then calls Issa the plumber to arrange a final contract for the work, with everyone's approval.

Scene 6. At the school.

   The town crier announces the opening of the pump at the school. President Tumka, the school director, and the **sous-préfet** make speeches praising the community's effort and the need for more such self-help projects.

Scene 7. At the home of Walwale.

   Burut visits Walwale to play draughts (**dara**). Walwale's wife Fatumata upbraids them for playing useless games instead of going to the town meeting. Walwale refuses to go. His son runs in, telling them of the water coming from the pump, and that there is a town meeting; of all the parents, they are the only ones who are not there. Walwale hits him and tells him he will not stand for his tricks. He then argues with Fatumata and announces that he will go to see Mai Gari.

Scene 8. At Mai Gari's compound.

   Walwale comes to apologize and asks Mai Gari to intercede on his behalf to Tumka. Mai Gari sends for Tumka, who accepts Walwale's apology and forgives him. Walwale announces that he will change his name to Muhammad and will donate 5,000 bricks to build a new wall around the school.

WALWALE
by Members of the Troupe Théâtrale d'Agadez

Character List

The village leaders:
    Sinadiri (metal solder)
    Mushe 1 (**monsieur**)
    Président Tumka (plaited, tied together), President of the Parents' Association
    Alhaji Korau
    Sassak'e (carpentered)
    Directeur (of the Primary School)
    Tubalaje (bricks)
    Maga-takarda (secretary)
    Mai Gari (the headman of the town)
    Walwale (unravelled)
    Fatumata, Walwale's wife

The townspeople:
    Mai Gangami (drummer, town crier)
    Inbiku ("I follow you"), Mai Gari's servant
    Sabkalkali
    Juma
    Men and Women at the town meeting

Sous-préfet
Arzika (wealth), the Sous-préfet's guard
Issa Plombier (the plumber)
Burut, Walwale's friend
Yaro (boy), Walwale's son

INDEX

acculturation 20
activity 132-3
Actors and Actresses:
  Bako, Kailou 78, 84-5, 100, 102-3, 112, 200, 271
  Begu, Chaibou 79, 96-7
  Garba, Ladi 89, 93
  Kassoum, Ali 78
  Lido, Mahamadou 73, 80-2, 88-91, 96, 114, 256
  Louché, Abdou 78, 84-5, 92, 102-3, 113, 188, 200, 270-1
  Manzo, Mamane 105, 107
  Nagondja, Abdou 78
  Nagondja, Dodo Abdou 112
  Nainou, Oumarou 83, 85, 101, 112-13, 213, 270-1
  Sanda, Sinni 77
  Tando, Ibrahim ("Gliss") 78, 191, 197, 198, 200, 113, 267-8, 271
Amicale des Fonctionnaires 29-30, 32, 35, 42; see fonctionnaires
animateur 61-2, 68, 86, 101, 256
Arrangement of Scenes 69-76
assimilation 20, 22, 25, 42
Authors:
  Aboubacar, Lobi 200, 203, 209
  Béart, Charles 23-4

Beckerman, Bernard 132-3, 239-40, 254
Beeman, William 184-5, 209, 213
Brink, James T. 191-2
Chaibou, Dan-Inna 12-19, 29, 30, 36, 40, 254, 267, 272
Cornevin, Robert 9, 21-33
Dadié, Bernard 28
Dandobi, Mahamane 30
Edgar, Frank 193
Frye, Northrop 165
Gidley, C.G.B 18-9
Graham-White, Anthony 7, 20, 21
Hakim, Tawfik al' 21
Idé, Oumarou 43
Johnston, H.A.S. 168
Ka, Abdou Anta 28
Kirby, E.T. 8
Kirk-Greene, Anthony 217
Mahamane, Aboubacar 3
Makward, Edris 93
Mariko, Babacar 254-5
Mariko, Kélitigui 253
McKee, Kenneth 166
Molière 31, 167
Nadao, Cheik Ahmed 28
Propp, Vladimir 165
Salifou, André 32-5
Schechner, Richard 154, 158
Scheub, Harold 16, 131, 141, 149
Shakespeare, William 21
Skinner, Neik 168, 249
Smith, M.G. 193
Sophocles 31
Soyinka Wole 15
Styan, J.L. 239

Traoré, Bakarky 22-7
Turner, Victor 152-8, 268
Yacouba, Alhassane 256
Yahaya, Ibrahim Yaro 9, 21
ballet 2, 3, 35, 37-9, 60, 67, 73, 147, 172, 243-4
blasphemy 2
boka 189-90, 198-200, 244, 267, 271-2
bori 13, 60, 93, 139
breach 152-7, 268
Center for Oral Traditions (CELHTO) 3
Central Characters 200-18
colonialism 19, 33-4, 76, 176
comedy 8-9, 17, 29, 44-6, 75, 111-14, 132-3, 136, 165, 167, 185, 215, 255, 257, 265-6, 272; see comic characters
Comic Characters 184-200; see comedy
Commedia dell' Arte 23, 166-7
community 67, 76, 93, 109, 133-4, 146, 148-51, 154-6, 173-4, 180-1, 204, 207, 209-10, 212, 239-40, 250, 257, 265, 272
competition 2, 23, 27-8, 31, 89, 172, 248, 251-2, 255
compositioin 75
corruption 70-1, 75, 103, 136, 143, 157, 175, 182-3, 191, 203-4, 209, 267-8
costumes 243-8, 252, 269, 271
crisis 152-7

culture 3, 39, 40, 61-2, 93
dance 7, 24, 29, 36, 37, 39, 93; see ballet
'dan kama 16-18
Development of a Theme 63-9
didacticism 45, 75, 111, 174, 180, 184, 197, 255
Directors:
  Adam, Alhaji Abdousalam 68, 77, 86-7, 105, 107-10, 249-50
  Bagoudou, Abdoullahi 37, 61
  Dogo, Yazi 45-6, 65, 72, 78-9, 84-5, 89, 91-2, 99-100, 102, 112-13, 155, 181, 198, 200, 214, 218, 243, 249, 270
  Lawal, Alhaji Zoubeirou 63, 73-4, 82-3, 89, 94, 96, 106, 113-4, 209, 252
  Na'Awa, Sani 68
  Nawaki, Abdou 61, 256
Distribution of Roles 76-82; see womens' roles and roles
doka 14, 177, 266
education 65, 74, 152, 257
elites 25, 29, 32, 240, 270
enactment 8
ethnic group 62, 102, 179, 192-3, 195-6, 199, 241, 251, 257
everyday life 135, 158, 167, 209, 270; see realism and Social Drama Form
FESTAC 104, 265

Index

fonctionnaire 60, 69, 73, 107, 182-3, 241-3, 266, 270; see Amicale des Fonctionnaires
French Theatre 29-35
griot 9, 16-17
images 132, 141
impersonation 18
improvisation 4, 7, 24, 35, 59, 89, 93-4, 96, 98, 101, 131, 167, 239, 248, 255, 257, 270; Improvisation in Performance 110-14
independence (national) 20-22, 31, 32
interpretation 75
irony 188
islam 110, 151, 157, 180, 189, 191, 210
keyword 89-90; see mot clef
kora 12
kunya 90-2, 102
Literary Drama 19-29
mai gurumi 15
mai komo 15-16
Maison des Jeunes 1, 3, 38, 87, 95, 257
malam 65, 80-1, 92, 103, 106-10, 150, 157, 179, 184, 187-9, 198, 200, 213, 267, 270
marabout 75, 187
masks 7, 24
metaphorical names 170-1
mot clef 89, 93; see keyword
music 7, 37
muslim 60, 68, 171, 180, 187, 189-90, 217, 244, 249,
mythology 7
Narrative Patterns 139-51
nationalism 25, 45, 100, 136, 143, 146, 151, 156, 173, 178, 197, 240, 251, 253-4, 257, 268
national festival 2, 38, 62-3, 81, 98, 113, 172, 241, 251
National Festival of Youth and Culture 3, 39, 40, 61-293
négritude 20
oral tradition 2, 26, 104, 131-2, 139, 141, 157-8, 165, 168, 265, 269
parody 2, 18
poets 15-16, 18, 217, 250
Plays:
  ALHAJI MAY BONDOL 44
  ALHAJI SHAGALI 73-5, 89, 133-5, 140, 146, 175-6, 200, 244, 272
  ALHAJI SHAIDAR MATA 105
  ANTIGONE 31
  ARMEE 43
  L'AVENTURE D'UNE CHEVRE 29-30
  BA GA IRINTA BA 65, 135, 138, 141, 154, 157, 168-9, 172, 181, 218, 245, 250, 272
  BABBAN RUMBU MATARSHI TUKUNYA 68-9, 138
  CALOO 43
  SI LES CAVALIERS ETAIENT LA 41
  DAJAR K'ASA AL'ADARTA 106, 137, 142, 144, 149, 157, 244, 248
  DU DAMAGARAM 32-4
  'DAN KWANGILA 64, 69-72, 75, 97, 98, 111, 134-5, 141, 146, 155, 157, 181, 185, 194-5, 205, 247-8, 272

LES FOURBERIES DE SCAPIN 31
GADO K'ARHIN ALLA 5, 15, 21, 37, 42, 104, 137, 139, 176, 186, 188, 190, 198, 200, 244-5, 265-6, 268, 270, 272
GIRMAN KAI RAWANIN TSIYA 111-2, 248-9
HANNU BIDI NA KANKA 42
L'IMPOT EST MORT 43
INDA NA SANII 42
KARA DA KIASHI 40
KOWA YA BUGI RUWA IDONAY 133, 136, 139, 154, 174, 192, 272
KUSKURE KARATU NE 143, 248
LAMPOO 41
LA LEGENDE DE KABRIN KABRA 30
LE MALADE IMAGINAIRE 31
RABAT 41
RIGA BA WUYA 247
RIKITTAA 44
SHEERIN KI, BUSHIA 43
SONNI ALI BER 41
TALALA MAI KAMAN SAKE 83, 98, 112, 136-8, 156, 169, 179-80, 186, 188, 193, 214, 245-7, 270, 272
TANIMOUNE ET L'EMANCIPATION 37
TCHIWAKE 41
WALAWALE 134, 248, 275
WASAN KARA 76-7, 106-7, 246, 248-9
YAKIN SHIHIRUN 41
'YAN ZAMINI 42
politics 63, 107, 137, 149, 151, 157, 94, 251, 265-7, 271
popular theatre 35
puppetry 9, 153

radio 18, 27, 40, 63-4, 67, 135, 138, 144, 201, 257, 265
realism 131, 133, 151; see everyday life and Social Drama Form
redress 152-7, 269
rehearsal 62, 69, 73, 76, 79, 82-3, 86-7, 111-13, 149, 167, 239, 246
  Actor Training in Rehearsal 87-93
  Rehearsal Process 93-110
religion 63, 65, 68, 107, 150-1
repetition 132, 138-41, 148, 157, 200, 269
roles 76, 78-9, 82, 87-8, 97, 99, 108-9, 168-9; see Distribution of Roles and womens' roles
Role of Director 82-7
sacred/secular theatre 12-19; see Chaibou
LE SAHEL 62, 255
samariyas 4, 29, 35-6, 38-40, 60, 62, 69, 77, 86, 94, 100, 102, 138, 168, 179, 210, 212, 242, 244, 256, 272
sarawniya 14
sarki 13, 18, 65, 67, 79, 81, 133, 137-9, 154, 168, 172-3, 175-8, 180-1, 185, 187, 199, 266-9, 271-2
sarkin bori 13
satire 140, 191, 249, 265, 267, 270
score 93-4, 97-8, 103, 105, 112, 114
Semaine de la Jeunesse 32, 252

Serious Characters 172-84
Shagari, Alhaji Shehu 77
Social Drama Form 151-8; see realism and everyday life
song 7, 18, 24, 36, 38, 39, 131; see ballet
sous-préfet and préfet 67, 75, 80-1, 95, 107-8, 133-4, 140, 146, 150, 154, 168, 172-77, 180-1, 185, 205, 241, 266-7, 269
spirits 13-15, 60, 265
tatsuniya 74
television 4, 18, 38-9, 70, 86-7, 105-7, 149, 152, 242, 248, 257, 265, 261
Le Théâtre Indigènede de la Cote-d'-Ivoire 28
Traditioinal Customs 9-11, 142
  bikin 'yar tsans 10
  bori 11, 265, 267
  dabo-dabo 11
  'dan akuyana 10
  langa 10
  kalankuwa 11
  wasannantashe 10
TRAITS d' UNION 27-8
Troupes:
  Amadou 'Dan Bassa 35, 45, 59, 64, 72, 77-8, 83, 85, 87, 98-105, 111, 168-9, 179, 241, 245, 265, 272
  Filingué 133, 154, 174, 192
  Gaya 61
  Mainé Soroa 63-4, 75, 79, 80-1, 83, 87-90, 92, 134, 140, 172, 189, 242, 252, 256

Maradi 69, 72, 96-8, 108, 113, 134, 138, 156-7, 181, 183
Nawaki Abdoui 61
ORTN of Zinder 40, 59, 67, 138
Radio Club of Zinder 35, 39-40, 59-60, 62, 67-8, 72, 76, 83, 86, 89, 105-111, 137-8, 142-3, 149, 151, 155, 157, 193, 241, 244, 246-7, 249
Tahoua 143
UNESCO 5
wasan kwaikwayo 3, 9
western drama 2, 20, 29, 31, 81, 131, 151, 265-6, 273
William Ponty School 20-30
womens' roles 60-2, 84, 87, 90-1, 108-9; see roles and Distribution of Roles
yankamanci 18